D0884524

PL/I FOR
SCIENTIFIC
PROGRAMMERS

Prentice-Hall
Series in Automatic Computation
George Forsythe, editor

ARBIB, *Theories of Abstract Automata*
BATES AND DOUGLAS, *Programming Language/One*
BAUMANN, FELICIANO, BAUER, AND SAMELSON, *Introduction to ALGOL*
BLUMENTHAL, *Management Information Systems*
BOBROW AND SCHWARTZ, EDS., *Computers and the Policy-Making Community: Applications to International Relations*
BOWLES, ED., *Computers in Humanistic Research*
CESCHINO AND KUNTZMANN, *Numerical Solution of Initial Value Problems*
CRESS, DIRKSEN, AND GRAHAM, *FORTRAN IV with WATFOR*
DESMONDE, *Computers and Their Uses*
DESMONDE, *A Conversational Graphic Data Processing System: The IBM 1130/2250*
DESMONDE, *Real-Time Data Processing Systems: Introductory Concepts*
EVANS, WALLACE, AND SUTHERLAND, *Simulation Using Digital Computers*
FIKE, *Computer Evaluation of Mathematical Functions*
FIKE, *PL/I for Scientific Programmers*
FORSYTHE AND MOLER, *Computer Solution of Linear Algebraic Systems*
GAUTHIER AND PONTO, *Designing Systems Programs*
GOLDEN *FORTRAN IV: Programming and Computing*
GOLDEN AND LEICHUS, *IBM 360: Programming and Computing*
GORDON, *System Simulation*
GREENSPAN, *Lectures on the Numerical Solution of Linear, Singular, and Nonlinear Differential Equations*
GRISWOLD, POAGE, AND POLONSKY, *The SNOBOL 4 Programming Language*
GRUENBERGER, ED., *Computers and Communications—Toward a Computer Utility*
GRUENBERGER, ED., *Critical Factors in Data Management*
HARTMANIS AND STEARNS, *Algebraic Structure Theory of Sequential Machines*
HULL, *Introduction to Computing*
HUSSON, *Microprogramming: Principles and Practices*
JOHNSON, *Structure in Digital Computer Systems: An Introduction*
KIVIAT, VILLANUEVA, AND MARKOWITZ, *The SIMSCRIPT II Programming Language*
LOUDEN, *Programming the IBM 1130 and 1800*
MARTIN, *Design of Real-Time Computer Systems*
MARTIN, *Programming Real-Time Computer Systems*
MARTIN, *Telecommunications and the Computer*
MARTIN, *Teleprocessing Network Organization*
MARTIN AND NORMAN, *The Computerized Society*
MCKEEMAN ET AL., *A Compiler Generator*
MINSKY, *Computation: Finite and Infinite Machines*
MOORE, *Interval Analysis*
PYLYSHYN, *Perspectives on the Computer Revolution*
PRITSKER AND KIVIAT, *Simulation with GASP II: A FORTRAN Based Simulation Language*
SAMMET, *Programming Languages: History and Fundamentals*
SNYDER, *Chebyshev Methods in Numerical Approximation*
STERLING AND POLLACK, *Introduction to Statistical Data Processing*
STROUD AND SECREST, *Gaussian Quadrature Formulas*
TAVISS, *The Computer Impact*
TRAUB, *Iterative Methods for the Solution of Equations*
VARGA, *Matrix Iterative Analysis*
VAZSONYI, *Problem Solving by Digital Computers with PL/I Programming*
WILKINSON, *Rounding Errors in Algebraic Processes*
ZIEGLER, *Time-Sharing Data Processing Systems*

PL/I FOR
SCIENTIFIC
PROGRAMMERS

C. T. FIKE

IBM SYSTEMS RESEARCH INSTITUTE

Prentice-Hall, Inc., Englewood Cliffs, N. J.

To My Mother

Current printing (last digit):

10 9 8 7 6 5 4 3 2

13-676502-5
Library of Congress Catalog Card Number: 76-104067
Printed in the United States of America

PRENTICE-HALL INTERNATIONAL, INC., *London*
PRENTICE-HALL OF AUSTRALIA, PTY. LTD., *Sydney*
PRENTICE-HALL OF CANADA, LTD., *Toronto*
PRENTICE-HALL OF INDIA PRIVATE LTD., *New Delhi*
PRENTICE-HALL OF JAPAN, INC., *Tokyo*

PREFACE

This book is intended for the experienced scientific programmer who wants to learn PL/I. It is different from most other currently available books on PL/I programming in two respects:

(1) It is not an introduction to programming, and the reader is assumed to have programmed previously in some language like FORTRAN or ALGOL.

(2) It has a scientific slant, and PL/I capabilities are discussed with scientific applications in mind.

The fact that the book is not introductory means that certain fundamental programming concepts are taken for granted and not explained. For example, there is no explanation of what loops are or why they are needed. Instead, it is assumed that the reader knows about the need for loops and wants to learn how to code them in PL/I. An entire chapter is devoted to explaining how they are coded.

The scientific slant of the book shows up in several ways:

(1) Many of the sample programs are based on elementary scientific applications. For instance, an iterative method for finding a root of an equation is used to illustrate one type of loop.

(2) Various PL/I capabilities less useful to scientific than to commercial programmers are not discussed. Thus, for example, PL/I record I/O, which is akin to COBOL I/O, is not described. The serious scientific PL/I user will of course want to learn record I/O some time, but he will probably not want to learn it first.

(3) Short sections are included in several chapters comparing PL/I and FORTRAN capabilities in order to help experienced FORTRAN programmers adapt themselves to PL/I rapidly.

(4) A chapter is included on FORMAC, which is a PL/I-related language used for programming certain algebraic and analytic operations.

This is not a reference book and does not deal with every aspect of PL/I. The omission of record I/O has already been mentioned. Various other topics, such as multitasking and object-code optimization, have been omitted because they need not concern the new PL/I user on his first encounter with the language. After he has had some practice with PL/I, then he can look into such topics on his own.

On the other hand, the book does deal with certain aspects of PL/I often treated sketchily or not at all in other textbooks. The serious programmer should appreciate, for example, the attention given to the PL/I precision and data-conversion rules. There is also an explanation of the use of complex arithmetic, together with a detailed example. An entire chapter of the book is devoted to the subject of debugging.

I have found it impractical to write about PL/I without referring to a particular implementation of it. Whenever I have made any remarks about implementation-dependent characteristics of the language, I have based those remarks on implementations for the IBM System/360 and on the F-level implementation in particular. Footnotes to the text indicate those places where implementation-dependent rules have been stated.

The PL/I language facilities described in this book are all available in the F-level implementation for the IBM System/360, except for some of the based-storage facilities discussed in Chapter 10. In particular, there are some restrictions on the uses of BASED, POINTER, and OFFSET variables. At the time of writing (Spring, 1969), the chief restrictions are the following:

(1) A BASED variable cannot be declared without an associated POINTER.

(2) A qualifier cannot be BASED or subscripted.

(3) OFFSET variables cannot be used as qualifiers.

The last chapter in the book is on FORMAC, which is a programming language used in conjunction with PL/I for programming various algebraic and analytic operations, of which differentiation is just one example. Although FORMAC is not a part of the PL/I language, I have devoted a chapter to it because I am convinced of its usefulness in scientific programming. In my opinion the reader will be well repaid for the time he takes to study the chapter.

Sample programs designed to illustrate various points about PL/I are distributed throughout the book. For the sake of brevity and clarity, these programs are often based upon greatly simplified assumptions, and they do not purport to be foolproof or to be suitable for practical applications.

I wish to express my thanks to Howard Edelson of the IBM Systems Research Institute and to Jackie Fike of the IBM World Trade Corporation for many long and invaluable discussions on PL/I.

Typesetting does not always preserve the spacing of characters in computer listings, of course. For some of the sample programs, the number of characters per line is, therefore, not always what it would be in computer printouts.

C. T. FIKE

New York

CONTENTS

1 FUNDAMENTALS   1

  1.1 Introduction 1
  1.2 Character Sets 2
  1.3 Identifiers; Keywords 3
  1.4 Writing PL/I Statements 4
  1.5 Main Programs 6
  1.6 PUT SKIP DATA 7

2 ARITHMETIC OPERATIONS   8

  2.1 Arithmetic Data Attributes 8
  2.2 DECLARE Statement 8
  2.3 Default Attributes for Arithmetic Variables 10
  2.4 Other Rules About DECLARE Statements 10
  2.5 Arithmetic Constants 11
  2.6 Floating-point Arithmetic in PL/I 12
  2.7 Initialization of Variables 13
  2.8 Sharing Storage Between Variables 14
  2.9 Assignment Statements 14
 2.10 Built-in Functions 16
 2.11 Expression Evaluation: Priority of Operations 17
 2.12 Expression Evaluation: Automatic Data Conversions 18
 2.13 Expression Evaluation: Precision of a Fixed-point Expression 20
 2.14 Expression Evaluation: Precision of a Floating-point Expression 23

2.15 Built-in Functions for Controlling the Attributes of Expressions 25
2.16 Fixed-point Pitfalls 27
2.17 Complex Arithmetic 28
2.18 PL/I and FORTRAN 29

3 **GO TO AND**
IF STATEMENTS   33

3.1 GO TO Statement; Label Variables 33
3.2 IF Statements 34
3.3 ELSE Clauses 35
3.4 Conditional Expressions 37
3.5 DO Groups in THEN and ELSE Clauses 38
3.6 Example 39
3.7 PL/I and FORTRAN 40

4 **DO LOOPS**   42

4.1 DO Statements 42
4.2 Additional Rules Concerning DO Loops 44
4.3 Example 46
4.4 WHILE Clauses 47
4.5 Example 48
4.6 Complex-arithmetic Example 49
4.7 PL/I and FORTRAN 50

5 **ARRAYS**   53

5.1 Array Variables 53
5.2 Additional Rules Concerning Arrays 54
5.3 The DEFINED Attribute for Arrays 56
5.4 Dynamic Storage Allocation 58
5.5 Array Arithmetic 59
5.6 Built-in Functions for Array Arithmetic 61
5.7 Cross Sections of Arrays 62
5.8 Example 64
5.9 Structures 65
5.10 PL/I and FORTRAN 68

6 INPUT/OUTPUT   71

6.1 Introduction 71
6.2 Printer Layout 72
6.3 The Stream Concept 73
6.4 List-directed Input/output 75
6.5 Data-directed Input/output 78
6.6 Edit-directed Input/output 80
6.7 Additional Rules About Formats 85
6.8 Picture Format Items 88
6.9 Program Interrupts 91
6.10 Nonstandard Files 93
6.11 PL/I and FORTRAN 96

7 PROGRAM
       INTERRUPTS   99

7.1 Introduction 99
7.2 Enabling and Disabling Interrupts 100
7.3 When an Interrupt Occurs 103
7.4 Additional Facts About On-units 105
7.5 Example 107
7.6 PL/I and FORTRAN 109

8 SUBPROGRAMS   111

8.1 Introduction 111
8.2 Subroutines 111
8.3 Functions 113
8.4 Argument and Parameter Attributes 116
8.5 Generic Functions 119
8.6 Recursive Procedures 120
8.7 Additional Facts About Subprograms 121
8.8 Array Arguments 123
8.9 Storage Allocation 126
8.10 Interrupts in Subprograms 128
8.11 EXTERNAL Variables 128
8.12 Internal Procedures 130
8.13 BEGIN Blocks 132
8.14 PL/I and FORTRAN 134

9 CHARACTER STRINGS
AND BIT STRINGS   **136**

9.1 Introduction 136
9.2 Character-string Constants 136
9.3 Character-string Variables 137
9.4 Input/output of Character Strings 139
9.5 Basic Character-string Operations 141
9.6 Conditional Expressions Involving Character Strings 142
9.7 Built-in Functions for String Manipulation 143
9.8 VARYING Character-string Variables 146
9.9 DEFINED Variables 148
9.10 Example 149
9.11 Subprograms 150
9.12 GET STRING and PUT STRING 153
9.13 Numeric-character Variables 154
9.14 Bit Strings 157
9.15 Bit-string Operators 160
9.16 Example 162
9.17 Data Conversions 163
9.18 Priority of Operators 167
9.19 PL/I and FORTRAN 168

10 BASED STORAGE AND
LIST PROCESSING   **171**

10.1 BASED and POINTER Variables 171
10.2 Building Lists 176
10.3 Example 179
10.4 AREA and OFFSET Variables 180
10.5 Additional Rules About BASED and Locator Variables 183
10.6 Example 185
10.7 Storage Classes 187

11 DEBUGGING   **190**

11.1 Introduction 190
11.2 Language Options 190
11.3 SUBSCRIPTRANGE and STRINGRANGE Conditions 191
11.4 SIZE Condition 193
11.5 FINISH Condition 194
11.6 CHECK Condition 195
11.7 Debugging List-processing Programs 197
11.8 Various Pitfalls 199
11.9 PL/I and FORTRAN 202

12 FORMAC

12.1 Introduction 205
12.2 FORMAC Fundamentals 206
12.3 Example 209
12.4 FORMAC Built-in Functions 210
12.5 Additonal Remarks About Built-in Functions 213
12.6 Mathematical Functions 216
12.7 Programmer-defined Functions 218
12.8 Exchanging Data Between PL/I and FORMAC 220
12.9 Example 221
12.10 Differentiation 223
12.11 Input/output of Formulas 224

INDEX 233

1 FUNDAMENTALS

1.1. INTRODUCTION

This book is for the programmer who has previous experience in scientific computing and who wants to learn how to use PL/I. The reader should already know what such things as loops, subprograms, and debugging are. He should previously have coded loops and subprograms in some other language, such as FORTRAN, and he should have debugged programs before. We shall assume that what he wants to do now is to learn how to do such things in PL/I.

PL/I is a rich language, richer than any other developed so far. We shall not describe all of the language, but we shall explain those parts of it that an experienced scientific programmer needs to know about in order to get started. Thus, for example, we shall describe PL/I stream-type input/output, which is analogous to FORTRAN formatted input/output, but we shall not describe PL/I record-type input/output, which is analogous to COBOL input/output. Once he has begun using PL/I, it should not be difficult for the reader to investigate on his own those topics that are not discussed here.

Throughout this book, we shall assume that the reader has access to a PL/I reference manual of some kind.[1] It will be necessary to refer to such a manual from time to time for details about PL/I not included in this book.

---

[1]Such a manual should be available for use with any particular PL/I compiler. For example, for the F-level PL/I compiler for the IBM System/360, the appropriate manual is *IBM System/360 Operating System: PL/I (F) Language Reference Manual*, IBM Form No. C28-8201.

1

1.2. CHARACTER SETS

A programmer may use either of two character sets in writing a PL/I program. The first is the 60-character set listed below:

Character	Name
	blank
.	period
<	less than
(	left parenthesis
+	plus
|	or
&	and
$	dollar mark
*	asterisk
)	right parenthesis
;	semicolon
¬	not
—	minus
/	slash
,	comma
%	percent
_	break (or underscore)
>	greater than
?	question mark
:	colon
#	number sign
@	at sign
'	single quote
=	equals
A-Z	letters of alphabet
0-9	digits

These 60 characters are classified as follows:

(1) Alphabetic characters, of which there are 29 (the 26 letters of the alphabet, together with the dollar mark, the number sign, and the at sign.[2]

(2) Digits, of which there are 10 (the integers 0–9).

---

[2]The dollar mark, the number sign, and the at sign are counted as "alphabetic" characters so that users whose alphabet contains more than 26 characters can make substitutions for these three characters.

(3) Special characters, of which there are 21 (all those characters that are neither alphabetic nor digital).

The collating sequence (the high-low relationship) of these 60 characters is not defined in PL/I and is therefore dependent on how the language is implemented.[3]

No characters but those 60 mentioned above can be used in a PL/I program, with the following exceptions: Any character can be used in a comment (Section 1.4) or in a character-string constant (Section 9.2), provided the character is valid in the computer being used.

The second character set that a programmer may use in writing PL/I programs is the 48-character set, which is a subset of the 60-character set. The characters that are *omitted* from the 60-character set are the following: break (underscore), number sign, question mark, colon, semicolon, less than, greater than, and, or, not, percent, at sign. In the 48-character set two-character combinations are used to substitute for certain of these missing characters. Thus, the composite symbol (..) consisting of two periods substitutes for the colon, and the composite symbol (,.) consisting of a comma and period substitutes for the semicolon. The interested reader should refer to his PL/I reference manual.

All the PL/I examples in this book are presented in the 60-character set.

1.3. IDENTIFIERS; KEYWORDS

In PL/I the term *identifier* is used to describe the name of data variables, program entry points (such as subroutine names), data files, and so forth. An identifier may contain one or more characters.[4] The first character must be alphabetic. Subsequent characters can be alphabetic characters, digits, or the break (underscore) character.

Examples:

X, K, Q6, NO__OF__POINTS, ROWSIZE

Statement labels are also classed as identifiers and so must be chosen in accordance with the rules above. As we shall illustrate in many examples later in this book, a statement label must precede the statement to which it applies and must be separated from the statement by a colon.

---

[3]The order in which the 60-character set is listed in this section is that of the collating sequence for the IBM System/360. Blank is low and 9 is high.

[4]In PL/I implementations for the IBM System/360 the maximum number of characters allowed in an identifier is 31.

Example:

$$\text{LOOP}: X = Y + \text{SQRT} (Z);$$

Like other programming languages, PL/I has a number of *keywords* used in the various types of PL/I statements. Two examples of keywords are DECLARE, which is used in declaring variables, and DO, which is used in writing loops. Some keywords have abbreviations which can be used interchangeably with the keywords they represent. For example, the abbreviation of the keyword DECIMAL is DEC, and the abbreviation of CHARACTER is CHAR. We shall discuss most of the PL/I keywords later in this book as we take up various topics. Usually we shall write keywords all in capital letters, as a reminder of their special status. In sample codes we shall use abbreviations wherever possible.

Neither keywords nor their abbreviations are *reserved* words in PL/I, so long as the 60-character set is used. That is to say, a programmer can use a keyword or the abbreviation of a keyword as one of his own identifiers, if he wishes, and no confusion results. Whether or not a word is interpreted as a keyword or as a programmer-defined identifier depends on the context in which the word is used. Because of this, the programmer can choose names like DECLARE, DO, DECIMAL, and DEC as identifiers.

When the 48-character set is used, there are some reserved words. Some of the composite symbols used as substitutes for special characters missing from the 48-character set are reserved. For example, GT, which substitutes for $>$, and LT, which substitutes for $<$, are reserved and cannot be used as programmer-specified identifiers. For a complete list of the reserved words associated with the 48-character set, the reader should consult his PL/I reference manual.

1.4. WRITING PL/I STATEMENTS

PL/I statements are written down on a coding pad and keypunched in free form. Any card columns can be used.[5] Statements are terminated by semicolons, and card boundaries have no significance. Several statements can be punched on a single card, and a statement can be continued from one card

---

[5]For a particular PL/I implemetation there may be restrictions on what card columns can be used. Thus, with the F-level implementation on the IBM System/360 it is customary, though not essential, to use only columns 2–72, and to reserve column 1 and columns 73–80 for other uses.

to another without the use of any special notation for continuation. A statement terminates only when a semicolon is encountered. There will be many examples in this book illustrating how statements can be written in a PL/I source program.

Blanks can be inserted more or less arbitrarily, with a few exceptions. Blanks are *not* permitted in programmer-specified identifiers or in PL/I keywords.[6] Composite operators, such as the exponentiation operator **, cannot contain blanks; and constants cannot contain blanks, except for character-string constants (alphabetic constants that we shall discuss in Chapter 9). Consider the following illustrations:[7]

Type	Right	Wrong
Variable name	ROWSIZE	ROWbSIZE
Keyword	DECLARE	DECbLARE
Operator	A**2	A*b*2
Constant	123456789.	123b456b789.

On the other hand, blanks are required as separators in certain situations. Identifiers, keywords, and constants must be separated from one another by at least one blank, if they are not otherwise separated by an operator, such as a plus sign or a minus sign, or by a punctuation mark, such as a comma or a left or right parenthesis.

Example: The statement

$$DO \quad K = 5;$$

is interpreted as a DO statement, which is the PL/I loop-control statement (Chapter 4). On the other hand, the statement

$$DOK = 5;$$

is interpreted as an assignment statement in which the value 5 is assigned to a data variable named DOK. Thus, the blank between DO and K in the first statement is a significant blank.

Wherever one blank can be used, an arbitrary number can be used. This fact permits the programmer to space out his statements neatly and to indent sections of code for the sake of clarity.

---

[6]There is one exception to this rule. The keyword GOTO may be written in the form GO TO, which is how it is written in this book.

[7]The symbol b denotes a blank.

A *comment* in a PL/I program is a string of characters set off on the left by the composite symbol /∗ and on the right by ∗/. Any characters valid in the computer being used can be inserted in a comment, even if the characters are not in the 60-character set. A comment can be inserted in a program anywhere that a blank can be inserted.

Example:

```
X = Y + Z;        /* COMPUTE NEW X VALUE. */
PUT DATA (X);     /* DEBUGGING STATEMENT */
```

1.5. MAIN PROGRAMS

The simplest type of PL/I program consists of a main program (or main *procedure*, as it is called in PL/I terminology), with no subprograms. We shall discuss subprograms in detail in Chapter 8. For the moment only the design of a main program will be considered.

A main program begins with a labeled PROCEDURE statement containing the keywords OPTIONS (MAIN); and it ends with an END statement, which may (and preferably does) contain the same label. Thus, if the label chosen is GO, we have the following framework for a PL/I main program:[8]

```
GO:   PROC OPTIONS (MAIN);
      . . .
      END GO;
```

(PROC is the PL/I abbreviation for the keyword PROCEDURE.) Program execution begins with the first executable statement in the main program.

A comment may precede the PROCEDURE statement.

The execution of a main program is terminated by executing the statement

```
RETURN;
```

This has the effect of returning control to the operating system. Any number of RETURN statements may be used in a program.

Until we take up subprograms in Chapter 8, most of our examples will have the following general layout:

---

[8]Use of the keywords OPTIONS (MAIN) to identify the main procedure is implementation dependent. It is the method used in PL/I implementations for the IBM System/360. Procedure labels in PL/I implementations for the IBM System/360 cannot contain more than seven characters.

```
/* NAME OF EXAMPLE */
GO: PROC OPTIONS (MAIN);
    . . .
    RETURN;
    END GO;
```

1.6. PUT SKIP DATA

In Chapter 6 we shall discuss in detail some of the PL/I input/output facilities. In the meantime, in order to be able to make examples, we shall use the PUT SKIP DATA statement to get printed output. The reader can also use this statement in practice codes in order to produce output. The statement is illustrated below:

PUT SKIP DATA (A, B, C);

The parentheses contain the names of one or more variables whose values are to be printed. The output is printed starting on a new line in the form of a series of equations terminated by a semicolon, such as

A = 3.14 B = 2.718 C = 1.57;

EXERCISES

1. Which of the following is a valid PL/I identifier?
   (a) NUMBEROFPOINTS
   (b) NUMBER__OF__POINTS
   (c) NUMBER OF POINTS
   (d) NUMBER.OF.POINTS
   (e) NUMBER—OF—POINTS
   (f) SQRT
   (g) PL/I
   (h) $#
   (i) X2
   (j) 2X

2 ARITHMETIC OPERATIONS

2.1. ARITHMETIC DATA ATTRIBUTES

In this chapter we shall deal with the characteristics of arithmetic constants and variables and explain some of the ways in which they can be used in PL/I to perform calculations. We begin by considering the *attributes,* or characteristics, of arithmetic data. Although other attributes will come up later, for the moment we shall consider just the attributes of *mode, base, scale,* and *precision,* which are the fundamental ones for the description of arithmetic data in PL/I.

The alternative specifications for these four attributes are

(1) Mode: real or complex.
(2) Scale: fixed-point or floating-point.
(3) Base: decimal or binary.
(4) Precision: the number of (decimal or binary) digits required for representation of the data.

2.2. DECLARE STATEMENT

The programmer can specify explicitly the attributes he wants for a PL/I variable, or he can allow certain attributes to be assumed on the basis of default rules. Explicit specification of attributes is done with the DECLARE (abbr.: DCL) statement.

Examples:

DCL A FLOAT DEC (16), B FIXED BIN (31);
DCL C FIXED DEC (8, 5);
DCL M CPLX FLOAT DEC (6), N FIXED BIN (15, 5);
DCL P FIXED, Q FLOAT, R BIN (21);

Any number of variables can be declared in a single DECLARE statement; the groups of specifications must be separated by commas. The keywords used to specify mode, scale, and base attributes are the following:

(1) Mode: REAL, COMPLEX (abbr.: CPLX).

(2) Scale: FIXED, FLOAT.

(3) Base: DECIMAL (abbr.: DEC), BINARY (abbr.: BIN).

The precision attribute appears only after one of the other attributes and has the form either (p, q) or (p). For a floating-point variable the precision specification must be (p), where p denotes the number of (binary or decimal) digits required to represent the mantissa of the variable. For a fixed-point variable the form should be either (p, q) or (p), where p denotes the number of (binary or decimal) digits required for the variable and q denotes the number of those digits to the right of the point.[1] The fixed-point specification (p) is a short form equivalent to $(p, 0)$. The maximum precisions allowed for both real and complex variables are the following:[2]

Fixed decimal	15
Fixed binary	31
Floating decimal	16
Floating binary	53

Example: The statement

DCL A REAL FIXED DEC (5, 3), B REAL FIXED BIN (5),
C REAL FLOAT DEC (6), D CPLX FLOAT DEC (16);

declares A to be a real, fixed-point, decimal variable of the form xx. xxx; B to be a real, fixed-point, binary variable of the form xxxxx.; C to be a real, float-

---

[1]Usually $p \geq q \geq 0$. Thus, the precision attribute $(3, 2)$ implies a number of the form x. xx. It is also permitted, however, to have $q > p$ or $q < 0$. Thus, the precision attribute $(2, 3)$ implies a number of the form .0xx, and $(2, -1)$ implies a number of the form xx0.

[2]The maximum precisions are implementation dependent. The values given are those for IBM System/360 implementations.

ing-point, decimal variable with a six-decimal-digit mantissa; and D to be a complex, floating-point, decimal variable with 16-decimal-digit mantissas for both its real and imaginary parts.

2.3. DEFAULT ATTRIBUTES FOR ARITHMETIC VARIABLES

When the attributes of a variable are not declared explicitly in a DECLARE statement, certain attributes are assumed automatically in accordance with the following default rules:

(1) If none of the mode, scale, and base attributes is specified, then these attributes depend on the first letter of the identifier (the name of the variable):

    (a) If the identifier begins with any of the letters I through N, then the attributes REAL FIXED BINARY are assumed.

    (b) If the identifier begins with any character other than one of the letters I through N, then the attributes REAL FLOAT DECIMAL are assumed.

(2) If at least one, but not all, of the mode, scale, and base attributes is specified, then the unspecified attributes are automatically selected from the list REAL, FLOAT, and DECIMAL.

(3) If no precision attribute is specfied, then a default precision is assumed as follows:[3]

Fixed decimal	(5, 0)
Fixed binary	(15, 0)
Floating decimal	(6)
Floating binary	(21)

Example: The statement

    DCL K FIXED, L DEC, M FLOAT, P FIXED BIN (31);

is equivalent to

    DCL K REAL FIXED DEC (5), L REAL FLOAT DEC (6),
        M REAL FLOAT DEC (6), P REAL FIXED BIN (31);

2.4. OTHER RULES ABOUT DECLARE STATEMENTS

Additional rules concerning DECLARE statements are these:

---

[3]Default values for precision attributes are implementation dependent. The values given are those for **IBM** System/360 implementations.

(1) A program can have more than one DECLARE statement.

(2) The most common position used for DECLARE statements in a program is at the start of the program, right after the PROCEDURE statement. Although a DECLARE can actually appear anywhere in a program, putting it anywhere except first can have special significance when an internal block structure is used, and so this should not be done carelessly. We shall explain internal block structures in more detail in Sections 8.12 and 8.13.

(3) The programmer can declare variables in groups when he intends them to have like attributes. Parentheses are used to indicate grouping; this is called *factoring* of attributes. The technique of factoring attributes can be used in declarations of other types of data attributes that we shall discuss in later chapters. We shall use it from time to time in examples.

Example: The statement

DCL (A, B, C) FLOAT (16);

is equivalent to

DCL A FLOAT (16), B FLOAT (16), C FLOAT (16);

2.5. ARITHMETIC CONSTANTS

Arithmetic constants, like variables, have mode, scale, base, and precision attributes, which depend on how constants are written.

Example:

Constant	Attributes
11. 001B	REAL FIXED BIN (5, 3)
11. 001E-3B	REAL FLOAT BIN (5)
3. 14	REAL FIXED DEC (3, 2)
3. 14E0	REAL FLOAT DEC (3)
11. 001BI	CPLX FIXED BIN (5, 3)
11. 001E-3BI	CPLX FLOAT BIN (5)
3. 14I	CPLX FIXED DEC (3, 2)
3. 14E0I	CPLX FLOAT DEC (3)
. 314159265E1	REAL FLOAT DEC (9)
052	REAL FIXED DEC (3, 0)
1. 1001001000011111110110101E3B	REAL FLOAT BIN (25)
3. 14159265E-2I	CPLX FLOAT DEC (9)
1. 1001001000011111110110101E3BI	CPLX FLOAT BIN (25)

The main rules concerning the attributes of constants are these:

(1) *Mode:* A complex constant contains the letter I; a real constant does not. The only complex constants are pure imaginary ones, and a number like $2 + 3i$ is regarded as a real constant plus a pure imaginary constant.

(2) *Scale:* A floating-point constant has an exponent of the form $E \pm n$ or En; a fixed-point constant does not. The exponent for a binary floating-point constant specifies a power of two, whereas the exponent for a decimal floating-point constant specifies a power of ten. The exponent is always a decimal integer (optionally signed), even if the constant itself is binary.

(3) *Base:* A binary constant ends with the letter B; a decimal constant does not. Except for the exponent, if there is one, a binary constant can contain only zeros and ones.

(4) *Precision:* The precision attribute of a constant can be deduced from its form. For the precision attribute (p, q) of a fixed-point constant, p is the number of digits in the constant, and q is the number of those digits to the right of the point. For the precision attribute (p) of a floating-point constant, p is the number of digits in the constant (the exponent not being counted). Zeros always count. The maximum precisions allowed for constants are the same as those for variables (see Section 2.2).

Most of the arithmetic constants that a programmer uses in PL/I are real, fixed-point, decimal constants. Other kinds of constants are often very helpful, however. For example, the programmer can assign a binary constant to a binary variable when he wants to specify the value bit for bit rather than to write a decimal constant and allow an automatic conversion to take place.

2.6. FLOATING-POINT ARITHMETIC IN PL/I

The PL/I language allows a programmer to declare floating-point variables (real or complex) to be (1) of either decimal or binary base, and (2) of any precision. In principle, floating-point data with an arbitrary combination of base and precision attributes might be implemented on any computer, although floating-point circuitry could probably be used for only a few combinations at most, and programming-simulated arithmetic would have to be used otherwise.

In practice, a PL/I implementation for a particular computer is not likely to provide floating-point arithmetic in more than one base and in more than two precisions. The base would be the number base of the computer's floating-point circuitry, and the precisions would probably correspond to single and double word lengths in the computer. Thus, for a computer having floating-point circuitry of two kinds, binary single precision and binary double precision (say), all floating-point calculations in a PL/I program would probably be done with one or the other of these two kinds, no matter what attributes a programmer specified for his variables and constants.

The F-level PL/I implementation on the IBM System/360 illustrates this point. All floating-point variables and constants in a PL/I program are represented internally as either (a) hexadecimal single precision (6 hexadecimal digits in a mantissa), and (b) hexadecimal double precision (14 hexadecimal digits in a mantissa), which are the two kinds of automatic floating-point arithmetic in the computer. Single precision is used if the base and precision attributes of a variable or constant are

(1) FLOAT BIN (p), where $p \leq 21$.

(2) FLOAT DEC (p), where $p \leq 6$.

Double precision is used when the attributes are

(1) FLOAT BIN (p), where $p > 21$.

(2) FLOAT DEC (p), where $p > 6$.

Therefore, in declaring floating-point variables, a PL/I programmer using the IBM System/360 may as well restrict his choice of attributes to FLOAT DECIMAL (6) for single precision and FLOAT DECIMAL (16) for double precision.

Many (and perhaps most) programmers will not care about these details, but they are important in certain types of work. Thus, an understanding of the explanation above would be important to any programmer told to code an application "in double precision," since he would then have to know what attributes of PL/I variables and constants resulted in the use of double-precision arithmetic internally.

2.7. INITIALIZATION OF VARIABLES

A constant value can be specified for automatic assignment to a variable when storage is allocated to the variable. If this is done, then the variable will already possess a value when it is used for the first time. Initialization is accomplished by specifying an INITIAL (abbr.: INIT) attribute for a variable in a DECLARE statement. Any variable not declared in this way has an undefined value initially and should not be assumed to have the value zero.

Example: The statement

DCL A FIXED DEC (8) INIT (0), B INIT (−1), K FLOAT;

causes A to be initialized to zero and B to be initialized to −1. The initial value of K is undefined. A and B are said "to have the INITIAL attribute."

The constant declared as an initial value for a variable can be signed and need not have the same attributes as the variable; an automatic conversion will be made if necessary. Thus, in the example, the number −1 is fixed rather than floating but will be converted automatically to the required floating-point form.

2.8. SHARING STORAGE BETWEEN VARIABLES

Under certain conditions variables can be assigned the same storage space by use of the DEFINED (abbr.: DEF) attribute in a DECLARE statement.

Example: The statement

DCL M FLOAT DEC (6), N FLOAT DEC (6) DEF M;

causes the two variables M and N to be assigned the same storage. N is said "to be defined on the base variable M."

Variables associated by means of the DEFINED attribute must have the same mode, scale, base, and precision attributes. Thus, a fixed-point variable could not be made to share storage with a floating-point variable.

A DEFINED variable cannot be initialized. In other words, a variable cannot have both the DEFINED and the INITIAL attributes. The base variable of a DEFINED variable can, however, be initialized.

As we shall explain in Chapter 10, there are other ways for a programmer to cause variables to share storage.

2.9. ASSIGNMENT STATEMENTS

The fundamental statement used to specify arithmetic operations in PL/I is the *assignment statement*. Its general form is

variable = expression;

The arithmetic expression on the right is evaluated, if necessary, and the result of the calculation is the value that is assigned to the variable on the left. Constants, variables, and functions can be used in forming the expression. (We shall discuss built-in functions in the next section and programmer-defined functions in Chapter 8.)

Examples:

$$A = B + C - D*E;$$
$$A = B**C - 2*D/E;$$
$$X = X - (Y/3)**2;$$
$$M = (P*N)**K;$$
$$Z = SQRT (B**2 - 4*A*C);$$

An arithmetic expression, like an arithmetic variable, has mode, scale, base, and precision attributes. Beginning in Section 2.11, we shall discuss the rules for evaluating an arithmetic expression and for determining its attributes.

The mode, scale, base, and precision attributes of the expression on the right side of an assignment statement may differ from the corresponding attributes of the target variable (that is, the variable on the left). After the value of the expression has been obtained, it is converted automatically to the attributes of the target variable. If the value of the expression has a base different from that of the target variable, the value is converted directly to the full precision of the target.[4]

Example:

```
DCL A REAL FIXED BIN (8, 8);
A = .1 ;
```

When this code is executed, the value assigned to A is the result of converting the fixed-decimal constant .1 to binary and truncating the converted value after the eighth binary place. Thus, the value assigned to A is .00011001B.

The conversion of the value of the expression on the right-hand side of an assignment statement to the precision of the target variable may result in the loss of nonzero high-order digits (those on the left). This constitutes a SIZE error, which is a type of error that is not detected automatically in PL/I but which can be detected by programming, as we shall explain in Section 11.4. In the preceding example, a SIZE error would occur if the assignment statement A = .1 were changed to A = 1, because the precision of A is insufficient for A to have a value as large as 1.

---

[4]In FORTRAN and some other programming languages, a number may first be converted to its new base in some intermediate precision and this value may then be truncated or filled out with zeros in order to give it the precision of the target. The PL/I method is more accurate.

Truncation of nonzero low-order digits (those on the right) occurs commonly in execution of assignment statements, and it is not considered to be an error.

When a variable is initialized by use of the INITIAL attribute, the kind of data conversion takes place as when an assignment statement is used. Thus, the statement

DCL A REAL FIXED BIN (8, 8) INIT (.1);

has the same effect as

DCL A REAL FIXED BIN (8, 8);
A = .1;

A value can be assigned to two or more variables at once by means of a *multiple assignment statement*. Thus, the statement

A, B = C;

is equivalent to the two statements

A = C;
B = C;

In such a case, the variables A and B can have different attributes.

2.10. BUILT-IN FUNCTIONS

Like other programming languages PL/I contains a number of built-in functions that can be used in arithmetic expressions. Some of the most important of these functions are ones used to evaluate mathematical functions. Thus, for example, SQRT is the built-in square-root function, LOG is the natural-logarithm function, and ABS is the absolute-value function. A reference to such a function has the general form

function name (expression)

The expression is called the function *argument*.

Example:

Y = SQRT (U∗V);

In this assignment statement the square root of U∗V is assigned to Y. U∗V is the argument for the square-root function.

The list of mathematical functions provided in PL/I includes various ones for evaluating trigonometric functions, hyperbolic functions, logarithms, and so on.

PL/I also has nonmathematical built-in functions that are used to facilitate certain programming operations. We shall discuss many of these functions in detail in later chapters. An illustration of such a function is SUBSTR, which is used to extract a substring from a given character string.

It is a general rule in PL/I with almost no exceptions that the arguments of built-in functions can be any type of data. Thus, for example, an argument for SQRT can be fixed or floating, decimal or binary, real or complex—in other words, whatever the programmer wishes. If a data conversion of some kind or other has to be performed on the argument before the function can actually be invoked, such a conversion will be performed automatically.

Many of the built-in functions are called *generic functions* in PL/I terminology. This means that they are really collections of functions, a particular one of which is invoked depending on how a function is referenced. SQRT and the other mathematical functions are all generic. If the argument for SQRT is a real number, such as the number 5, then a real square root is calculated. On the other hand, if the argument is a complex number, such as $5 + 6i$, then a complex square root is calculated. Similarly, if the argument is single precision, the square root is single precision; and if the argument is double precision, the square root is double precision. Thus a number of basically different calculations are possible when SQRT is invoked, and which one is used depends on what the argument is.

As we have said, certain built-in functions will be discussed in later chapters. Others will be introduced as necessary in examples. For a complete list of the available built-in functions and for additional information on their use, the reader should refer to his PL/I reference manual.

2.11. EXPRESSION EVALUATION: PRIORITY OF OPERATORS

The PL/I arithmetic operators are the following:

Operator	Use
**	exponentiation
*	multiplication
/	division
+	addition
—	subtraction

By inserting parentheses, one can always specify unambiguously the order in which operations are performed in an arithmetic expression. When parentheses are omitted from an arithmetic expression, the evaluation order is based on the following priority scheme:[5]

Priority level 1 (highest) **, prefix + , prefix −
Priority level 2 *, /
Priority level 3 (lowest) infix + , infix −

Level 1 operations are performed first, and level 3 operations last. If two or more level 1 operators appear in an expression, the order of priority of those operators is from right to left. If two or more operators of a level other than level 1 appear in an expression, the order of priority of those operators is from left to right.

Examples:

Expression	Equivalent meaning
A + B − C	(A + B) − C
A + B*C	A + (B*C)
A/B − C	(A/B) − C
A*B**C	A*(B**C)
A*B/C	(A*B)/C
A** − B	A**(−B)
− A**B	− (A**B)
A**B**C	A**(B**C)

2.12. EXPRESSION EVALUATION: AUTOMATIC DATA CONVERSIONS

There are no restrictions in PL/I on the mixing of mode, scale, base, and precision attributes in an arithmetic expression. Automatic conversions are made whenever necessary for evaluation of an expression. Thus, for example, both binary and decimal variables can appear in an expression. For many kinds of work it is not necessary to know in detail what automatic data conversions can occur, but knowledge of conversion rules can sometimes be important. In this section we shall explain briefly the rules for mode, scale, and base conversion. Precision will be discussed separately in the next two sections.

Consider what happens in the evaluation of A (op) B, where (op) can mean any of the operators + , − , *, or / (that is, any arithmetic operator but **). Both A and B can be real or complex, fixed or floating, and binary or decimal.

---

[5]A plus or minus sign is said to be a *prefix* operator if it precedes a single expression and is said to be an *infix* operator if it joins two expressions. Thus the minus sign in − X is a prefix sign, whereas that in X − Y is an infix sign.

(1) If real and complex are mixed, the real element is converted to complex, and the expression A (op) B is complex.

(2) If fixed and floating are mixed, the fixed element is converted to floating, and the expression A (op) B is floating.

(3) If binary and decimal are mixed, the decimal element is converted to binary, and the expression A (op) B is binary.

The same rules apply for exponentiation (the evaluation of A∗∗B) with the following exceptions:

(1) If A is complex and B is fixed-point real with a precision attribute of the form $(p, 0)$, then B is not converted to complex, but A∗∗B is still complex.

(2) If A is floating and B is fixed with a precision attribute of the form $(p, 0)$, then B is not converted to floating, but A∗∗B is floating.

(3) Even if both A and B are fixed, one or both of them will be converted to floating and A∗∗B will be floating unless B happens to be an unsigned nonzero real integer constant and the precision of A∗∗B does not exceed the maximum allowed precision (see Section 2.13).

The rules for mode, scale, and base conversion that were summarized above are applied as necessary when an arithmetic expression appearing on the right-hand side of an assignment statement is evaluated. The mode, scale, and base attributes of the target variable on the left-hand side of the assignment statement are irrelevant so far as evaluation of the expression is concerned. After the expression has been evaluated, then its value is converted to have the attributes of the target variable, and only then are the target attributes relevant.

Example: Consider the following code:

```
DCL A FIXED DEC, B FIXED BIN, C FIXED DEC;
. . .
C = 5 + A∗B;
```

The assignment statement is executed as follows: (1) A is converted to binary; (2) the product A∗B is formed and is fixed binary; (3) the fixed-decimal constant 5 is converted to fixed binary; and (4) the sum 5 + A∗B is formed in fixed binary. Finally, the value of 5 + A∗B is converted to fixed decimal for assignment to C. (We shall explain in the next section how the precisions involved in this example would be determined.)

When a built-in function is used in an expression, the attributes of the function value depend on what the function is and on the attributes of its argument. For SQRT and the various transcendental functions, such as EXP, LOG, COS, and SINH, the scale of the function value is always floating, and the mode is the same as that of the argument.

The absolute-value function ABS, to take a different type of example, always has the real mode, but its scale and base are the same as those of its argument. Thus ABS is fixed decimal if its argument is fixed decimal, fixed binary if its argument is fixed binary, and so on.

Example: The expression $2 + \text{LOG}(2)$ is floating, but the expression $2 + \text{ABS}(-2)$ is fixed.

It would require too much space here to list all the PL/I built-in functions and describe their attributes. In cases where he is doubtful about the attributes of a built-in function, the programmer should consult his PL/I reference manual.

2.13. EXPRESSION EVALUATION:
PRECISION OF A FIXED-POINT EXPRESSION

In a fixed-point calculation it is often important (and sometimes crucial) for the programmer to know the precision of each expression involved in the calculation, if he is to obtain an accurate result. The precision of a fixed-point expression depends on a series of rules and may not be obvious at all. We shall briefly summarize below these rules for fixed-point expressions. With floating-point arithmetic, matters are somewhat simpler, since the possibilities for precision are limited in practice, and the rules are not so complicated. This will be explained in the next section.

The rules by which the precision of a fixed-point expression is determined are given below. As we shall explain in Section 2.14, there are built-in functions that the programmer can use to exert explicit control over the precision of an expression.

(1) The precision of a fixed-point expression can never exceed the maximum value allowed for fixed-point data: 15 for fixed decimal and 31 for binary.[6] These limits apply to intermediate results as well as final results.

(2) If a number is converted from one base to another when an expres-

---

[6]These maximum precisions are implementation dependent. The values given are those for IBM System/360 PL/I implementations. Compare Section 2.2.

sion is evaluated, then a new precision appropriate to the new base is determined automatically. Roughly, the precision is converted at 3.32 bits per decimal digit (because $\log_2 10 = 3.32$). The full rule is the following:

(a) If the conversion is from decimal to binary,[7] the old attribute (p, q) is converted to (r, s), where r is the least integer $\geq 1 + 3.32p$ and s is the least integer $\geq 3.32q$.

(b) If the conversion is from binary to decimal,[8] the old attribute (p, q) is converted to (r, s), where r is the least integer $\geq 1 + p/3.32$ and s is the least integer $\geq q/3.32$.

(3) If the value computed for r in (2a) or (2b) exceeds the implementation maximum (a practical possibility in the conversion of decimal to binary), then the value of r is taken to be the maximum allowed precision. This could cause the loss of significant digits (those to the left) in the conversion. Such an occurrence constitutes a SIZE error, which is not detected automatically but can be detected by programming; we shall discuss SIZE errors in more detail in Section 11.4.

(4) The precision of the expression A (op) B, where (op) can be any one of the operators $+$, $-$, $*$, $/$, or $**$, depends on what the operation is and on the precisions of the operands A and B. In the summary below, we assume that A and B are either both fixed binary or both fixed decimal. (Otherwise, the rules of Section 2.11 would apply.) We let (p_1, q_1) denote the precision of A, and (p_2, q_2), that of B.

(a) *Addition* and *subtraction*. A $+$ B or A $-$ B has the precision attribute (r, s), where $r = 1 + \max(p_1 - q_1, p_2 - q_2) + \max(q_1, q_2)$ and $s = \max(q_1, q_2)$.

(b) *Multiplication*. A$*$B has the precision attribute (r, s), where $r = 1 + p_1 + p_2$ and $s = q_1 + q_2$.

(c) *Division*. A$/$B has the precision attribute (r, s), where $r = N$ and $s = N - (p_1 - q_1 + q_2)$. The value of N is the maximum allowed precision. If A and B are binary, N is 31; if decimal, N is 15.[9]

(d) *Exponentiation*. A$**$B has the precision attribute (r, s), where $r = (p_1 + 1)B - 1$ and $s = qB$. Here B is assumed to be a nonzero real integer constant, for otherwise A$**$B would be floating rather than fixed.

---

[7]If $q < 0$ (which the language allows), then s is the largest integer $\leq 3.32q$.

[8]If $q < 0$, then s is the largest integer $\leq q/3.32$.

[9]The maximum precisions 31 and 15 are implementation dependent. The values given are those for IBM System/360 PL/I implementations.

(5) If the value computed for r in (4a) or (4b) exceeds the implementation maximum, then the value of r is taken to be the maximum allowed precision. This might mean that for certain values of A and B the precision of the expression A (op) B would be too small for its value and that significant digits would be lost when the expression was evaluated. Such an occurrence constitutes a FIXEDOVERFLOW (abbr.: FOFL) error, which is detected automatically; we shall discuss FIXEDOVERFLOW errors in more detail in Section 11.4.

(6) If the value computed for r in (4d) exceeds the implementation maximum, then A is converted to floating, and A**B is evaluated according to the rules for floating-point expressions. (This is also what happens if B is not a nonzero real integer constant.)

The precision of the target variable in an assignment statement does not influence the way an expression appearing on the right side of the assignment is evaluated. Only when the expression has been evaluated and its value is ready to be converted to the attributes of the target variable is the precision of the target variable taken into account.

Rule (2) given above applies only when base conversion is required for expression evaluation and not when it is required in order to give a data value the attributes of the target variable in an assignment statement. When a number is converted from one base to another in the process of crossing the equals sign in an assignment statement, the target precision for the conversion is always the full precision of target variable (see Section 2.9).

The reader should be able to see after some study that the rules in (4) are not merely arbitrary. For example, consider the expression A + B when A has precision attribute (5, 2) and B the attribute (4, 3).

$$A = \quad xxx.xx$$
$$B = \quad x.xxx$$
$$A + B = xxxx.xxx$$

To represent A + B exactly, three digits are needed to the right of the point and four to the left, the leftmost digit being included to provide for a possible carry into that position. In other words, the precision of A + B should be (7, 3). This is exactly what is obtained with the rule in (4a).

Example:

```
DCL (A, B, C) FIXED BIN (15, 0), R FIXED DEC (7, 5);
. . .
R = .5* (A + B/C);
```

The assignment statement in this code is executed as follows:

(a) B/C is computed as FIXED BINARY (31, 16).

(b) A + B/C is computed as FIXED BINARY (31, 16). The precision of the expression would be (32, 16), but 32 exceeds the maximum of 31. A FIXEDOVERFLOW error might occur when the addition is performed.

(c) The fixed-decimal constant .5, whose precision is (1, 1), is converted to binary with precision (5, 4).

(d) .5*(A + B/C) is computed as FIXED BINARY (31, 20). The precision would be (37, 20), but 37 exceeds the maximum. A FIXEDOVERFLOW error might occur when the multiplication is performed.

(e) Finally, the value of .5*(A + B/C) is converted to FIXED DECIMAL (7, 5) for assignment to R. A SIZE error would occur if the result were larger than 99. 99999, which is the largest value that R can have.

2.14. EXPRESSION EVALUATION:
PRECISION OF A FLOATING-POINT EXPRESSION

In principle, the rules for determining the precision attribute of a floating-point expression should be just as complicated as those for a fixed-point expression. In practice, the floating-point rules are much simpler than the fixed-point ones. As we explained in Section 2.6, a PL/I implementation is not likely to provide floating-point arithmetic in more than one base and two precisions, and so there are normally only two kinds of floating-point data. Therefore, the possibilities for the precision attribute of a floating-point expression can be thought of as limited to only two alternatives for practical purposes. In order to make the explanations in this section as simple as possible, we shall call the two types of floating-point data *single precision* and *double precision*.[10]

Consider the arithmetic expression A (op) B, where (op) can be +, −, *, /, or **; and suppose that this expression has a floating-point value by the rules explained in Section 2.12. The precision of the expression can be determined from the following rules:

(1) If both A and B are floating and if one of them, say A, is double precision, then the calculation is performed in double precision and the result is double precision; if B is not double, it is converted to double by affixing zeros. If both A and B are single precision, then the calculation is performed in single precision, and the result is single precision.

(2) If either A or B is fixed, it may have to be converted to floating (see

_____

[10]Strictly speaking, this terminology is foreign to PL/I, but it accurately describes how the language is actually implemented in the F-level PL/I compiler for the IBM System/360. As we explained in Section 2.6, in PL/I implementations for the IBM System/360, a variable is single precision if it is declared FLOAT DEC (6) or FLOAT BIN (21) and is double precision if it is declared FLOAT DEC (16) or FLOAT BIN (53).

Section 2.11). Suppose that B is fixed and has to be converted to floating. The conversion is to double precision[11] if either (a) A is double-precision floating, or (b) B is FIXED DEC (p, q), where $p > 6$, or FIXED BIN (p, q), where $p > 21$. Otherwise, the conversion is to single precision. After both A and B are expressed in floating-point form, then rule (1) given above determines the precision of the expression A (op) B.

When an expression is evaluated, subexpressions are themselves evaluated as if they were separate entities. Thus, a complicated expression might have a floating-point value but contain a subexpression with a fixed-point value; the subexpression would be evaluated in fixed-point arithmetic in such a case.

Example: Consider the following code:

```
DCL (X, Y, Z) FLOAT DEC (6);
. . .
Z = X*Y+X**(1/3);
```

When this code is executed, the quotient 1/3 is FIXED DECIMAL (15, 14). Since X is floating, this quotient must be converted to floating; it is converted to double precision because $15 > 6$. Then X is converted to double precision itself, because its exponent is now double precision, and the expression X**(1/3) is then computed in double-precision floating-point. The product X*Y is formed in single precision, and this result is then converted to double precision (by affixing zeros) for addition to X**(1/3). Thus, X*Y + X**(1/3) is obtained in double precision. It is truncated to single precision for assignment to Z.

It may be noted that, when fixed-point data is converted to floating, the accuracy of the conversion depends on the precision of the converted result and not on the precision of the fixed-point data itself. Thus, for the expression X + .1, where X is double-precision floating-point, when the constant .1 is converted to double-precision, the converted result is accurate to full double precision.[12] Likewise, if we have the assignment statement X = .1, where X is double precision, the conversion of .1 to double precision is accurate to full double precision.

When a built-in function is used in an expression, the precision of the function value depends on what the function is and on the argument used. For SQRT and the various transcendental functions, such as LOG, SIN, and COSH,

---

[11]This rule holds for PL/I implementations for the IBM System/360.

[12]This may be implementation dependent. It is true, at any rate, in the F-level PL/I implementation for the IBM System/360.

the argument is converted to floating-point automatically, if it is not floating to start with. The function value is single precision if the (converted) argument is single precision and is double precision if the argument is double precision.

For many (and perhaps most) applications, programmers are not particularly concerned about the precision of floating-point operations; calculations may be nominally in single precision, but there is no harm done if some double precision is used unintentionally. If a programmer wants to be sure that he uses nothing but single precision in his floating-point calculations, then he should be careful not to declare floating-point variables with precisions larger than six decimal digits and not to use constants containing more than six decimal digits in floating-point expressions. If, on the other hand, a programmer wants double precision exclusively, he should declare all his floating-point variables with the decimal precision attribute (16). With only a few possible exceptions (notably those involving exponentiation), fixed-point data in a floating-point expression will be "attracted" to double precision by context.

2.15. BUILT-IN FUNCTIONS FOR CONTROLLING THE ATTRIBUTES OF EXPRESSIONS

PL/I has a number of built-in functions that the programmer can use to exert explicit control over the attributes of expressions, both fixed-point and floating-point ones. We shall describe in this section some of these functions and their main uses.

(1) DECIMAL (abbr.: DEC) and BINARY (abbr.: BIN) can be used to control base conversions. Thus, if N is fixed-binary, then the value of DEC(N, p, q) is the result of converting N to fixed-decimal with the target precision (p, q). The BINARY function has an analogous interpretation.

(2) FIXED and FLOAT can be used to control scale conversions. Thus, if X is floating-point, then the value of FIXED(X, p, q) is the result of converting X to fixed-point with target precision (p, q). Similarly, if N is fixed-point, then the value of FLOAT(N, p) is the result of converting N to floating-point with the target precision (p).

(3) PRECISION (abbr.: PREC) can be used to adjust the precision of a data value. Thus, if N is fixed-point, then the value of PREC(N, p, q) is the result of adjusting the precision of N to (p, q). Similarly, if X is floating-point, then the value of PREC(X, p) is the result of adjusting the precision of X to (p).

(4) MULTIPLY can be used to form a product with a specified precision. Thus, if M and N are fixed-point, the value of MULTIPLY(M, N, p, q) is the product M*N expressed in precision (p, q). Similarly, if X and Y are floating-point, the value of MULTIPLY(X, Y, p) is the product X*Y expressed in precision (p). The new precision is maintained throughout execution of the function.

In addition to the functions just described, there are also the functions DIVIDE and ADD, which are analogous to MULTIPLY, and the functions REAL and COMPLEX (abbr.: CPLX) for controlling mode conversions.

Many of these functions have short forms. For example, FIXED(X, p) is a short form equivalent to FIXED(X, p, 0). Likewise, DEC(N) is a short form equivalent to DEC(N, r, s), where r and s are determined by rule (2b) of Section 2.13. The reader can consult his PL/I reference manual for more information on these short forms.

A general principle concerning all these functions is that attributes of the data involved are not changed unless they have to be. For example, if N is fixed-point and complex, then the value of DEC(N, p, q) is also fixed-point complex. Another general principle is that the precision specified in the arguments of a function is a decimal precision if the function value is decimal and a binary precision if the value is binary. For example, for the function PREC(N, p, q) the arguments p and q specify a decimal precision if N is decimal and a binary precision if N is binary.

Example:

```
DCL (X, Y) FLOAT DEC (6), Z FLOAT DEC (16);
...
Z = Z + X*Y;
```

Here the expression X*Y would be evaluated in single precision, and the product would be converted to double precision (by affixing zeros) for addition to Z. If the assignment statement were changed to

```
Z = Z + MULTIPLY(X, Y, 16);
```

then X and Y would be converted to double precision, and the product X*Y would be formed in double precision.[13] Likewise, if the statement were changed to

```
Z = Z + X*PREC(Y, 16);
```

---

[13]This use of MULTIPLY is convenient, for example, when it is necessary to compute a double-precision inner product of single-precision vectors.

then Y would be converted to double precision; X would be attracted to double precision by context; the multiplication would again be in double precision; and the product would be a double-precision value.

The programmer can cause a SIZE error during program execution by specifying too small a precision when he uses certain of the built-in functions described in this section. The precision specified among the function arguments must be sufficient to allow the function value to be represented without loss of significant digits (that is, digits on the left of the result). Thus, MULTIPLY (7, 5, 1, 0) would cause a SIZE error because the product 35 cannot be represented with precision (1, 0). Such an error is not detected automatically but can be detected by programming (see Section 11. 4).

2.16. FIXED-POINT PITFALLS

The fixed-point precision rules (Section 2.13) are often a source of difficulty to new PL/I programmers. The effects of these rules have to be studied carefully and cannot be ignored. A simple example will illustrate this point.

Example:

```
DCL M FIXED DEC (10, 5), N FIXED BIN (15);
N = 0;
M = N + .1;
```

By the rules of Sections 2.12 and 2.13, the decimal constant .1 is converted to binary with the precision (5, 4). Since the binary representation of .1 is .0001100110011..., the result of this conversion is 0. 0001B, which equals $\frac{1}{16}$ rather than $\frac{1}{10}$. Therefore, the value assigned to M by this code is $\frac{1}{16}$. (In decimal form this would be .0625, of course.)

Problems like this usually are associated with base conversions and can often be avoided by avoiding base conversions—in other words, by using only one number base in each fixed-point calculation. Use of the built-in functions described in the preceding section can also be helpful, because they allow explicit control of conversions and precisions. Thus, if the last statement in the preceding example were changed to the following, the value computed for M would be correct:

$$M = DEC(N) + .1 ;$$

Fixed-point expressions involving division are also sometimes sources of difficulty, and such expressions deserve close examination. A fixed-point quotient in PL/I always has maximum precision. *There is therefore more chance of a* FIXEDOVERFLOW *error in an expression that involves a fixed-point quotient than in one that does not.* Use of the DIVIDE function to control the precision of a quotient is often a convenient solution to this problem. Another solution is to assign the value of a fixed-point quotient to another variable temporarily.

Example:

```
DCL A FIXED DEC (8, 5), (B, C, D) FIXED DEC (2);
...
A = B + C/D;
```

In the last statement the quotient C/D has precision (15, 13). The expression B + C/D would have precision (16, 13). Since 16 exceeds the maximum, however, the precision is actually (15, 13). Consequently FIXEDOVERFLOW error is possible when the addition is performed. (For example, it would occur if B = 75, C = 50, and D = 2.) There would be no possibility of overflow if the last statement were changed to the following:

```
A = B + DIVIDE(C, D, 7, 5);
```

Alternatively, the code could be changed to the following:

```
DCL A FIXED DEC (8, 5), (B, C, D) FIXED DEC (2),
      TEMP FIXED DEC (7,5);
...
TEMP = C/D;
A = B + TEMP;
```

2.17. COMPLEX ARITHMETIC

Some specific points about complex arithmetic are briefly summarized below. We shall give an illustration of the use of complex arithmetic in Section 4.6.

(1) If A is real and B is complex, the statement

```
A = B;
```

assigns the real part of B to A. Similarly, if A is complex and B is real, the same statement assigns B to the real part of A and makes the imaginary part of A equal to zero.

(2) It is impossible to slip accidentally from real into complex arithmetic,

because no calculation can produce a complex result unless a complex data element is involved in the calculation. Thus, trying to evaluate $(-1)**.5$, which contains no complex data, merely produces an error condition, whereas evaluating $(-1 + 0I)**.5$ produces the complex result $0 + 1I$.

(3) There are several built-in functions that facilitate work with complex arithmetic: REAL and IMAG, which extract the real and imaginary parts of a complex number; COMPLEX (abbr.: CPLX), which constructs a complex number from its real and imaginary parts; and CONJG, which forms the complex conjugate of a complex number.

(4) The built-in functions COMPLEX, REAL, and IMAG are also pseudo-variables, which means that they can appear on the left side of assignment statements. (A handful of built-in functions can be used as pseudovariables; we shall encounter some others later.)

Example:

```
DCL A CPLX FLOAT DEC (6) INIT (0);
IMAG(A) = 1;
```

This causes the imaginary part of A to be assigned the value one, without a change in the real part of A.

(5) A complex constant like $2 + 3I$ can be specified by means of the INITIAL attribute as an initial value for a complex variable, even though $2 + 3I$ is not a pure constant, strictly speaking, and is actually considered to be an expression. Expressions are not ordinarily allowed in INITIAL attributes.

(6) Programmers writing expressions involving complex arithmetic must resist the temptation to write the symbol I for $\sqrt{-1}$ instead of $1I$. Thus, for $\cos z + i \sin z$, the expression COS(Z) + 1I*SIN(Z) would be correct, whereas COS(Z) + I*SIN(Z) would not, unless I happened to be a complex variable with the value $1I$.

2.18. PL/I AND FORTRAN

The following remarks are intended for FORTRAN programmers who want to draw analogies between PL/I and FORTRAN. Sections similar to this one will also be included at the end of later chapters.

(1) The terms for various language elements differ in PL/I and FORTRAN.

For example, names of variables are usually called *labels* in FORTRAN but are called *identifiers* in PL/I. In PL/I labels are the names of statements. FORTRAN programmers learning PL/I are advised to adapt themselves to the new terminology quickly, for otherwise they will not be able to use a PL/I reference manual properly.

(2) The I–N default rule (Section 2.3) for the naming of fixed-point and floating-point variables in PL/I is analogous to the FORTRAN rule for naming integer and floating-point variables. It should be remembered however, that PL/I fixed-point arithmetic is not like FORTRAN integer arithmetic.

(3) The PL/I DECLARE statement fulfills the functions of the FORTRAN-type declaration statements like REAL and COMPLEX. There is no counterpart in PL/I, however, to the FORTRAN IMPLICIT statement.

(4) There are several differences between constants in PL/I and FORTRAN. Some notable illustrations are these: (a) A constant like 3.14 is fixed in PL/I but floating in FORTRAN. (b) There are no D-type exponents in PL/I such as that in the FORTRAN double-precision floating constant 3.14D0. (c) There are no octal or hexadecimal constants in PL/I.

(5) The PL/I INITIAL attribute is analogous to the FORTRAN DATA statement. Unlike a FORTRAN variable, however, a PL/I variable can be re-initialized (for example, on successive entries to a subprogram). This distinction is not of critical importance in simple applications of the INITIAL attribute; we shall explain it further in Chapter 8.

(6) The PL/I DEFINED attribute is analogous to the FORTRAN EQUIVALENCE statement. A PL/I DEFINED variable and its base variable must, however, have the same attributes (see also Sections 10.1 and 10.4).

(7) Certain arithmetic expressions are valid in PL/I that are invalid in FORTRAN, such as K**A, where K is real fixed and A is complex floating.

(8) Certain difficulties in PL/I arising from mixing attributes in arithmetic expressions have no counterparts in FORTRAN. For example, problems resulting from the mixing of binary and decimal data cannot arise in FORTRAN.

(9) Many PL/I built-in functions are analogous to FORTRAN built-in functions. For example, the PL/I FIXED, FLOAT, and PREC functions have counterparts in the FORTRAN IFIX, FLOAT, DFLOAT, SNGL, and DBLE functions.

(10) Constants converted to double precision in PL/I because of their context are sometimes converted more accurately than they would be in analogous situations in FORTRAN. Thus, in the expression $X + .1$, where X is double precision, the constant would be converted accurately to double precision in PL/I. To get an accurate conversion in FORTRAN it would be necessary to write $X + .1D0$.

(11) When a FORTRAN integer is converted to floating because of its context, it is never converted to anything but single precision. In PL/I the conversion of fixed-point data to floating can also be to double precision.

EXERCISES

1. Suppose that variables A, B, C, D, and E are declared as follows:

DCL A FIXED, B BIN, (C, D) FLOAT (16), E CPLX (16);

What are the mode, scale, base, and precision attributes of these variables?

2. State the mode, scale, base, and precision attributes for each of the following constants:

(a) .0001B   (b) 2.718
(c) .2718E-1   (d) 47
(e) 1I   (f) 376E0I

3. Which of the following DECLARE statements are invalid?

(a) DCL A, B DEF A;
(b) DCL B DEF A;
(c) DCL A FLOAT DEC (6), B FLOAT BIN (21) DEF A;
(d) DCL A INIT (5), B DEF A;
(e) DCL A FIXED, B FIXED DEF A INIT (5);

4. Suppose that variables A, B, and C are declared as follows:

DCL (A, B) FIXED DEC (10), C FIXED BIN (15);

State the mode, scale, base, and precision attributes of the expressions listed below, and identify those expressions in which a FIXEDOVERFLOW or SIZE error is possible.

(a) A + 5   (b) C + 5
(c) DEC (C, 5) + 5   (d) A*B + 5
(e) MULTIPLY (A, B, 10, 0) + 5   (f) A/B + B
(g) DIVIDE (A, B, 10, 0) + B

5. Suppose that variables A, B, and C are declared as follows:

$$\text{DCL (A, B) FLOAT DEC (6), C FLOAT DEC (16);}$$

State which of the following expressions are single precision and which are double precision.

(a) A*B   (b) A + C
(c) A**(1/4)   (d) A**(.25)
(e) C + 5   (f) A + 1/5
(g) A + DIVIDE (1, 5, 5, 5)   (h) A + PREC(C, 6)/B

6. Suppose that N is FIXED DEC (5). What is the value of the expression

$$N - 2*(N/2)$$

for (a) even values of N, and (b) odd values of N?

3 GO TO AND IF STATEMENTS

3.1. GO TO STATEMENT; LABEL VARIABLES

The GO TO statement causes a branch (transfer or jump) in the sequence of program steps. The general form of the statement is

GO TO label;

In the simplest cases the label is a statement label that appears somewhere in the program, but it can be a *label variable*. A label variable is a nonarithmetic variable specified to have the LABEL attribute in a DECLARE statement. It can be assigned statement-label values and thus used to construct program switches.

Example:

```
        DCL X LABEL;
        . . .
        X = L2;
L1:     R = T/2;
        GO TO X;
        . . .
L2:     X = L3;
        GO TO L1;
L3:
```

When the label variable X has the value L2, the statement GO TO X is equivalent to GO TO L2 and thus causes a branch to the statement labelled L2.

33

Similarly, when X has the value L3, the statement GO TO X causes a branch to L3.

A label variable can be initialized by use of the INITIAL attribute. Thus, in the preceding example we could have initialized X to the value L2 by writing the DECLARE statement as follows:

DCL X LABEL INIT (L2);

In PL/I, labels are a type of *program control data*. (Arithmetic data, by contrast, is a type of *problem data*.) The constants associated with this type of data are called *statement label constants*, and these are merely the statement labels that can be used in PL/I programs. The associated variables are the label variables described in this section.

3.2. IF STATEMENTS

Tests for various conditions can be made with the IF statement, which has the basic form

IF conditional expression THEN statement;

The statement in the THEN clause specifies action to be taken if the condition tested is true.

Examples:

IF A < B THEN P = Q + R;

IF K ¬ = L THEN GO TO X;

IF P + 2 > = Q + R THEN RETURN;

IF K = 5 THEN PUT DATA (X);

Simple conditional expressions like those in this example can be formed by separating two arithmetic expressions by one of the following comparison operators:

Comparison Operator	Meaning
=	is equal to
<	is less than
>	is greater than
< =	is less than or equal to
> =	is greater than or equal to
¬ =	is not equal to
¬ <	is not less than
¬ >	is not greater than

In Sections 3.4 and 3.5 we shall explain how to form more complex IF statements by using compound conditional expressions and by specifying more than one action statement in the THEN clause.

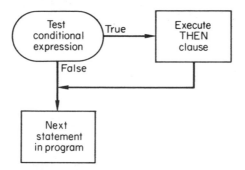

Figure 1. Flowchart of IF statement. Control would not necessarily pass to the next statement (as is shown) if the THEN clause contained a GO TO leading in some other direction.

If two arithmetic expressions having different attributes are used together in a comparison, automatic data conversions are performed just as they are when an expression involving mixed attributes is evaluated. Thus, for a test of the condition $A < B$, where A is binary and B is decimal, B would be converted to binary.

Because of the effect of rounding errors, a test made in an IF statement may be satisfied in practice when it is not satisfied mathematically. For example, the condition $A/B = 1$ should be true if and only if $A = B$. In practice, the machine-computed quotient would not generally be the same as the true quotient. For a particular value of A there might be several values of B for which the machine-computed quotient would equal one, and so the condition might be satisfied even though A and B were unequal.

3.3. ELSE CLAUSES

An ELSE clause can be used with an IF statement. The ELSE clause is put in a separate statement, as shown below:

IF conditional expression THEN statement;

ELSE statement;

The statement in the ELSE clause specifies action to be taken if the condition tested in the IF statement is false.

Examples:

IF A $>$ B THEN A $= 0$;
ELSE A $= 1$;
IF K $\neg= $ L $+$ N THEN J $=$ K/L;
ELSE J $=$ L/K;

In Section 3.5 we shall explain how more than one action statement can be included in an ELSE clause.

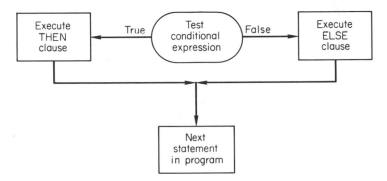

Figure 2. Flowchart of IF statement with an ELSE clause. Control would not necessarily pass to the next statement (as is shown) if either the THEN clause or the ELSE clause contained a GO TO statement leading in some other direction.

IF statements, together with their associated ELSE clauses, can be nested. In a sequence of nested IF statements, ELSE clauses pair off with IF statements just as right parentheses pair off with left parentheses in arithmetic expressions.

Example: Suppose that we want to compute y, where y is defined piecewise by the following relations:

$$\begin{aligned} y &= ax + b & \text{for } x \leq 1 \\ &= cx + d & \text{for } 1 < x \leq 2 \\ &= ex + f & \text{for } 2 < x \leq 3 \\ &= gx + h & \text{for } x > 3 \end{aligned}$$

The code might be as follows:

IF X $<=$ 1 THEN Y $=$ A$*$X $+$ B;
ELSE IF X $<=$ 2 THEN Y $=$ C$*$X $+$ D;
    ELSE IF X $<=$ 3 THEN Y $=$ E$*$X $+$ F;
        ELSE Y $=$ G$*$X $+$ H;

Successive lines of code are indented to show the ELSE clauses pair off with their respective IF statements.

Ordinarily one has the choice of whether or not to use an ELSE clause after an IF statement, but it is possible to have a situation in which an ELSE clause is essential. It may even be necessary to use in a program a null ELSE clause, that is, one of the form

> ELSE;

Example: Consider the code

> IF A > B THEN IF C < D THEN P = Q;
> ELSE P = R;

The ELSE clause belongs to the immediately preceding IF (the one beginning IF C < D); the outer IF has no associated ELSE clause. Therefore, no action results from this code unless A > B. If A > B, then P is set equal to Q if C < D and is set equal to R otherwise. The need for a null ELSE clause would arise if the ELSE clause in the code were supposed to belong to the outer IF. In such a case, the code could be written as follows:

> IF A > B THEN IF C < D THEN P = Q;
> ELSE;
> ELSE P = R;

Of course, the action resulting from this code would be different from the action resulting from the original code.

3.4. CONDITIONAL EXPRESSIONS

The conditional expressions permitted in IF statements can be more complex than the simple ones used as illustrations in Sections 3.2 and 3.3. As was explained in Section 3.2, simple conditional expressions are formed by joining two arithmetic expressions with one of the eight conditional operators listed in that section. Three logical operators analogous to operators in Boolean algebra can be used to combine simple conditional expressions and form compound conditional expressions. The logical operators are

> ¬ not
>
> & and
>
> | or

Examples:

$$\text{IF } (A + 1 < B) \And (C = D + E) \text{ THEN } P = Q;$$
$$\text{IF } ((K = 5) \mid (K = 6)) \And (L = J + 1) \text{ THEN } P = Q;$$
$$\text{IF } (K < 25) \And \lnot (L = 15) \text{ THEN } P = Q;$$
$$\text{IF } \lnot (K = 5) \text{ THEN } P = Q;$$

By inserting parentheses, one can always specify unambiguously the order in which logical operations are performed in a conditional expression. If the order of logical operations is not specified by parentheses, then the logical operators are applied in the order in which they are listed above. We shall discuss in Section 9.18 the priority rules that determine the order of operations in an unparenthesized expression containing logical and arithmetic operators. In the meantime, it is recommended that arithmetic expressions used in a conditional expression be enclosed in parentheses, as those were in the example above. This is probably a good practice to follow in any case, since it is clear and helps to prevent misunderstandings.

PL/I does not allow compound subjects or predicates, and the programmer must resist the temptation to use them when writing IF statements. For example, for testing whether or not A is less than either B or C, the proper conditional expression is $(A < B) \mid (A < C)$, and not $A < B \mid C$. Similarly, for testing whether or not $A = B = C$, the proper expression is $(A = B) \And (A = C)$, and not $A = B = C$. The expressions $A < B \mid C$ and $A = B = C$ actually do have meanings in PL/I, as we shall explain in Chapter 9, but these meanings are not relevant to the tests just mentioned.

Strictly speaking, conditional expressions in IF statements are expressions with bit-string values, and the three logical operators are bit-string operators. It is usually unnecessary for the programmer to be aware of this, however, in order to use IF statements correctly. We shall discuss this point in more detail in Section 9.15.

3.5. DO GROUPS IN THEN AND ELSE CLAUSES

The action specified in a THEN or ELSE clause can be more than just a single statement. For either type of clause the action can consist of several statements made into a DO group. This means that the action statements must be bracketed by the two statements

$$\text{DO};$$

and

$$\text{END};$$

(This DO statement is actually a degenerate form of the loop-control statement that we shall discuss in Chapter 4.)

Example:

```
IF A > B + C THEN DO; P = Q; X = Y + Z; END;
ELSE DO; P = R; X = Y − Z; END;
```

When a long DO group is used, one can enhance the clarity of the program by attaching a label to the DO statement and naming the label in the END statement, to show that the END statement matches with the DO. Although it is not particularly important when DO groups are short, this technique has much to recommend it generally. PL/I programs often contain very many END statements, and it is not always easy to know what to match them with.

Example:

```
        IF A > B + C THEN
L1 : DO;
        P = Q;
        X = Y + Z;
        END L1;
        ELSE
L2 : DO;
        P = R;
        X = Y − Z;
        END L2;
```

3.6. EXAMPLE

The code given below is a complete program for finding the root of the equation

$$\exp(-x) - x = 0$$

by means of the Newton-Raphson iteration method. The method consists of computing numbers in the sequence $x_0, x_1, x_2, x_3, \ldots$ defined by the relations

$$x_0 = 1$$
$$x_k = x_{k-1} + \delta_k \qquad \text{for } k = 1, 2, 3, \ldots$$

where

$$\delta_k = (\exp(-x_k) - x_k)/(\exp(-x_k) + 1)$$

The iteration continues so long as $k \leq 20$ and $10^{-6} \leq |\delta_k| < |\delta_{k-1}|$. In this code, EXP and ABS are the built-in exponential and absolute-value functions, respectively.

```
/* FIND ROOT OF EXP(− X) − X = 0 BY NEWTON − RAPHSON METHOD */
GO : PROC OPTIONS (MAIN);
        DCL EPSILON INIT (1E−6);
        X, K = 1;
        OLD__DELTA = 1E10;
LP : DELTA = (EXP (− X) − X)/(EXP (− X) + 1);
        X = X + DELTA;
        PUT SKIP DATA (K, X);
        IF (K < = 20) & (ABS (DELTA) ¬< EPSILON) & (ABS (DELTA) <
            ABS (OLD__DELTA)) THEN DO;
                    OLD__DELTA = DELTA;
                    K = K + 1;
                    GO TO LP;
                    END;
        RETURN;
        END GO;
```

3.7. PL/I AND FORTRAN

The following remarks are intended for FORTRAN programmers who want to draw analogies between PL/I and FORTRAN.

(1) The use in PL/I of a GO TO with a label variable as its object (such as was illustrated in Section 3.1) is analogous to the use of an assigned GO TO statement in FORTRAN.

(2) There is no computed GO TO statement in PL/I like that in FORTRAN. An analogous result can be obtained, however, by use of a GO TO with a subscripted label variable (Section 5.2) as its target, such as

```
GO TO LBL(K);
```

(3) There is nothing in PL/I like the FORTRAN arithmetic IF statement.

(4) The IF statement in PL/I is analogous to the logical IF in FORTRAN. FORTRAN, however, has no ELSE clause. Also, FORTRAN allows only one action statement after an IF, whereas PL/I allows an arbitrary number organized in a DO group.

EXERCISES

1. What are the values of A and B after the following code is executed?

```
DCL A FIXED BIN (15) INIT (0);
B = 0;
IF A = B THEN GO TO LBL;
    B = 1;
LBL: A = 2;
```

2. What are the values of P and Q after the following code is executed?

```
I, J = 1;
P, Q, K = 2;
IF I ¬ < K THEN DO; P = 0; Q = 1; END;
ELSE IF ¬ (J > K) THEN P, Q = 2;
ELSE Q = 4;
```

3. What is the value of C after the following code is executed?

```
DCL B INIT (0);
A = 1;
IF A = 0 THEN IF B = 0 THEN C = 0;
ELSE DO; C = 1; GO TO LBL; END;
C = 2;
LBL:
```

4. Suppose that the value to be assigned to C depends on the signs of A and B, as shown in the table below. Write code to assign the correct value to C for any combination of values of A and B.

	$A = 0$	$A > 0$	$A < 0$
$B = 0$	$C = 1$	$C = 2$	$C = 3$
$B > 0$	$C = 2$	$C = 1$	$C = 5$
$B < 0$	$C = 4$	$C = 6$	$C = 1$

5. Rewrite the following code so that the value assigned to X is the same as before and there are no nested IF's.

```
IF A > 0 THEN IF B > 0 THEN IF C > 0 THEN X = 4;
ELSE X = 5;
ELSE X = 1;
ELSE X = −1;
```

4 DO LOOPS

4.1. DO STATEMENTS

The loop-control statement in PL/I is the DO statement, which has several forms. Simple loops can often be controlled by a DO of the form

$$DO \text{ variable} = e_1 \text{ TO } e_2;$$

where e_1 and e_2 denote arbitrary arithmetic expressions. The "variable" (usually called the *control variable*) is an arithmetic variable with arbitrary attributes (for example, fixed or floating).

Examples:

```
DO K = 0 TO N;
DO I = −1 TO 5;
DO K = 2*L TO N + 1;
DO X = .5 TO 12.5;
```

The DO statement controlling a loop goes at the beginning of the loop, and a matching END statement goes at the end of the loop. Just before the start of execution of the loop, the control variable is set equal to e_1. After each time through the loop, the control variable is incremented by one. A test of the value of the control variable is made each time through (at the "top" of the loop). If the programmer does not stop the loop early by branching out of it, then execution of the loop terminates when the test shows that the control variable has become larger than e_2.

A more general from of the DO statement is

$$\text{DO variable} = e_1 \text{ TO } e_2 \text{ BY } e_3;$$

With this type of DO statement, the control variable is incremented (in the algebraic sense) by e_3 after each time through the loop. A test of the value of the control variable is made each time through (at the top of the loop). Execution of the loop terminates (1) when the control variable becomes larger than e_2, if $e_3 \geq 0$, or (2) when the control variable becomes smaller than e_2, if $e_3 < 0$.

Examples:

$$\text{DO K} = 1 \text{ TO } 99 \text{ BY } 2;$$
$$\text{DO K} = 25 \text{ TO } -1 \text{ BY } -1;$$
$$\text{DO X} = 1 \text{ TO } 2 \text{ BY } .01;$$

Note that because the test of the control variable occurs at the top of the loop for each of the two types of DO loops described above, the statements in a loop could be skipped over completely without being executed even once. Thus, any statements in the range of the DO statement

$$\text{DO K} = 1 \text{ TO } 0;$$

would be skipped.

Still another form of the DO statement is

$$\text{DO variable} = e_1, e_2, \ldots, e_n;$$

In this case the control variable takes on successively the values $e_1, e_2, \ldots, e_n$.

Examples:

$$\text{DO K} = 1, 5;$$
$$\text{DO K} = 1, 3, 6, 2.5, -4;$$
$$\text{DO U} = \text{X, Y, Z} + 1, 3.14;$$

The three ways mentioned above for specifying values of the control variable in a DO loop, namely (1) a TO phrase, (2) a TO ... BY phrase, and (3) a list of values, can be used repeatedly and in any combination in a single DO statement.

Example:

$$\text{DO K} = 1 \text{ TO } 4, 6 \text{ TO } 8, 11, 9, 12 \text{ TO } 18 \text{ BY } 2;$$

This statement causes the control variable K to take on the values 1, 2, 3, 4, 6, 7, 8, 11, 9, 12, 14, 16, and 18.

When a DO loop contains a large number of statements, it is a good practice for the programmer to label the DO statement and include that label in the END statement that matches the DO. This helps to avoid confusion for anyone studying the program by making it clear what statement the END is supposed to match up with.

4.2. ADDITIONAL RULES CONCERNING DO LOOPS

In this section we summarize briefly some additional facts and rules about DO loops.

(1) Branching (by means of a GO TO) into the range of a DO loop from outside of it is not permitted. On the other hand, branching from a point inside the loop to another point inside the loop or to a point outside of it is permitted.

(2) The control variable of a DO loop can be used in statements inside or outside the loop. If the loop is terminated early by branching out of it, then the value of the control variable after the exit from the loop is its value at the time of exit.

(3) Program control must reach the END statement of a DO loop each time through the loop. If some statements inside the loop are to be branched over by means of a GO TO, then in order to meet this requirement it may be necessary to label the END statement and use that label as the target of the GO TO.

Example: The following code computes

$$\sum_{\substack{k=1 \\ k \neq 5}}^{n} k^2$$

```
        SUM = 0;
L1 :    DO K = 1 TO N;
        IF K = 5 THEN GO TO L2;
        SUM = SUM + K**2;
L2 :    END L1;
```

(4) Expressions (like e_1 and e_2 in the preceding section) defining values of the control variable in a DO statement are evaluated just before execution of the loop begins and are not reevaluated while the loop is

being executed. Therefore, calculations during execution of the loop that alter the values of those expressions do not affect the number of times the loop is repeated. The value of the control variable itself, however, can be altered by an assignment statement inside the loop, and doing this could affect the number of times the loop would be repeated.

(5) When DO loops are nested, one END statement can sometimes be used to close more than one loop. The rule is that, if an outer DO statement is labeled, then every unclosed inner DO is automatically closed when an END statement containing that label is encountered. This is called *multiple closure*.

Example: The following code computes

$$\sum_{i=1}^{n} \sum_{j=i}^{n} ij$$

```
        SUM = 0;
LB:  DO I = 1 TO N;
        DO J = I TO N;
        SUM = SUM + I*J;
        END LB;
```

(6) Specifying control-variable values that cannot be calculated exactly in computer arithmetic can sometimes lead to unexpected results because of the accumulation of rounding errors. For example, the loop

```
        DCL X FLOAT;
        DO X = 1 TO 2 BY .0005;
        END;
```

is executed 2002 times (rather than the expected number 2001) in PL/I implementations for the IBM System/360. The problem is that the increment actually used is not .0005 exactly, but some slightly smaller floating-point approximation to that value, say $.0005(1 - \varepsilon)$. After 2001 times through the loop, the control variable is not equal to 2 exactly but instead to $2 + (.0005 - 2001\varepsilon)$, which turns out to be still less than 2, so the loop is cycled one extra time. This difficulty is inherent in the use of computer arithmetic and is not peculiar to PL/I. The simplest way to avoid it is to use only control variables whose values can be computed exactly in computer arithmetic, such as fixed-point integers.

(7) Another valid form of DO statement is the following:

$$\text{DO variable} = e_1 \text{ BY } e_2;$$

This merely causes the control variable to be initialized to e_1 and then to be incremented indefinitely by e_2 each time through the loop. There is no test on the value of the control variable.

(8) A DO loop defined by a DO statement of the following form will terminate when the control variable exceeds e_2:

$$\text{DO variable} = e_1 \text{ TO } e_2;$$

If the loop is not terminated early by branching out of it, then the value of the control variable after termination of the loop is its first value that exceeds e_2. An analogous rule holds when the DO statement has the form

$$\text{DO variable} = e_1 \text{ TO } e_2 \text{ BY } e_3;$$

4.3. EXAMPLE

The code given below is another complete program for finding the real root of the equation

$$\exp(-x) - x = 0$$

The algorithm is the same one that was used in the related example in Section 3.6, but a DO loop is now used to control the iteration. EXP and ABS are the built-in exponential and absolute-value functions, respectively.

```
/*   FIND ROOT OF EXP(− X) − X = 0 BY NEWTON−RAPHSON METHOD */
GO : PROC OPTIONS (MAIN);
     DCL EPSILON INIT (1E−6);
     X = 1;
     OLD__DELTA = 1E10;
  A: DO K = 1 TO 20;
     DELTA = (EXP(− X) − X)/(EXP(− X) + 1);
     X = X + DELTA;
     IF (ABS(DELTA) < EPSILON) | (ABS(DELTA) >=
         ABS(OLD__DELTA)) THEN GO TO B;
     ELSE OLD__DELTA = DELTA;
     END A;
  B: PUT SKIP DATA (K, X);
     RETURN;
     END GO;
```

4.4. WHILE CLAUSES

Another form of the DO statement is the following:

DO WHILE (conditional expression);

The conditional expression in the WHILE clause is like a conditional expression in an IF statement. Just before each cycle through the loop, the condition is tested, with current values used for all the variables in the expression; repetition of the loop continues as long as the condition is true. The statements in the loop are skipped over completely if the condition is false the first time it is tested.

Example: The following code computes

$$\sum_{k=1}^{n} k$$

```
SUM = 0;.
K = 1;
DO WHILE (K <= N);
SUM = SUM + K;
K = K + 1;
END;
```

WHILE clauses can also be used in conjunction with control variable specifications. Thus, a DO statement can have the form

DO variable = e_1 TO e_2 WHILE (conditional expression);

The effect of this statement is to cause the loop to be performed with the control variable running from e_1 to e_2 so long as the condition is true. Repetition of the loop stops when either the control variable becomes larger than e_2 or when the condition ceases to be true.[1] The conditional expression is tested after the control variable has been incremented and tested. Therefore, if looping terminates because the conditional expression has become false, the value of the control variable is what it would have been on the next time through the loop.

Example:

```
DO K = 1 TO 25 WHILE (K < 15);
END;
```

Here the value of K is 15 when looping terminates.

---

[1] It is important to realize that this type of DO statement does *not* cause the loop to be repeated while *either* the control variable runs from e_1 to e_2 *or* the condition is true.

Some of the other valid types of DO statements involving WHILE clauses are illustrated in the next example.

Examples: The following are all valid DO statements:

```
DO WHILE (I < J & I = K);
DO K = 1 TO 15 BY 2 WHILE (X**2 > = Y);
DO K = 1 BY 1 WHILE (X > = Y);
DO K = 1 TO 5 WHILE (I < J), 6 TO 24 BY 2 WHILE (I < L);
```

An application of a DO statement with a WHILE clause is given in the next section.

4.5. EXAMPLE

The code given below is a complete program for finding a root of the equation

$$P(1 + x)^{n/12} [(1 + x)^{1/12} - 1] - R [(1 + x)^{n/12} - 1] = 0$$

by the method of bisection, where P, R, and n are given constants and x is the unknown. (The root sought is the effective annual interest rate for an automobile loan for which the principal is P, the monthly payment is R, and the number of monthly payments is n.) The method is an iterative one. On each iteration an interval (L, U) is bisected that is known to contain a sign change (and therefore a zero) of the function on the left side of the equation. A sign change is then found in one or the other of the two subintervals, and that subinterval becomes the interval (L, U) for the next iteration. The process terminates when $U - L \leq 10^{-6}$.

Note that some of the floating-point calculations are in double precision (see Section 2.14).

```
/* CALCULATE EFFECTIVE INTEREST RATE */
GO: PROC OPTIONS (MAIN);
     DCL (I, L, M) FLOAT, EPSILON INIT (1E—6);
     P = 1485.90; R = 130.00; N = 12;
     L = .05; U = .5;
     FL = P* ((1 + L) ** (N/12)) * ((1 + L) ** (1/12) — 1) — R*
          ((1 + L) ** (N/12) — 1);
     FU = P* ((1 + U) ** (N/12)) * ((1 + U) ** (1/12) — 1) — R*
```

```
               ((1 + U) ** (N/12) — 1);
   LP: DO WHILE ((U — L) > EPSILON);
        M = (L + U)/2;
        FM = P* ((1 + M) ** (N/12)) * ((1 + M) ** (1/12) — 1) — R*
             ((1 + M) ** (N/12) — 1);
        IF FM = 0 THEN GO TO FOUND;
        IF ((FL > 0) & (FM < 0)) | ((FL < 0) & (FM > 0)) THEN
             DO; U = M; FU = FM; END;
        ELSE DO; L = M; FL = FM; END;
        END LP;
FOUND: I = M;
        PUT SKIP DATA (I);
        RETURN;
        END GO;
```

4.6. COMPLEX-ARITHMETIC EXAMPLE

The code given below is a complete program for finding a complex root of the equation

$$z^z + ie^{iz} \ln z = 0$$

The method used is the Newton-Raphson iteration method, and the arithmetic is complex floating point.

The method consists of computing numbers in the sequence $z_0, z_1, z_2, z_3, \ldots$ defined by the relations

$$z_0 = .5 + .8i$$
$$z_k = z_{k-1} + \delta_k \qquad \text{for } k = 1, 2, 3, \ldots$$

where

$$\delta_k = - \frac{z^z + ie^{iz} \ln z}{z^z(1 + \ln z) + e^{iz}\left(\dfrac{i}{z} - \ln z\right)}$$

The value $.5 + .8i$ is used for a starting value because a root is known to lie near there. The iteration continues so long as $k \leq 20$ and $10^{-5} \leq |\delta_k| < |\delta_{k-1}|$.

In this code EXP and LOG are the built-in exponential and natural-logarithm functions, and ABS is the built-in absolute-value function. All three of these functions are used with complex arguments. EXP and LOG have complex values, and ABS has a real value.

```
/* FIND COMPLEX ROOT OF Z**Z + 1I*EXP (1I *Z)*LOG (Z) = 0. */
GO: PROC OPTIONS (MAIN);
    DCL ETA FLOAT (16) INIT (1E—15), (Z, DELTA, OLDDELTA) CPLX (16);
    Z = .5 + .8I;
    OLDDELTA = 1E10;
L1: DO K = 1 TO 20;
    DELTA = — (Z**Z + 1I*EXP(1I*Z)*LOG(Z))/(Z**Z* (1 + LOG(Z)) +
        EXP(1I*Z) * (1I/Z — LOG(Z)));
    Z = Z + DELTA;
    PUT SKIP DATA (K, Z);
    IF (ABS(DELTA) < ETA) | (ABS(DELTA) >= ABS(OLDDELTA))
        THEN GO TO L2;
    OLDDELTA = DELTA;
L2: RETURN;
    END GO;
```

4.7. PL/I AND FORTRAN

The following remarks are intended for FORTRAN programmers who want to draw analogies between PL/I and FORTRAN.

(1) The first two types of DO statements described in Section 4.1 are analogous to FORTRAN DO statements. The other PL/I DO statements, such as those involving WHILE clauses, have no counterparts in FORTRAN. It should be noted that the PL/I statement

$$DO K = 1, 5;$$

causes a loop to be executed twice, once with $K = 1$ and once with $K = 5$. A FORTRAN programmer might misconstrue the statement above, thinking it to have the effect of the PL/I statement

$$DO K = 1 TO 5;$$

(2) The use of an END statement to terminate a loop in PL/I is analogous to using a CONTINUE statement for the same purpose in FORTRAN. The use of an END is mandatory in PL/I, however, whereas a CONTINUE is not always necessary in FORTRAN.

(3) Arbitrary arithmetic expressions (including, for example, negative constants) are allowed in the specifications of limits for control variables in PL/I, whereas such specifications are severely restricted in FORTRAN.

(4) A "backward" DO (i. e., a DO with a negative increment of the control variable) is permitted in PL/I, whereas it is not in FORTRAN.

(5) Problems in PL/I involving the accumulation of rounding error in a control variable (see Section 4.2) cannot arise in FORTRAN, because a control variable in a FORTRAN DO must always be an integer.

(6) FORTRAN, in certain cases, allows branching out of and back into a DO loop, whereas PL/I never does.

(7) Unlike a FORTRAN DO loop, a PL/I DO loop may be executed zero times (in other words, it may be skipped). See Section 4.1.

EXERCISES

1. Write code to evaluate the continued fraction given below for $x = .5$.

$$\cfrac{x}{1 + \cfrac{x^2}{3 + \cfrac{x^2}{5 + \cfrac{x^2}{7 + \cfrac{x^2}{9 + \cfrac{x^2}{11 + \cfrac{x^2}{13 + \cfrac{x^2}{15}}}}}}}}$$

2. Assume $n \geq 1$. Write code to compute

$$\sum_{i=0}^{n-1} \sum_{j=i}^{n-1} (1 + ij)$$

3. Write code to compute

$$\sum_{\substack{k=1 \\ k \neq 9}}^{25} k^3$$

4. What is the value of K after the following code is executed?

```
T = 0;
DO K = 15 TO .1 BY −1;
T = T + K;
END;
```

5. Write code to find the least value of n such that

$$\sum_{k=1}^{n} k^5 < 2500$$

5 ARRAYS

5.1. ARRAY VARIABLES

An array variable can be declared in PL/I by specifiying a *dimension attribute* for the variable in a DECLARE statement. The dimension attribute gives the number of dimensions in the array and the bounds for each dimension.

Example:

DCL A(5), B(− 2 : 6), K(5, 0 : 12) FLOAT,
X(2 : 11, − 1 : 5, 6 : 15) FIXED BIN (31);

For each dimension of the array, the bounds of the dimension are expressed in the form (1) $p:q$, or (2) q. For the form (1), p and q must be signed or unsigned integers such that $p \le q$; in this case, the lower bound of the dimension is p, and the upper bound is q. The short form (2) is equivalent to $1:q$, so in this case q must be an integer such that $1 \le q$. The number of bounds specifications in the dimension attribute is the number of dimensions of the array.

Any particular element in an array can be referenced by means of subscript notation. Thus, the (3, 2) element in a two-dimensional array A would be A(3, 2). The subscripts must lie within the bounds specified for their respective dimensions.

Example: The statement

DCL A(15), B(2 : 11, − 1 : 5) FIXED DEC (12);

declares two array variables A and B. Array A has the dimension attribute (15) and is therefore one-dimensional. The Ith element in the array is $A(I)$, where I must satisfy $1 \leq I \leq 15$. Since only the dimension attribute is specified for A, its other attributes are determined by the default rules of Section 2.3, so the elements of A have the attributes REAL FLOAT DECIMAL (6). Array B has the dimension attribute $(2:11, -1:5)$ and is therefore two-dimensional. The (I, J) element of the array is $B(I, J)$, where I and J must satisfy the inequalities $2 \leq I \leq 11$ and $-1 \leq J \leq 5$. The elements of B have the attributes REAL FIXED DECIMAL (12).

The reader must distinguish between the terms *bounds* and *extent*, which are used in PL/I terminology to describe dimension attributes. In the specification $p:q$ of a dimension for an array, the integers p and q are the *bounds* of the dimension, and $q - p + 1$ is the *extent* of the dimension.

Example: A fifth-degree polynomial

$$P(x) = a_0 + a_1 x + a_2 x^2 + a_3 x^3 + a_4 x^4 + a_5 x^5$$

can be evaluated conveniently by expressing it in the form

$$P(x) = a_0 + x(a_1 + x(a_2 + x(a_3 + x(a_4 + xa_5))))$$

This evaluation method is called *nested multiplication*. The code for computing $P(x)$ for $x = 3$ could be as follows:

```
DCL A(0:5);
. . .
X = 3;
P = A(5);
DO K = 4 TO 0 BY -1;
P = A(K) + X*P;
END;
```

5.2. ADDITIONAL RULES CONCERNING ARRAYS

Some additional rules and facts concerning array variables are summarized below.

(1) A dimension attribute must appear in a DECLARE statement after the name of the variable and ahead of any other attributes. The reason for this is to prevent confusion between dimension and precision attributes, which can look alike.

(2) There is nominally no limit to the number of dimensions an array can

have, although for a particular PL/I implementation some high number might be set as a practical limit.[1]

(3) Using a subscript whose value lies outside the bounds declared for the corresponding dimension results in a SUBSCRIPTRANGE (abbr.: SUBRG) error during program execution. Such an error is not detected automatically but can be detected by programming. We shall discuss this in more detail in Section 11.3.

(4) An arbitrary expression can be used as a subscript. A noninteger value is reduced automatically to an integer by *truncating* its fractional part. Thus, A(3.6) becomes A(3), and A(−3.6) becomes A(−3).

(5) An array can be initialized by use of the INITIAL attribute in a DECLARE statement. A list of constant values must be provided for assignment to elements in the array. The order in which elements are assigned values from the list is *row-major* order, that is, in order with the last subscript varying most rapidly and the first subscript varying least rapidly. If the number of constants is less than the number of elements in the array, the unmatched array elements are left with undefined values. An *iteration factor* written in parentheses before a constant can be used to save writing one constant repeatedly in a list. Thus, writing (5)1 is equivalent to writing 1, 1, 1, 1, 1.

Example: Consider the statement

    DCL A(2, 2, 2) INIT (1, 2, 3, 4, 5, 6, 7), B(5) INIT ((5)0);

Every element in array A is initialized except A(2, 2, 2), which is left undefined initially. Thus, A(2, 1, 1) is initialized to 5, and A(2, 2, 1) to 7. Every element in array B is initialized to 0.

(6) A subscripted label variable can be used as a statement label. (This is exceptional. Ordinarily it would be wrong to use a label *variable* as a statement label *constant*.) Suppose, for example, that LBL were declared as follows:

    DCL LBL(3) LABEL;

Then LBL(1), LBL(2), and LBL(3) could be used as statement labels, and a statement like GO TO LBL(K) could be used as a three-pronged branch.

---

[1]For the F-level PL/I implementation on the IBM System/360, the maximum number of dimensions allowed is 32.

5.3. THE DEFINED ATTRIBUTE FOR ARRAYS

One array can be made to share storage with another array by use of the DEFINED (abbr.: DEF) attribute (cf. Section 2. 8).

Example:

DCL A(5, 5), B(5, 5) DEF A, C(75) FIXED DEC (6),
D(75) FIXED DEC (6) DEF C ;

The array having the DEFINED attribute is called the *defined array*, and the array it is defined on is called *base array*. Thus, in the preceding example, A is the base array for the defined array B. Array variables associated by means of the DEFINED attribute must have the same mode, scale, base, and precision attributes. Their dimension attributes need not be the same, but these attributes are subject to certain restrictions that will be explained below. Two other restrictions are (1) that a variable cannot have both the DEFINED and INITIAL attributes, and (2) that a base array cannot have the DEFINED attribute itself.

To understand the effect of using the DEFINED attribute for an array, one must understand that the result of specifying the attribute is to establish a correspondence between all the elements of the defined array and some or all of the elements in the base array. In the absence of specifications to the contrary (a possibility discussed later), the correspondence is always the obvious one based on correspondence of subscripts. Suppose, for example, that B is a two-dimensional defined array and that A is its base array. Then $B(I, J)$ is made to correspond to $A(I, J)$, and these two elements have the same storage location. One consequence of this rule is that the base array A must have the same number of dimensions as the defined array B and that the bounds for each dimension of B must lie within the bounds of the corresponding dimension of A. The $B(I, J) \rightarrow A(I, J)$ rule applies in each of the following declarations, all of which are valid:

DCL A(10, 10), B(10, 10) DEF A ;
DCL A(10, 10), B(5, 5) DEF A ;
DCL A(10, 10), B(5, 10) DEF A ;
DCL A(10, 10), B(2 : 6, 5 : 10) DEF A ;

On the other hand, each of the following declarations is *invalid*, because in each case the $B(I, J) \rightarrow A(I, J)$ correspondence rule fails somehow to associate each element of the defined array with an element in the base array:

DCL A(10, 10), B(20, 5) DEF A ;
DCL A(10, 10), B(0 : 9, 0 : 9) DEF A ;
DCL A(10, 10), B(100) DEF A ;

One can specify a correspondence rule more elaborate than the simple B(I, J)→A(I, J) type of rule described above by using dummy variables called *i*SUB's with the DEFINED attribute. The dummy variable *i*SUB refers to the *i*th subscript of the defined array. For instance 2SUB would refer to the second subscript of a defined array. These *i*SUB's can be used in formulas which prescribe how to calculate from the subscripts of an element in the defined array the subscripts of its corresponding element in the base array. Such formulas are given in a *base subscript list*, which follows the name of the base array in the DEFINED attribute specification.

Example:

```
DCL A(10, 10),
    B(10, 10) DEF  A(2SUB, 1SUB),
    C(0 : 9, 0 : 9) DEF A(1 +1SUB, 1 +2SUB),
    D(10) DEF A(1SUB, 1SUB),
    E(5, 6 : 10) DEF A(1SUB, 2SUB—5);
```

The DEFINED attribute for B specifies that B(I, J) "maps" onto A(J, I) so that those two elements have the same storage location. Similarly, we have C(I, J) →A(I+1, J+1), D(I)→A(I, I), and E(I, J)→A(I, J—5). In matrix terminology, B is the transpose of A, and D is the diagonal of A.

As implied in the foregoing example, defined and base arrays need not have the same number of dimensions when the correspondence between their elements is defined by means of *i*SUB formulas in a base subscript list.

The *i*SUB formulas that define the mapping of the defined array into the base array can be quite elaborate. Thus, the following declaration is valid:

```
DCL A(10, 10), B(100) DEF A((1SUB +9)/10, MOD(1SUB—1, 10) + 1);
```

This declaration causes the one-dimensional array B to be mapped onto the rows of the two-dimensional array A. (The MOD function is a built-in function used in this context to find the remainder when 1SUB—1 is divided by 10.) Variables can also be used in these base-subscript-list formulas.

The reader should now be able to see what the restrictions are on the dimension attributes of base and defined arrays: Suppose that A is the base array and B is the defined array. If no base subscript list is specified with the DEFINED attribute for B, then A and B must have the same number of dimensions, and the bounds of each dimension of B must lie within the bounds of the corresponding dimension of A. If a base subscript list is used to define the mapping of B into A, these restrictions do not apply. What is required is that the mapping match each element of B with a valid element of A, that is, with an element whose subscripts lie within the bounds prescribed for A. If this requirement is not satisfied, a SUBSCRIPTRANGE (abbr.: SUBRG) error can occur during program execution. Such an error is not detected automatically but can be detected by programming; we shall discuss this in more detail in Section 11. 3.

Among the numerous practical uses of DEFINED arrays are (1) to partition matrices into submatrices, and (2) to store special types of matrices—such as triangular, symmetric, and band matrices—in the minimum of space.

> **Example:** Consider the problem of storing the elements of an $n \times n$ upper-triangular matrix T ($T_{ij} = 0$ if $i > j$). T can be stored in $\frac{1}{2}n(n + 1)$ locations if only those elements T_{ij} are stored for which $i \leq j$. Such a storage arrangement for an array T is specified in the following DECLARE statement. The value of n used is $n = 10$.
>
> $$\text{DCL A(55), T(10, 10) DEF A(10*(1SUB-1)-}$$
> $$\text{1SUB*(1SUB-1)/2+2SUB);}$$
>
> An element T(I, J) can be referenced if $I \leq J$ but not if $I > J$.

5.4. DYNAMIC STORAGE ALLOCATION

To achieve greater flexibility and economy in the handling of storage, the programmer can make use of dynamic storage allocation. In the absence of specifications to the contrary, PL/I causes storage to be allocated to the variables used in a (main) program at the start of execution of the program. The programmer can alter this situation and cause storage for a variable to be allocated and released upon his explicit commands. There is more than one way to do this in PL/I; the easiest way is to declare the variable to have the CONTROLLED (abbr.: CTL) attribute. When this is done, the variable can be referenced in ALLOCATE and FREE statements, which cause the allocation and release of storage for the variable.

> **Example:** Consider the code
>
> ```
> DCL A CTL;
> ...
> ALLOCATE A;
> ...
> FREE A;
> ```

The variable A is allocated storage when the ALLOCATE statement is executed. The storage is released for possible reuse in some other way after the FREE statement has been executed.

Although, as was illustrated in the preceding example, a CONTROLLED variable does not have to be an array, the most important applications of the CONTROLLED attribute involve arrays, since the quantity of storage required for them is often considerable. In the DECLARE statement for a CONTROLL-ED array, the bounds in the variable's dimension attribute can be replaced by asterisks. Actual bounds can then be specified in an ALLOCATE statement. Variables or expressions, as well as constants, can be used to define such bounds.

Example:

```
DCL A(*, *) CTL, B(*) CTL;
...
N = 5;
ALLOCATE A(N + 1, 0 : N), B(8);
...
FREE B;
...
FREE A;
```

An INITIAL attribute for a variable can also be included in an ALLOCATE statement in order to initialize the variable when storage allocation takes place.

Example:

```
ALLOCATE A(2, 3) INIT (1, −2, 3, 4, 0), B(N) INIT((N)0);
```

Repeated use of the ALLOCATE statement to allocate storage to a variable, without intermediate use of the FREE statement, causes a "pushdown" storage stack to be created for the variable. Each time that ALLOCATE is used after the first time, new storage is allocated to the variable, and the old storage is saved or "pushed down" in a last-in, first-out stack. Use of the FREE releases the storage most recently allocated to the variable and allows storage pushed down previously to become available again after having been dormant temporarily. Data values retained in pushed-down storage are not destroyed.

A restriction on the use of CONTROLLED variables is that a variable cannot have both the DEFINED and CONTROLLED attributes.

Other methods of dynamic storage allocation in PL/I will be discussed in Section 8.13 and Chapter 10.

5.5. ARRAY ARITHMETIC

The programmer can reference array variables without subscripts in arithmetic expressions and assignment statements in order to perform operations on

entire arrays. Array operations are just ordinary operations performed elementwise on array variables. The following example illustrates this and shows
how nonarray elements, such as constants, are handled in array operations.

Example: Consider the following code:

```
DCL A(6, 12), B(6, 12), C(6, 12);
. . .
A = 2*B + C;
B = C**2 + 5;
C = 0;
```

Each element of B is multiplied by 2, the result is added to the corresponding
element of C, and this sum is then stored in the corresponding position of A.
Next, each element of C is squared, the result is added to 5, and this sum is
then stored in the corresponding position of B. Finally, each element of C is
assigned the value 0.

The general rules for evaluation of expressions, such as those on the priority of
operators, apply for array arithmetic just as they do for ordinary arithmetic.

An array can be used as an argument for built-in functions like SQRT
and LOG, and these functions are applied to the array elementwise.

The dimensions of two arrays used together in array operations must be
compatible in the following ways:

(1) The arrays must have the same number of dimensions.
(2) For each dimension the bounds of the dimension must be the same in
both arrays. It is not sufficient for dimensions to have the same extent;
they must have the same bounds. Thus, the following code is *invalid:*

```
DCL A(5), B(0:4);
A = B;
```

The usefulness of array arithmetic is enhanced by the fact that it can be
used on CONTROLLED array variables. Suppose, for example, that array arithmetic is to be used in certain matrix calculations, where the order of the
matrices varies and is a parameter in the program. By using CONTROLLED
variables and ALLOCATE statements, the programmer can adjust the bounds
of the arrays in the program on the basis of the parameter value. Then his
array arithmetic can be always on arrays of the exact size he needs in the
calcuations.

Using array arithmetic is a substitute for writing a loop in a program.
The actual calculations are in fact performed inside a loop generated automat-

ically by PL/I. If this fact is not appreciated, misunderstandings can arise about what programs will do.

Example: Suppose an array A is declared with the statement

```
DCL A(5);
```

Then the single statement

```
A = A/A(1);
```

is equivalent to

```
DO K = 1 TO 5;
A(K) = A(K)/A(1);
END;
```

Note that A(1) is changed on the first time through the loop. Therefore, the result is *not* the same as it would be if the code were

```
T = A(1);
DO K = 1 TO 5;
A(K) = A(K)/T;
END;
```

To conclude this section, it should be pointed out that the product obtained by multiplying two square arrays in PL/I array arithmetic is not the product in the matrix algebra sense. The PL/I product is formed elementwise, whereas the matrix product is formed by a row-by-column process. (The PL/I type of product is rarely used in matrix algebra, where it is called the *Hadamard product*.) Although PL/I facilities that we shall describe in Section 5.7 greatly facilitate the calculation of a matrix product, the programmer must still write a loop in order to perform the calculation.

More illustrations of array arithmetic are given in the next section and in Section 5.8.

5.6. BUILT-IN FUNCTIONS FOR ARRAY ARITHMETIC

PL/I has several built-in functions that are often useful in applications of array arithmetic. These functions take arrays as their arguments.

The functions SUM and PROD find the sum and product, respectively, of the elements in an array. A number of commonplace mathematical calculations can be conveniently expressed in terms of these two functions.

Example: Consider the two arrays X and Y declared as follows:

DCL X(5), Y(5);

The arithmetic mean of the elements of X is SUM(X)/5, and the geometric mean is PROD(X)∗∗(1/5). Thinking of X and Y as vectors in matrix algebra, we can express the Euclidean norm of X as SQRT(SUM(X∗∗2)) and the inner product of X and Y as SUM(X∗Y). If we wanted to obtain the inner product of X and Y in double precision (even though X and Y are single precision), we could write SUM(MULTIPLY(X, Y, 16)).

The next example is similar to the preceding one, except that CONTROLLED arrays are used.

Example: To calculate the chi-square statistic for a chi-square goodness-of-fit test in statistics, one must evaluate a sum of the form

$$\sum_{k=1}^{n} \frac{(O_k - E_k)^2}{E_k}$$

The code for this calculation might be as follows:

DCL O(∗) CTL, E(∗) CTL;
...
ALLOCATE O(N), E(N);
CHISQUARE = SUM(((O − E)∗∗2)/E);

The built-in functions ANY and ALL can be used in tests on arrays in IF statements. Suppose that A and B are arrays with compatible dimensions. Then ANY(A < B) is a conditional expression that is true if any element of A is less than its corresponding element in B. Similarly, ALL(A <= B) is a conditional expression that is true if every element of A is less than or equal to its corresponding element in B. An illustration of the use of these functions is given in Section 5.8.

5.7. CROSS SECTIONS OF ARRAYS

The programming of array operations can sometimes be simplified by using *cross sections* of arrays. A cross section might be, for example, an entire row or column of a two-dimensional array. The notation for a cross section is a subscripted array variable with one or more subscripts replaced by asterisks.

Example: Suppose an array A is declared by the statement

DCL A(4, 5);

The cross section A(∗, 3) is a one-dimensional array consisting of the elements A(1, 3), A(2, 3), A(3, 3), and A(4, 3). Similarly, the cross section A(K, ∗) is a one-dimensional array consisting of the elements A(K, 1), A(K, 2), A(K, 3), A(K,4) and A(K, 5). The two-dimensional cross section A(∗, ∗) is the same as A itself.

A cross section should always be thought of as an array itself whose number of dimensions is equal to the number of asterisks used as subscripts. Since a cross section is an array, it can be used together with other arrays in array arithmetic.

Example: Consider the code

```
DCL A(5, 5), B(5, 4), C(5, 7);
. . .
A(*, 3) = B(*, 3) + C(*, 4);
B(*, 4) = 0;
```

The second statement in this code is effectively equivalent to the following loop:

```
DO K = 1 TO 5;
A(K, 3) = B(K, 3) + C(K, 4);
END;
```

The statement B(∗, 4) = 0 causes the elements B(1, 4), B(2, 4), B(3, 4), B(4, 4), and B(5, 4) to be set equal to zero. Note that the statement

```
A(3, *) = B(3, *) + C(4, *);
```

would be invalid because the cross sections involved in it do not have compatible dimensions.

Readers familiar with matrix algebra may wonder whether or not certain combinations of cross sections are valid in array expressions. Consider the code

```
DCL A(5, 5), B(4, 5), C(5);
. . .
C = A(*, 3) + B(4, *);
```

If we think of A(∗, 3) and B(4, ∗) as column and row vectors, respectively (the third column of A and the fourth row of B), then we might suspect that the code above is invalid, since it involves adding a 5×1 matrix to a 1×5 matrix. The code is valid, however. So far as PL/I is concerned, A(∗, 3) and B(4, ∗) are both just one-dimensional arrays, and the code above is merely equivalent to

```
DO K = 1 TO 5;
C(K) = A(K, 3) + B(4, K);
END;
```

Cross sections can be useful in the programming of certain matrix operations.

Example: Suppose that three matrices A, B, and C are declared as follows:

DCL A(25, 25), B(25, 25), C(25, 25);

The following code will form the matrix product of A and B and store the result in C.

```
LB: DO I = 1 TO 25;
DO J = 1 TO 25;
C(I, J) = SUM(A(I, *)*B(*, J));
END LB;
```

Cross sections can also be used as arguments for the array-handling built-in functions, such as SUM and PROD.

5.8. EXAMPLE

The code given below is a complete program for computing the dominant eigenvalue of a certain 3×3 positive matrix by the power method. Let the matrix be denoted by A. The power method is an iterative one that consists of computing concurrently vectors in the two sequences $u^{(1)}$, $u^{(2)}$, $u^{(3)}$, ... and $v^{(1)}$, $v^{(2)}$, $v^{(3)}$, ... defined as follows:

$$u^{(0)} = \text{vector of all ones}$$
$$\left. \begin{array}{l} v^{(k)} = Au^{(k-1)} \\ u^{(k)} = v^{(k)}/v^{(k)}_{\max} \end{array} \right\} k = 1, 2, 3, \ldots$$

where $v^{(k)}_{\max}$ denotes the maximum element of the vector $v^{(k)}$. The $u^{(k)}$ sequence converges to the eigenvector corresponding to the dominant eigenvalue of A, and the sequence of numbers $v^{(1)}_{\max}$, $v^{(2)}_{\max}$, $v^{(3)}_{\max}$, ... converges to the dominant eigenvalue of A. A convergence test is made on the elements of the elements of the $u^{(k)}$ vectors; the iteration is stopped as soon as for each element $u^{(k)}_i$ the condition

$$\left| \frac{u^{(k)}_i - u^{(k-1)}_i}{u^{(k)}_i} \right| < 10^{-5}$$

is satisfied.

For convenience the data has just been built into the code instead of being read into it from data cards. The function ABS is the built-in absolute-value function.

```
/* COMPUTE DOMINANT EIGENVALUE OF POSITIVE MATRIX BY POWER
     METHOD. */
GO: PROC OPTIONS (MAIN);
      DCL (A(*, *), U(*), V(*), OLDU(*)) CTL, MAX FLOAT, EPSILON INIT(1E−5);
      N = 3;
      ALLOCATE A(N, N) INIT (5, 4, 3, 1, 2, 2, 7, 8, 6, 1), U(N), V(N), OLDU(N);
      U = 1;
L1:   DO K = 1 TO 20;
      MAX = 0;
L2:   DO I = 1 TO N;
      V(I) = SUM(A(I, *)*U);
      IF V(I) > MAX THEN MAX = V(I);
      END L2;
      OLDU = U;
      U = V/MAX;
      IF ALL(ABS((U − OLDU)/U) < EPSILON) THEN GO TO L3;
      END L1;
L3:   PUT SKIP DATA (K, MAX, U);
      RETURN;
      END GO;
```

5.9. STRUCTURES

In PI/I terminology arrays are said to be *data aggregates*. *Structures* are a second type of data aggregate. We shall briefly describe a few properties of structures in this section.

A *structure variable* (structure, for short) is a collection of variables. A variable in the collection can be an ordinary element variable, an array variable, or another structure. The fact that a structure can contain another structure implies that there is a hierarchical relationship among the variables in a structure. A structure and the hierarchy of its variables is defined by listing the structure variable and the variables it contains in a DECLARE statement and specifying a level number for each variable to show its relative position in the hierarchy. The level number precedes the name of a variable and must be separated from it by a blank.

Example:

```
DCL 1 A,
      2 B(10) FIXED (15),
      2 C,
         3 D FIXED BIN (15),
         3 E,
      2 F FLOAT (16),
      G FIXED BIN (31), H FIXED ;
```

Here the structure A contains B, C, and F, where C is a structure itself that contains D and E. B is an array; and D, E, and F are element variables. G and H, which do not have level numbers, are not part of the structure A. The variables do not have to be listed on separate lines, as they are here, but this is often done for clarity.

The topmost variable in a structural hierarchy is called the *major structure variable;* its level number must be 1. Other structure variables in the hierarchy are called *minor structure variables.* Any variable at any level can be dimensioned, but other attributes can be specified only for variables in a structure that are not themselves structures. In other words, attributes like FIXED and FLOAT can be specified only at the deepest level of a data hierarchy.

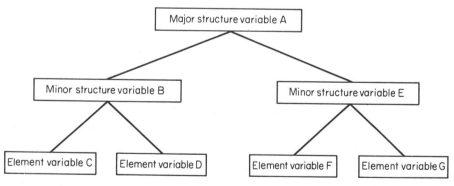

Figure 3.   Tree representation of a structure.

Two or more variables in different structures can have identical names. One of them can be identified by qualifying its name with that of a structure that contains it or, if necessary, with the names in a hierarchy of structures that contain it. A qualifying name precedes the variable's name and is separated from it by a period as in A.B.

Example:

DCL 1 A, 2 B, 3 C, 3 D, 2 E, 3 F, 3 G,
1 P, 2 B, 3 C, 3 F, 2 E;

The two F's in this DECLARE are E. F and B. F; by itself the name F is ambiguous and therefore invalid. The two C's are A.B.C and P.B.C; the name B.C is ambiguous.

When subscripting is required along with qualification, they can be *interleaved* with the variable names, as in A(I).B(J).C(K), or they can be grouped together, as in the equivalent expression A.B.C(I, J, K).

A simple way to define one structure so that it contains the same subfields and has the same hierarchy as another structure is to use the LIKE attribute as illustrated in the next example.

Example:

DCL 1 A, 2 B(5), 2 C, 3 E FIXED, 3 F, 1 P LIKE A;

This DECLARE statement is equivalent to the following:

DCL 1 A, 2 B(5), 2 C, 3 E FIXED, 3 F,
1 P, 2 B(5), 2 C, 3 E FIXED, 3 F;

Structure assignments and structure arithmetic are permitted when all structures involved have identical structuring (such as might be obtained with the LIKE attribute). Names do not have to be identical, only hierarchical relationships. Thus, if A, B, and C are structure variables with identical structuring (perhaps with A declared first, then B LIKE A and C LIKE A), the statement

$$A = B + C;$$

causes corresponding variables in B and C to be added and assigned to corresponding variables in A. Such a statement is equivalent to a series of assignment statements involving the variables at the deepest levels of the three structures. Conversions, if they are required, are all automatic.

Structural assignments and arithmetic can also be performed with the variables in different structures matched on the basis of variable names rather than on the basis of positions in data hierarchies. This type of structure operation is specified by including the key words BY NAME, preceded by a comma, at the end of an assignment statement. Operations BY NAME do not require identical structuring of the variables involved. Variables are considered to match BY NAME when their names and those of all their qualifiers match except for the names of major structure variables.

Example:

$$\text{DCL 1 A, 2 B, 2 C, 3 D, 3 E, 1 P LIKE A,}$$
$$\text{1 Q, 2 C, 3 E, 3 D, 2 F;}$$
$$\text{A = P;}$$
$$\text{Q = A, BY NAME;}$$

Here the statement A = P is equivalent to the following:

$$\text{A.B = P.B;}$$
$$\text{A.C.D = P.C.D;}$$
$$\text{A.C.E = P.C.E;}$$

The second assignment statement is equivalent to

$$\text{Q.C.E = A.C.E;}$$
$$\text{Q.C.D = A.C.D;}$$

The reader interested in more details about structures should refer to his PL/I reference manual. We shall not use them again in this book until we get to Chapter 10, where we need them in list-processing work. Structure variables, because of their special character as data aggregates, sometimes are subject to rules different from those for other variables. For the sake of brevity, we shall not make a point of this in subsequent chapters, and the reader should not assume that we are referring to structure variables unless we say so explicitly.

5.10. PL/I AND FORTRAN

The following remarks are intended for FORTRAN programmers who want to draw analogies between PL/I and FORTRAN.

(1) Array terminology is not the same in PL/I and FORTRAN. The PL/I terms *extent*, *bound*, and *dimension* all correspond in a general way to the FORTRAN term *dimension* (see Section 5. 1).

(2) The PL/I DECLARE statement fulfills the function of the FORTRAN DIMENSION statement. In fact, as the reader has probably noticed already, the DECLARE statement performs functions analogous to those of several FORTRAN statements, such as DIMENSION.

COMMON, EQUIVALENCE, and the various type-declaration statements, such as DOUBLE PRECISION and INTEGER.

(3) PL/I subscripts can be zero or negative, as well as positive, whereas FORTRAN subscripts must be positive.

(4) PL/I allows any number of dimensions in an array, whereas the maximum number in a FORTRAN array is seven.

(5) The PL/I DEFINED attribute works somewhat like the FORTRAN EQUIVALENCE statement, in the sense that its use causes variables to share storage. There is, however, a fundamental difference between DEFINED and EQUIVALENCE. A FORTRAN programmer mainly uses EQUIVALENCE to conserve storage, by using a storage area for two or more sets of data (at different times, of course). A PL/I programmer mainly uses the DEFINED attribute so that he can reference *one* set of data in more than one way.

(6) The adjustable-dimension feature in FORTRAN is the only FORTRAN facility that is similar to the PL/I dynamic storage allocation facilities. This comparison is a poor one, though, because the PL/I storage allocation capabilities are much more powerful and flexible than those of FORTRAN.

(7) FORTRAN has no array arithmetic or array cross sections.

EXERCISES

1. Write a DECLARE statement to define a 4×4 matrix T partitioned as shown below into four 2×2 submatrices A, B, C, and D. It should be possible to reference any element of a submatrix or of T itself. Use the DEFINED attribute and base subscript lists.

$$T = \begin{pmatrix} A & B \\ C & D \end{pmatrix}$$

2. The (i, j) element of a tri-diagonal matrix is zero unless $|i - j| \leq 1$. Therefore, only 28 storage locations have to be used to store a 10×10 tri-diagonal matrix. Write a DECLARE statement to define a 10×10 tri-diagonal matrix A so that only 28 storage locations are used and the (i, j) element of A can be referenced in the form A(I, J). Use the DEFINED attribute and a base-subscript list.

3. Twenty-five numbers are stored in a one-dimensional array A. Exactly one of these numbers is zero. Write code to find the zero and replace it with the number one. Try to use a DO statement with a WHILE clause.

4. Write a DECLARE statement to declare a 3×3 matrix A and to initialize its elements to the values shown below:

$$A = \begin{pmatrix} 1 & 4 & 7 \\ 2 & 5 & 8 \\ 3 & 6 & 9 \end{pmatrix}$$

5. Consider the following code:

```
DCL A(25, 25), B(25, 25);
...
A = 2*B + 3*A(1, 4);
```

write DO loops to replace the assignment statement so that the values assigned to the elements of A are the same as before but no array operations are used.

6. For a stochastic matrix it should be true that every element of the matrix is positive and that, for each row, the sum of the elements in the row equals one. Declare a two-dimensional CONTROLLED array named P, and allocate storage for it. Use the asterisk notation in the DECLARE statement, and specify dimensions 5×5 in the ALLOCATE statement. Then, assuming that values have been assigned to the element of P, code tests to verify that every element is positive and that all the row sums lie between .999999 and 1. 000001. Assign the variable FLAG the value zero if these tests are satisfied and the value one if they are not.

7. Assume that sample data values are stored in X(1), X(2), ..., X(100), where X is declared as follows:

```
DCL X(100);
```

Write code to compute the sample variance s^2 defined by the formula

$$s^2 = \frac{n(\sum x_k^2) - (\sum x_k)^2}{n(n-1)}$$

where n is the sample size and where each summation is for values of k from 1 to n.

6 INPUT/OUTPUT

6.1. INTRODUCTION

In this chapter we shall describe some of the PL/I input/output facilities. A thorough discussion of this topic would be too long for this book, so we shall restrict ourselves to a limited view of the subject. Mainly we shall be dealing with the two standard PL/I files SYSIN and SYSPRINT.

(1) SYSIN is the standard file for card input. In a small computer configuration, it normally corresponds to a card reader. In a large configuration it may correspond instead to a tape or disk unit, in which case the "cards" are actually card images.

(2) SYSPRINT is the standard file for high-speed printer output. In a small computer configuration it normally corresponds to a printer. In a large configuration it may correspond to a tape or disk unit, in which case the "print lines" are actually line images.

Both SYSIN and SYSPRINT are described in PL/I terminology as STREAM files. Input and output on STREAM files are executed by means of the GET and PUT statements. The reason for the term "stream" will become apparent later.

Besides the STREAM file, PL/I has another type of file called the RECORD file, for which the input and output statements are READ and WRITE. In scientific programming, RECORD files are not as important as STREAM files; and, since the subject of RECORD files would require a full chapter to itself, we shall omit it.

Nonstandard files (that is, files other than SYSIN and SYSPRINT) have numerous programming applications, of course. They are used, for example, for punching cards, for auxiliary print files, and for scratch files. In Section 6.10 we shall explain briefly how to use certain types of nonstandard STREAM files, but until then the discussion will apply only to the standard files SYSIN and SYSPRINT. In this chapter we shall also restrict our attention to the problem of input/output for arithmetic data. The subject of input/output for alphabetic data fits naturally into our discusson of character strings in Chapter 9, and we shall return to it then.

6.2. PRINTER LAYOUT

The two parameters LINESIZE and PAGESIZE associated with the file SYSPRINT affect the page layout of printer output. (Every STREAM file used for printing has such parameters associated with it.) The default value for LINESIZE is 120 characters.[1] This means that 120 print positions are available for use on each line. The default value for PAGESIZE is 60 lines. The standard PL/I action is to eject the form automatically after this number of lines has been printed on one page and to advance the form to line one of the next page. As we shall explain, the programmer can arrange alternative end-of-page action if he wishes.

The programmer can specify his own values for the LINESIZE and PAGESIZE parameters associated with SYSPRINT by using the OPEN statement, which is the PL/I statement for opening files.

Example: The statement

    OPEN FILE (SYSPRINT) LINESIZE (132) PAGESIZE (55);

causes the parameters LINESIZE and PAGESIZE associated with SYSPRINT to be set equal to 132 characters and 55 lines, respectively.

Both SYSIN and SYSPRINT will be opened and closed automatically, so programmers usually do not need to use the OPEN statement or the related CLOSE statement. SYSPRINT must be opened explicitly, however, if values for the page-layout parameters are to be specified for it.

If he wishes, the programmer can override the automatic form eject that occurs when a page is complete. The process for doing this and setting up

---

[1]The LINESIZE and PAGESIZE default values are implementation dependent. The values given are those for the F-level PL/I implementation on the IBM System/360.

alternative end-of-page procedures involves use of the ENDPAGE interrupt, which we shall discuss briefly in Section 6.9 and in more detail in Chapter 7.

Control of page format is sometimes facilitated by use of the built-in function LINENO, which takes the name of a print file as an argument and has as its value the number of the current print line for that file. (The line-number count starts from one every time the form is ejected to the top of a new page.) An example of the use of LINENO is given at the end of the next section.

6.3. THE STREAM CONCEPT

As we said in Section 6.1, the two standard files SYSIN and SYSPRINT are both STREAM files. The term *stream* is used because such files are thought of in PL/I as consisting of continuous streams of data without record boundaries. Specifically, card boundaries in SYSIN input and line boundaries in SYSPRINT output have no special significance. This does not mean that card and line boundaries cannot be taken into account in programming but only that they are not taken into account automatically.

A GET statement used to read data from SYSIN does not cause input to be read from a new card, except by chance. The processing of input is merely resumed wherever it was left off previously. If all the data required for a GET statement has not been read in when an input card has been processed completely, then another card is read automatically and the processing of input continues with the new card.

Similarly, a PUT statement does not cause output on SYSPRINT to begin on a new line, except by chance. Output is merely "added on" wherever a previous PUT statement left off with its output, possibly in the middle of a line. When one line is full, another line is started automatically.

It is obviously necessary for the programmer to be able to take card and line boundaries into account, and PL/I provides ways in which this can be done. When reading from SYSIN, the programmer can write GET SKIP instead of merely GET, in order to ensure that the next input data comes from column one of a new card.[2]

When writing on SYSPRINT, the programmer has three options that he can use to control page layout. Instead of writing merely PUT, he can use

---

[2]The SKIP means, in effect, "new card." If the next input would come from column one of a new card anyway, the SKIP has no effect and can optionally be omitted. There is one exception to this rule: GET SKIP cannot be used to read the first data card, because the SKIP would cause the first data card to be bypassed.

PUT PAGE, PUT SKIP(n), or PUT LINE(n). These forms of the PUT statement can be used anywhere that PUT alone can be used.

(1) PUT PAGE causes the form to be ejected to line one of the next page.

(2) PUT SKIP(n) causes the form to be advanced n lines. PUT SKIP is a short form equivalent to PUT SKIP(1). PUT SKIP and PUT SKIP(2) statements are commonly used to obtain single and double spacing, respectively. PUT SKIP(0) causes space suppression (i.e., a "carriage return" without form movement).

(3) PUT LINE(n) causes the form to be advanced to line n of the current page, if that line has not already been passed. If the line has been passed, then PUT LINE(n) has the same effect as PUT PAGE. Thus, PUT LINE(31) is in effect a command to advance the form to the next half page.

When any of these options is used, the next available print position is the first position in the new line. In other words, there is always a "carriage return." We shall explain in Section 6.9 what happens if the value of n in PUT SKIP(n) or PUT LINE(n) is such that the line number is advanced beyond the value of PAGESIZE.

The most common applications of the GET and PUT options described above are in input and output statements that cause transmission of data. (These will be discussed in ensuing sections.)

Examples:

```
GET SKIP LIST (A, B);
PUT PAGE DATA (X, Y, Z);
PUT SKIP(2) LIST (U, V);
PUT LINE(25) EDIT (P, Q) (F(6, 2), X(5), E(12, 6));
```

The following are, however, complete statements in themselves:

```
GET SKIP;
PUT PAGE;
PUT SKIP(n);
PUT LINE(n);
```

The PUT PAGE statement, for example, causes the form to be advanced to the top of a new page, without transmission of any output for printing.

Example: The statement

IF LINENO(SYSPRINT) $>$ 50 THEN PUT PAGE;

causes the form to be ejected to the top of a new page if the current line number on SYSPRINT is greater than 50.

6.4. LIST-DIRECTED INPUT/OUTPUT

PL/I has three kinds of input/output for STREAM files: (1) list-directed, (2) data-directed, and (3) edit-directed. In this section we shall describe the use of list-directed input/output on SYSIN and SYSPRINT. The other two types of input/output will be explained in subsequent sections.

The basic form of the GET statement for list-directed input on SYSIN is

GET LIST (data list);

The data list is a list of variables, which may include ordinary element variables, subscripted array variables, or unsubscripted array variables. Numbers are read in sequentially from cards and assigned in sequence to the variables in the data list. For unsubscripted array variables, as many input numbers are assigned to the variable as there were elements in the array; it is as if all the elements in the array are actually listed in the data list in "row-major" order (last subscript varying most rapidly).

Example: Consider the statements

DCL X(3), Y(4);

. . .

GET LIST (A, X, Y(2), K);

Six numbers are read from the input stream and assigned in order to A, X(1), X(2), X(3), Y(2), and K.

Constants in the SYSIN input stream can have any of the valid forms for PL/I constants that were described in Section 2.5, and they can be signed. Furthermore, complex numbers like $-2.5 + 7I$ and $3 - 5I$ are allowed, even though such numbers strictly are not constants in PL/I. Consecutive input constants must be separated by either a comma or a blank, and extra blanks between numbers are ignored. A complex number in the input stream must be written without a blank before its interior sign, since such a blank would be interpreted as a field separator.

The attributes of the input constants do not have to be the same as the attributes of the data-list variables to which they are assigned; automatic conversions will be made when necessary. It is as if the constants being read in were assigned to data-list variables by means of ordinary assignment statements in the program.

Example: Suppose that the GET statement is

GET LIST (X, Y, Z);

and that the next data in the input stream is[3]

314bbb—16.2E—5bbb12.2

Then the effect of the GET LIST is the same as that of the statements

$$X = 314;$$
$$Y = -16.2E-5;$$
$$Z = 12.2;$$

Since SYSIN is a STREAM file, there is great latitude in the way data constants can be punched in cards. No special number of input fields has to be punched in any card, and fields can be spaced out in any way that seems convenient to the programmer.

Example: Suppose that 100 numbers are punched in data cards and that there is no other data in the cards. The numbers might be read in by means of the following code:

```
DCL A(100);
DO K = 1 TO 100;
GET LIST (A(K));
END;
```

The numbers could be punched in the cards one to a card, two to a card, or without any regular scheme at all, provided they were separated by blanks or commas.

A *repetitive specification* is a special form of DO loop designed to be used in a data list.

Example: The statement

GET LIST ((A(K), B(K) DO K = 1 TO 4));

---

[3]The symbol b denotes a blank.

is equivalent to

GET LIST (A(1), B(1), A(2), B(2), A(3), B(3), A(4), B(4));

A repetitive specification in a data list must be enclosed in parentheses, which are in addition to any other parentheses that may be required for other reasons. It is easy to make a mistake when one is writing a repetitive specification by omitting an apparently superfluous set of parentheses that is actually needed.

The various DO options, such as the WHILE clause, can all be used in repetitive specifications. Nested repetitive specifications are also allowed; these are useful when multidimensional arrays are used in a program.

Example: The statement

GET LIST (((A(I, J) DO J = 1 TO 3) DO I = 1 TO 3));

is equivalent to

GET LIST (A(1, 1), A(1, 2), A(1, 3), A(2, 1), A(2, 2),
          A(2, 3), A(3, 1), A(3, 2), A(3, 3));

The basic form of the PUT statement for list-directed output on SYSPRINT is

PUT LIST (data list);

The data list is like a data list for a GET LIST statement, except that it can include constants and expressions as well as variables. The values of the data list are printed in order at certain "tab" positions, normally five numbers to a 120-character print line.[4] If the data list contains an unsubscripted array variable, then the elements of the array are printed in row-major order. Repetitive specifications can also be used for output of arrays.

Example: The following code causes a table of powers of two to be printed:

```
PUT PAGE;
DO K = 1 TO 100;
PUT SKIP LIST (K, 2**K);
END;
```

The table starts on a new page and is printed in two columns, with K in the

---

[4]The tab locations are implementation dependent. For the F-level PL/I implementation on the IBM System/360, they are at print positions 1, 25, 49, 73, 97, and 121. The tab at 121 is not used in 120-character print lines.

first column and 2^K in the second column. Lines are single spaced. Double spacing could be obtained by changing PUT SKIP LIST to PUT SKIP(2) LIST.

The appearance of the printed output for variables in the data list of a PUT LIST statement is not under the programmer's control, except indirectly; it depends on the attributes of the variables. Thus, for example, the number of digits printed in an output number depends on the precision of the corresponding variable. Output values are *not* rounded.

The last example in this section illustrates the use of a repetitive specification for output.

Example: Suppose that 100 numbers $A(1), A(2), \ldots, A(100)$ are to be printed in four columns, with $A(1)$ through $A(25)$ in column one, $A(26)$ through $A(50)$ in column two, and so on. The code for doing this might be as follows:

```
PUT PAGE;
DO I = 1 TO 25;
PUT SKIP LIST ((A(I + J) DO J = 0 TO 75 BY 25));
END;
```

6.5. DATA-DIRECTED INPUT/OUTPUT

The form of the GET statement for data-directed input on SYSIN is

GET DATA (data list);

The data list is like a data list for a GET LIST statement, with certain exceptions that we shall explain below. The data read in by a GET DATA statement is also like the data read in by a GET LIST statement, except that it is self-identifying. The input data consists of a set of assignment statements of the form

variable = constant

Consecutive assignment statements in this set are separated by either a comma (*not* a semicolon) or a blank, and the entire set is terminated by a semicolon. Extra blanks between statements are ignored.

Example: Input for the statement

GET DATA (A, B);

might be, say,

A=123.45, bbB=.314E1 ;

For each variable in the data list, there can be (but does not have to be) an assignment statement in the input stream assigning a value to the variable. The order in which variables appear in the input stream does not have to be the order in which they appear in the data list. The semicolon at the end of the set of assignment statements stops the input and determines how much data in the input stream is processed by the GET DATA statement.

Constants in the input stream for a GET DATA statement can have the same forms as constants used as input for a GET LIST. That is, they can have any of the forms valid for PL/I constants, and they can be signed. Complex constants are also allowed. The constants do not have to have the same attributes as the variables to which they are assigned; automatic conversions will be made when necessary.

Example: Consider the code

```
GET DATA (A, B);
GET DATA (X, K, Y);
```

Suppose that the data in the input stream on SYSIN is

$$A=3.14bB=-12;bbY=17E-3bK=5;$$

Then the first GET DATA statement reads in values for A and B, and the second one reads in values for Y and K (but not in data-list order). The value X is left unchanged, because no assignment statement for X appeared in the input data

The data list for a GET DATA statement cannot include either a DEFINED variable or a subscripted variable. An unsubscripted array name can be included, however, in which case the input assignments can include subscripted references to the array. Unsubscripted array names are never allowed in the input data.

Example: Suppose that it is necessary to read in the nonzero elements of a sparse 5×5 matrix. (A sparse matrix is one most of whose elements are zero.) The code might be as follows:

```
DCL A(5, 5) INIT ((25)0);
. . .
GET DATA (A);
```

The data in the input stream might be, say,

$$A(2,1)=5, bbA(3,4)=-17, bbA(4,4)=12, bbA(5,1)=2;$$

The basic form of the PUT statement for data-directed output on SYSPRINT is

PUT DATA (data list);

The data list can include ordinary element variables, both subscripted and un-subscripted array variables, and repetitive specifications for arrays. Constants, expressions, and DEFINED variables, all of which could be used in the data list of a PUT LIST statement, are not allowed in the data list of a PUT DATA. The form of the output is analogous to the form of the input for a GET DATA. It consists of a series of equations giving the values of the variables in the data list; the output terminates with a semicolon.

Example: The statement

PUT DATA (A, B);

might produce as output, say,

$$A = 3.14126E-01 \qquad B = -1.25672;$$

Output equations from a PUT DATA statement are printed at the same implementation-dependent "tab" positions that are used for output from a PUT LIST (see Section 6.4). Output values are *not* rounded.

Data-directed output is not very useful for printing reports because control over the format of the output is quite limited. It is very useful, however, for printing small amounts of output and was used for this purpose in the examples in Sections 3.6 and 4.5. Data-directed output is also extremely useful when "quick and dirty" output is needed for debugging purposes, since PUT DATA statements can be written quickly and with only small risk of clerical errors, and the output is automatically labeled.

6.6. EDIT-DIRECTED INPUT/OUTPUT

Edit-directed input/output is the most versatile kind of input/output in PL/I. We shall devote this section and the two succeeding sections to describing its use.

The form of the GET statement for edit-directed input from SYSIN is

GET EDIT (data list) (format list);

The data list is like a GET LIST data list. It can contain ordinary element variables, both subscripted and unsubscripted array variables, and repetitive specifications. As in the case of GET LIST, inclusion of an unsubscripted array variable is equivalent to listing all the array elements in row-major order. The format list is a series of edit and control specifications that describe how the input is to be processed; we shall describe these format specifications in detail below.

Example:

GET EDIT (A, B, Z(3)) (SKIP, F(5,2), X(3), E(12,6), COL(45), F(6));

As input is read from the SYSIN input stream, the format is processed one item at a time. *Data-format items*, such as E(12,6) and F(6), match up with data-list variables and describe how input numbers to be assigned to the variables should be interpreted. *Control-format items*, such as SKIP and COL(45), do not match up with data-list variables but are inserted in the format in order to specify information about the location of data fields in the input stream.

The principal data-format items for arithmetic input data are given below. A third type of data-format item will be described in Section 6.8.

(1) $F(w, d)$ is used to describe an input field that can contain a (signed or unsigned) fixed-decimal constant, such as 3.14159. $w =$ the number of columns in the input field; $d =$ the number of digits in a constant that are to be construed to be to the right of an understood decimal point if the constant itself contains no decimal point. $F(w)$ is a short form equivalent to $F(w, 0)$.

(2) $E(w, d)$ is used to describe an input field that can contain a (signed or unsigned) floating-decimal or fixed-decimal constant, such as .314159E1 or 1.570296. $w =$ the number of card columns in the input field; $d =$ the number of digits in a constant (not counting the exponent if there is one) that are to be construed to be to the right of an understood decimal point if the constant itself contains no decimal point.

For both E- and F-format items, if a constant contains a decimal point, then the value of d in the format item is ignored. In other words, a decimal point in the data overrides the specification of d in the format item.

The control-format items for *input* are given below:

(1) $X(n)$ specifies that the next n columns in the input stream are to be skipped.

(2) SKIP specifies that the next input card is to be read (if necessary) so that the next input will come from column one of a new card.[5] (Putting SKIP first in the format of a GET EDIT statement has the same effect as using GET SKIP EDIT.)

(3) COL(n) specifies that the next input is to come from column n of the current input card, if that column has not already been processed as input. If column n has already been processed, then the next input card is read automatically, and the COL(n) control-format item applies to the new card.[6] (COL is an abbreviation for COLUMN.)

Input numbers read in by means of a GET EDIT do not have the same attributes as the data-list variables to which they are assigned; automatic conversions will be made whenever necessary. Thus, for example a floating-point constant specified by an E-format item could be read in and assigned to a fixed-point variable.

Example: Suppose that the statement

GET EDIT (A, B, K) (F(6,3), X(3), F(6), COL(20), E(10,4));

is used to read in a data card that contains, beginning in column one, the data below. The symbol b denotes a blank column.

123456bbbb12.34bbbb3.592E2bbb

(1) Columns 1-6 are read in under the format item F(6,3), and the constant 123.456 is assigned to A. The position of the understood decimal point is obtained from the format item.

(2) The control-format item X(3) specifies that the next three columns (7-9) are to be skipped.

(3) Columns 10-15 are read in under the format item F(6), and the constant 12.34 is assigned to B. The decimal point in the data overrides the format specification for an understood decimal point.

(4) The control-format item COL(20) specifies that the next input will come from column 20, with the result that columns 16-19 will be skipped.

---

[5]If the next input would come from column one of a new card anyway, a SKIP has no effect. There is one exception to this rule: A statement like GET EDIT (...)(SKIP,...) cannot be used to read the first data card, because the SKIP would cause the first data card to be bypassed. See the remarks in the footnote in Section 6.3.

[6]Although they appear to have similar functions, the SKIP and COL(1) control-format items are different. COL(1), unlike SKIP, cannot cause the first data card to be bypassed. Programmers should acquire the habit of using COL(1) rather than SKIP.

(5) Columns 20–29 are read under the format item E(10,4), and the constant 3.592E2 is assigned to K. (Note that the constant can be floating, even if the variable is fixed.)

In the process of matching data-format items with data-list variables, if the format items should run out before the data list does, the format is merely rescanned from the beginning. If the data list runs out first, the unused part of the format is ignored.

Example: The statement

GET EDIT ((A(K) DO K = 1 TO 100)) (F(5));

processes the next 500 card columns in the input stream on SYSIN and reads in 100 numbers, one number for each five columns; the first column processed is not necessarily column one of a card. The statement

GET SKIP EDIT ((A(K) DO K = 1 TO 100)) (F(5));

processes input in the same way, except that a new input card is started and the input starts with column one of the new card. The statement

GET EDIT ((A(K) DO K = 1 TO 100)) (COL(1), F(5));

reads in 100 five-column numbers, one number from columns 1-5 in each of 100 different cards.[7]

The form of the PUT statement for edit-directed output of SYSPRINT is

PUT EDIT (data list) (format list);

In this case the data list can contain element variables, both subscripted and unsubscripted array variables, repetitive specifications, constants, and expressions. The interpretation of a PUT EDIT is analogous to that of a GET EDIT, except that it initiates output instead of input. Data-list variables match up with data-format items that describe how the numbers are to be printed. Control-format items specify line-spacing and other page-format information.

Example:

PUT EDIT (X, Y, Z) (PAGE, F(5,3), X(3), E(10,4), COL(1), F(10));

---

[7]See the remarks given earlier in this section on the COL(1) and SKIP control-format items.

The principal data-format items for output of arithmetic data are given below. A third type of data-format item will be described in Section 6.8.

(1) F(w, d) specifies that the output is to be in the form of a (possibly signed) fixed-decimal constant. w = the number of print positions in the output field; d = the number of digits to be printed to the right of the decimal point. F(w) is a short form equivalent to F(w, 0).

(2) E(w, d) specifies that the output is to be in the form of a (possibly signed) floating-decimal constant. w = the number of print positions in the output field; d = the number of digits to be printed to the right of the decimal point in the mantissa of the number.

For both the E- and F-format items, leading zeros are suppressed, and output numbers are right justified in the fields allocated to them.

The control-format items for output are the following:

(1) X(n) specifies that the next n print positions are to contain blanks.

(2) PAGE specifies that the form is to be advanced to line one of the next page and that the next available print position is the first position in that line.

(3) SKIP(n) specifies that the form is to be advanced so that the line number is increased by n and that the next available print position is the first position of the new line. The format item SKIP is a short form equivalent to SKIP(1).

(4) LINE(n) specifies that the form is to be advanced to line n of the current page and that the next available print position is the first position of the new line. If line n has already been passed on the current page, then LINE(n) has the same effect as PAGE.

(5) COL(n) specifies that the next output is to begin in print position n of the current line and that blanks are to fill the intervening print positions. If position n of the current line has already been filled, then there is an automatic carriage return, and the next output begins in position n of the new line.[8]

We shall explain in Section 6.9 what happens if a control-format item causes the line number to be advanced beyond the value of PAGESIZE.

---

[8]The SKIP and COL(1) control-format items, though similar, do not have identical functions. In particular, SKIP can cause a carriage return before the first line of printing starts. This could lead to one less line of printing on the first page of output than on subsequent pages. (This output phenomenon is the counterpart to the input phenomenon of bypassing the first data card. See the remarks in footnotes in Section 6.3 and 6.6.) COL(1) is recommended for general use in preference to SKIP.

The process of scanning a format list for a PUT EDIT statement is the same as that for a GET EDIT. If the format items run out before the data list does, the format is rescanned from the beginning (without an automatic carriage return). If the data list runs out first, the unused part of the format list is ignored.

Example: Suppose that it is desired to print a 4 × 4 matrix at the top of a new page. The four rows are to be double spaced, say, and the four columns are to start in print positions 1, 21, 41, and 61, respectively. The code might be as follows:

PUT PAGE EDIT (((A(I,J) DO J = 1 TO 4) DO I = 1 TO 4)) (F(10,5), COL(21),
    F(10,5), COL(41), F(10,5), COL(61), F(10,5), SKIP(2));

6.7. ADDITIONAL RULES ABOUT FORMATS

Additional rules and facts concerning formats in GET EDIT and PUT EDIT statements are summarized briefly below.

(1) Another type of control-format item is the *remote-format* item, which has the form R(label). It can be used by itself or with other items in a GET EDIT or PUT EDIT format. The *label* is the statement label of a FORMAT statement that contains format items to be treated as if they were actually part of the format list in which the remote-format item appears.

Example: The code

                PUT EDIT (A, B, C) (F(6,2), R(L3), E(15,5));
        L3: FORMAT (COL(1), F(5));

is equivalent to

                PUT EDIT (A, B, C) (F(6,2), COL(1), F(5), E(15,5));

(2) A special C-format item can be used to read in and print out values for COMPLEX variables. Its form is

                C(real format item, real format item)

where the real format items are ordinary format items suitable for describing REAL data. The first real format item describes the real part of the complex number, and the second one describes the imaginary part of the number. If the second real format item is omitted, it is assumed to be the same as the first one.

Example: Suppose that a card contains a complex number, with the real part in columns 1-10 and the imaginary part (without an I) in columns 11-20. The number might be read in by means of the following code:

```
DCL X CPLX;
GET EDIT (X) (COL(1), C(F(10)));
```

The real part and the imaginary part will each be read under an F(10) format.

(3) A format list is never scanned any further than is necessary for processing the input or output data. This means that a control-format item, such as a SKIP, at the end of a format is not processed unless the format list has to be rescanned.

Example: Consider the code

```
PUT PAGE EDIT (A) (E(15,8), SKIP);
PUT EDIT (B) (E(15,8));
```

The SKIP at the end of the first format list is not processed because the format list does not have to be scanned that far for the value of A to be printed. Therefore, the value of B is printed on the same line as the value of A.

(4) An E-format or F-format input field can contain blanks, both to the left and to the right of a constant in the field. Blanks to the right do not count as zeros. When the constant contains no decimal point, right-hand blanks do not affect the position of the understood decimal point. Because of this, a constant can be left-justified in its input field.

Example: Suppose that the statement

```
GET EDIT (A) (F(6,2));
```

is used to read the data b123bb, where the symbol b denotes a blank. Then the value 1.23 is assigned to A.

(5) If an F-format input field contains all blanks, the value assigned to the data-list variable is zero. If an E-format input field contains all blanks, a CONVERSION error results; in Section 6.9 we shall discuss CONVERSION errors briefly and again in Section 7.5.

(6) Output numbers are rounded automatically when they are printed under control of E- and F-format items, provided that the internal precision of the output data exceeds the external precision with which

it is printed. No other rounding of output occurs automatically any-where in PL/I.

(7) An *iteration factor* can be used to show that a format item is to be repeated. The iteration factor precedes the format item and is enclosed in parentheses.

Example: The item

$$(3)F(5)$$

is equivalent to

$$F(5), F(5), F(5)$$

Applying an iteration factor to a group of format items enclosed in paren-theses causes the entire group to be repeated.

Example: The item

$$(2)(SKIP, F(5), E(12,6))$$

is equivalent to

$$SKIP, F(5), E(12,6), SKIP, F(5), E(12,6)$$

(8) Besides constants, both variables and expressions can be used in a for-mat, either as iteration factors or as field-width specifiers.

Example: Suppose that it is desired to print an $n \times n$ matrix A at the top of a page, single spaced with n numbers per line, where n is a variable in the pro-gram. The code might be as follows:

PUT PAGE EDIT (((A(I,J) DO J = 1 TO N) DO I = 1 TO N)) ((N)F(8,5), SKIP);

If an iteration factor has the value zero, then the format item to which it applies is ignored when the format list is scanned, and the item does not match up with a data-list variable.

Example: If $N = 0$, then the format item (N) F(6, 2) is ignored, and the for-mat list is processed just as if the item were not present at all.

(9) Conditional expressions like those used in IF statements can be used in formats. They are mainly used as iteration factors. For example, the format item $(K>2)F(5)$ is treated as F(5) if $K > 2$ and is ignored if $K \leq 2$.

Example: The following code prints a four-place normal probability table for arguments running from 0 to 2.99 by steps of .01.

```
DCL X FIXED DEC (3,2);
PUT PAGE EDIT ((.5*ERF (X/1.41421E0) DO X = 0 TO 2.99 BY .01))
              ((10)F(8,4), SKIP, (MOD(100*X, 50) = 0) SKIP);
```

The output is single spaced, ten numbers per line, with an extra space after every fifth line. The MOD function is a built-in function used here to compute the remainder when 100*X is divided by 50. The condition MOD(100*X, 50) = 0 is true every time 50 numbers (i. e., five lines) have been printed and is false at other times. The ERF function is the built-in error function, which happens to be useful here for computing probabilities for the standard normal distribution.

(10) Input can be read and reread repeatedly under different formats by use of the STRING option of the GET statement. This will be described in Section 9.12 in connection with our discussion of character strings.

6.8. PICTURE FORMAT ITEMS

An important type of data-format item not discussed in Section 6.7 is the picture, or P-format, item. It is extremely versatile and can be used to process all sorts of input and output data formats that would be difficult or impossible to handle with E- and F-format items.

The general form of a P-format item is

P'picture characters'

The picture characters are a series of control characters that specify the external form of the input or output data field; they can be thought of as a symbolic picture of the data.

Examples:

```
GET EDIT (A, B) (P'999V99', P'Z9V999');
PUT EDIT (X, Y) (P'SSSV.99', P'Z,ZZZV.99');
```

The number of picture characters available is quite large, and we shall describe only a few of the most important ones in this section. In the description of picture characters given below, we explain the interpretation of the characters as they are used for *output*. Their interpretation for *input* will be discussed further below. Throughout this discussion, the symbol b will be used to indicate a blank in an input or output field.

Picture Character	Meaning
9	Print a digit (0-9). Do not suppress (change to blank) a leading zero. *Example*: Under the format P'999' the number 12 would print as 012.
Z	Print a digit, but suppress a leading zero. *Example*: Under the format P'ZZZ' the number 10 would print as b10.
	Insert a comma. *Example*: Under the format P'9,999' the number 1234 would print as 1,234.
Y	Print a nonzero digit and change a zero to a blank, no matter where the zero appears. *Example*: Under the format P'YYY' the number 120 would print as 12b.
B	Insert a blank. *Example*: Under the format P'9B9' the number 12 would print as 1b2.
S	Print the sign (+ or −) of the number. *Example*: Under the format P'S99' the number 12 would print as +12.
−	Print a blank if the number is nonnegative and a minus if the number is negative. *Example*: Under the format P'−99' the number 12 would print as b12 and the number −12 would print as −12.
V	Specifies the position in which the decimal point of the number being printed is understood to fall, but does not cause printing of a decimal point. If no V picture character is included in a P format, one is automatically assumed at the right of the picture. *Example*: Under the format P'9V99' the number 1.2 would print as 120. Under the format P'99' the number 2.5 would print as 02.
	Insert a decimal point. Although this picture character specifies where a decimal point will be printed, it does not specify the position of the decimal point for arithmetic purposes. An arithmetically significant decimal point is specified by the V picture character, which does not cause printing. *Example*: Under the format P'9.99' the number 1.2 would print as 0.01. (The 2 would be dropped off.) Under the format P'9V.99' the number 1.2 would print as 1.20.

To illustrate a few of the numerous possibilities for use of P formats, we summarize very briefly some applications.

(1) Printing a number without suppressing leading zeros (as might be desirable for printing a table). See the example given for the picture character 9.

(2) Printing a number without its decimal point (as is often done in the printing of log tables, for example).

Example: Under the format P′V9999, the number .0123 would print as 0123.

(3) Printing a number with a space inserted periodically for the sake of readability.

Example: Under the format P′V.99999B99999B99999′ the number .123456789012345 would print as .12345b67890b12345.

(4) Printing a number with comma insertion to set off thousands, millions, etc., for the sake of readability.

Example: Under the format P′Z,ZZZ,ZZZV.99′ the number 1234.56 would print as 1,234.56.

(5) Printing of plus signs as well as minus signs. See the example given for the picture character S.

(6) Printing a number in the European style in which a comma is used instead of a decimal point.

Example: Under the format P′ZZV,99′ the number 1.23 would print as b1,23.

Unlike E- and F-format output, P-format output is *not* rounded automatically.

To understand how input is processed under a P format, one should think of the input process as the inverse of the output process with the same format. A number written out under a P format could be read back in correctly under the same format. Not only is this true, but for an input field to be valid for processing under a P format, the field must have exactly the form it would have had if it had been written out under the same format. Let us consider a simple example that emphasizes some of the implications of this situation. Suppose that a five-column input field is to be read in under the format P′B99Y.′, say. The first column of the input field must contain a blank, and the fifth column must contain a decimal point. (Since a V picture character is automatically understood on the right-hand side of the picture, the position of the decimal point in the card in this example is also the position of the decimal point for arithmetic purposes.) The second and third columns must contain digits and cannot contain blanks. The fourth column must contain one of the digits 1–9 or a blank; if it does contain a blank, the blank is interpreted as a zero. Thus, if the input field were b12b., the number read in would be 120.

If an input field read in under a P format does not have the required form, a CONVERSION error results; we shall discuss this type of error briefly in Section 6.9 and again in Section 7.5. The programmer can use the fact that invalid data causes an error to do validity checking of input data.

> **Example:** Suppose that a number is to be read in from an input card and that the number is to be punched in five columns with leading zeros punched and without a decimal point. If the field is read in under the format P'99999', the occurrence of any nondigital character in one of the columns would result in a CONVERSION error. Thus, an invalid blank and similar errors would be detected.

Note that for input under a P format, just as for output, the position in which the decimal point is to be understood to fall is specified by a V picture character. The decimal point (.) picture character specifies the actual appearance of a decimal-point input character, but this decimal point has no arithmetic significance.

> **Example:** If the data field 123 were read in under the format P'9V99', the value read in would be 1.23. The input field 1.23 could be read in under the format P'9V.99', and the value read in would also be 1.23.

The picture formats that have been described in this section are called *numeric-character formats*. The external input and output fields that they describe cannot contain letters of the alphabet. It is appropriate to mention here that two other picture characters, A and X, can be used to describe alphabetic data. A P-format item that contains either of these picture characters is called a *character-string format*. We shall discuss such pictures in Section 9.4 in connection with our study of character strings.

6.9. PROGRAM INTERRUPTS

Several exceptional conditions can cause interrupts to occur during the execution of GET and PUT statements in a PL/I program. Although we shall not discuss interrupts in detail until the next chapter, it is appropriate to mention them briefly here because of their importance for proper understanding of PL/I input/output operations.

An ENDFILE interrupt occurs when an end-of-file is encountered during the processing of input. (An ENDFILE condition is said to be *raised* for the input file.) In the absence of specifications to the contrary by the programmer, the standard system action taken in such a case is to terminate program execution. The programmer can, however, recover control after an end-of-file has been encountered by using the ON statement, which is the PL/I statement that defines the action to be taken after an interrupt occurs. For example, if the statement

ON ENDFILE(SYSIN) GO TO LBL2;

is executed *before* an end-of-file is encountered on SYSIN, then it will cause a branch to the statement labeled LBL2 when an end-of-file is eventually read.

We shall discuss the use of ON statements in detail in the next chapter and shall illustrate how important types of interrupts can be dealt with. We defer further discussion of this subject until then.

It is not possible to read past an end-of-file without first closing and re-opening the file. Once the ENDFILE condition has been raised, until the file has been closed a subsequent attempt to read the file merely causes another ENDFILE interrupt to occur.

An ENDPAGE interrupt occurs when the programmer attempts to write on a line whose number is larger than the value of PAGESIZE for the print file involved (see Section 6.2). The standard system action taken automatically when an ENDPAGE interrupt occurs is to advance the form to line one of the next page and to reset the line count to one (in other words, to skip over the crease). As we shall explain in Chapter 7, the programmer can, if he wishes, inhibit the standard system action and can execute steps of his own choosing when an ENDPAGE interrupt occurs. Programmers often do this in order to print page totals and page headings.

An ENDPAGE interrupt is most likely to occur as one tries to print past the end of a page, but it can also be caused by a forms-movement command, such as PUT SKIP(n) or PUT LINE(n) or by the SKIP(n) and LINE(n) control-format items. Thus, for example, if PAGESIZE were less than 61, the statement PUT LINE (61) would cause an ENDPAGE interrupt.

Programmers, particularly beginners, sometimes find it advantageous to control page layout without bothering with the ENDPAGE interrupt. One can do this as follows:

(1) Inhibit the standard system action for ENDPAGE by executing at the

beginning of the program the following statement, which says in effect "do nothing":

ON ENDPAGE(SYSPRINT);

(2) Test the LINENO built-in function in order to detect the end of a page by using a statement like

IF LINENO(SYSPRINT) > 50 THEN ...

A CONVERSION interrupt occurs when invalid data is encountered during the processing of input. Thus, a CONVERSION interrupt would result from trying to read under the format P'999' an input field containing a blank. The standard system action taken after such a CONVERSION error is to terminate program execution. The programmer can, however, inhibit this action and can sometimes even correct the invalid data and resume normal program execution. A CONVERSION interrupt can also occur under certain conditions during the writing of output.

Other types of interrupts can occur as the result of errors during the execution of input/output operations, such as the NAME and UNDEFINEDFILE interrupts. We shall not discuss these interrupts.

6.10. NONSTANDARD FILES

So far in this chapter, we have discussed only the two standard PL/I files, SYSIN and SYSPRINT. Nonstandard files are, of course, also needed frequently in programming, and in this section we shall explain how to use them in several typical applications. Although we shall now be discussing nonstandard files, we still limit ourselves to the subject of STREAM files.

To use a nonstandard file in a PL/I program, one must do two things that are not usually required when SYSIN or SYSPRINT is used: (1) define the file name in a DECLARE statement, and (2) include the file name in every GET or PUT statement referring to the file. It is also often necessary to open and close files explicitly by means of the OPEN and CLOSE statements. The illustrations in this section will show how these things are done.

To explain the use of nonstandard files we shall take three simple problems and discuss them individually: (1) how to write out an auxiliary print file, (2) how to punch cards, and (3) how to use a scratch file for temporary storage. Our discussion of these problems does not include any explanation of what has to be done outside of a PL/I program in order to use a nonstandard file. Usually it is necessary to provide monitor control cards defining the file.

Such cards vary from system to system, of course, and their study is beyond the scope of this book.

(1) *Auxiliary print files.* Suppose that it is desired to have two output files for printing, SYSPRINT and a second, nonstandard file that we shall call AUXPRT. This file might be declared and opened by means of the following statements:

```
DCL AUXPRT PRINT FILE;
OPEN FILE(AUXPRT) PAGESIZE (55);
```

The DECLARE statement defines AUXPRT to be the name of a file with the PRINT attribute.[9] The chief significance of the PRINT attribute is that it causes the output records to be suitable for printing, which they might not otherwise be.[10] The OPEN statement opens the file and defines PAGESIZE for the file to be equal to 55; a LINESIZE value could also be specified in this OPEN statement. When PAGESIZE or LINESIZE is not specified for a PRINT file, the value assumed is the same default value that is used for SYSPRINT (see Section 6.2). The OPEN statement in this illustration can be omitted if the default values for LINESIZE and PAGESIZE are acceptable. Output can be written on AUXPRT just as it would be written on SYSPRINT, but the file name AUXPRT must be stated explicitly in PUT statement, as in the following examples:

```
PUT FILE(AUXPRT) PAGE;
PUT FILE(AUXPRT) EDIT (X, Y) ((2)F(8,5));
PUT FILE(AUXPRT) SKIP LIST (A, B);
```

The file is closed automatically when the program terminates, although it can be closed explicitly by means of the statement

```
CLOSE FILE(AUXPRT);
```

(2) *Punched-card output.* Since there is no standard file for punched-card output in PL/I, it is necessary to define a nonstandard file whenever card output is desired. Suppose that such a file is named PUNCH. The file might be declared and opened by means of the following statements:

---

[9]In PL/I implementations for the IBM System/360, file names are limited to at most seven characters. The name SYSPRINT is allowed as an exception.

[10]For example, in the F-level PL/I implementation for the IBM System/360, carriage-control characters are automatically included in the output only if the file has the PRINT attribute.

```
DCL PUNCH OUTPUT FILE;
OPEN FILE(PUNCH) LINESIZE(80);
```

The DECLARE statement defines PUNCH to be the name of an output file. The OPEN statement opens the file and defines its LINESIZE value to be 80.[11] Making LINESIZE equal to 80 has two results: (1) A SKIP option in a PUT statement (or, equivalently, a SKIP format item) causes the current card to be filled out through column 80 with blanks and a new card to be started. (2) If no SKIP is used to force the start of a new card, then a new card is started automatically when all 80 columns of one card are full. Output can be written on the file PUNCH by means of PUT LIST, PUT DATA, and PUT EDIT statements. The file name must be stated explicitly, as in these examples:

```
PUT FILE(PUNCH) EDIT (X) (COL(10), P'99V99');
PUT FILE(PUNCH) SKIP LIST (A, B, C);
```

Because PUNCH is not specified in the DECLARE statement to be a PRINT file, output from PUT LIST and PUT DATA statements is not written at the "tab" positions mentioned in Section 6.4; instead, consecutive output fields from these statements are merely separated by a blank. The file can be closed with a CLOSE statement or left to be closed automatically when the program terminates.

(3) *Scratch files for temporary storage.* Suppose that it is necessary in a program to write out data on a scratch file and then read it back in again later. To be specific, let us say that we need to write out a 25×25 matrix A and read it back in transposed form (that is, with rows and columns interchanged). Let the name of the file be SCRATCH. Then the code might be as follows:

```
DCL A(25, 25), SCRATCH FILE;
. . .
OPEN FILE(SCRATCH) OUTPUT;
PUT FILE(SCRATCH) LIST (A);
CLOSE FILE(SCRATCH);
. . .
OPEN FILE(SCRATCH) INPUT;
GET FILE(SCRATCH) LIST (((A(I,J) DO I = 1 TO 25) DO J = 1 TO 25));
CLOSE FILE(SCRATCH);
. . .
```

The DECLARE statement defines SCRATCH to be a file name. The first OPEN statement opens the file as an *output* file. The elements of the array are then

---

[11]The term LINESIZE may not seem appropriate when print lines are not involved. In such cases LINESIZE can be thought of as the *logical record length.*

written out row-major order (that is, by rows) by means of a PUT LIST statement. (Data-directed or edit-directed output could also be used, but there
would hardly be any point to doing so since the output is not supposed to be
printed.) The file is then closed and reopened, this time as an *input* file. (Ordinarily it is not necessary to open and close a file explicitly. In this case it is
necessary because the file is first used as an output file and then as an input
file.) The GET LIST statement reads the matrix back by columns so that it
comes into storage in transposed form. Afterwards, the file is closed for a
second time; this second CLOSE statement could be omitted. The output on
file SCRATCH is a stream of decimal numbers separated by blanks. (For
reasons that we have not explained, there are no "lines" or "tab" positions.)

6.11. PL/I AND FORTRAN

The following remarks are intended for FORTRAN programmers who want
to draw analogies between PL/I and FORTRAN. There are so many differences
between the PL/I and FORTRAN input/output facilities that we will mention
only some of the most important points. It should be remembered that besides
the STREAM file PL/I has another file type called the RECORD file, which
we have not discussed.

(1) Edit-directed input/output in PL/I is similar to FORTRAN formatted
input/output. The stream concept does not apply, however, in
FORTRAN formatted input/output operations.

(2) Many PL/I format items are analogous to FORTRAN format items.
Thus, there are E, F, and X items in both languages, although the
notation for them is not identical. There are other analogies, too: The
PL/I SKIP control-format item is like the FORTRAN slash; PAGE is
like the carriage-control character 1; and COL is like a T format. On
the other hand, FORTRAN has no P format, and PL/I has no D, I, or
Z formats. The PL/I E-format item does the work of Fortran E and
D; and the PL/I F-format item, that of FORTRAN F and I.

(3) Trailing blanks in an input field are sometimes treated differently in
PL/I and FORTRAN. Thus, if the input field b3b is read in under the
format item F(3) in PL/I, the value read in is 3. If the field is read
under F3.0 in FORTRAN, the value read in is 30.

(4) A data-format item in PL/I can be selected without consideration of
the attributes of the corresponding data-list variable. Thus, a value
for a fixed-point variable can be read in under an E format. In FOR-
TRAN a value for an integer variable cannot be read in under an E
format.

(5) There are several differences between the format-scanning rules in PL/I and FORTRAN. In PL/I a format is not scanned any further than is necessary for processing the data list. Thus, a SKIP at the end of a format is ignored unless the format has to be rescanned. In FORTRAN a slash at the end of a format can be processed even if the format is not rescanned. When a PL/I format is rescanned, it is rescanned from the beginning, and there is no automatic "carriage return." A FORTRAN format is rescanned from the last open parenthesis, and there is an automatic "carriage return."

(6) Carriage-control characters like those in FORTRAN formats are not used in PL/I, but certain control-format items fulfill equivalent functions. Thus, PAGE starts a new page, SKIP causes single spacing, SKIP(2) causes double spacing, and SKIP(0) causes space suppression.

(7) A data list for a PL/I PUT LIST or PUT EDIT statement can include constants and expressions. In FORTRAN a data list for a WRITE statement can contain only variables.

(8) Using the PL/I ENDFILE interrupt to recover control after reading an end-of-file is analogous to using the END option of the FORTRAN READ statement for the same purpose.

(9) PL/I has no ENDFILE, BACKSPACE, or REWIND statements; the CLOSE statement is a substitute for ENDFILE and REWIND.

(10) Variables and conditional expressions can be used in PL/I formats but not in FORTRAN formats.

Example: The item

$$(K>2)F(2*N,N)$$

is a valid format item in PL/I.

(11) A complete format list cannot be read in during execution of a PL/I program, as it can in FORTRAN. This drawback is offset, to a great extent, by other features of PL/I formats.

(12) PL/I has no format item directly comparable to the FORTRAN H-format item.

(13) FORTRAN has more than two standard files. It has, for example, a standard file for punched-card output.

(14) The nearest counterpart in PL/I to unformatted FORTRAN input/output is list-directed input/output like that illustrated in the third problem in Section 6.10.

(15) PL/I data-directed input/output is similar in some ways to FORTRAN NAMELIST input/output.

(16) If an unsubscripted array name appears in the data-list of a PL/I GET or PUT statement, the array is processed by *rows*. In a comparable situation in FORTRAN, an array is processed by *columns*.

EXERCISES

1. The (i, j) element of a tri-diagonal matrix is zero when $|i - j| > 1$. (a) Write code to print the elements of a 5×5 tri-diagonal matrix T as a 5×5 array with double spacing between rows. (b) Same as (a), except print blanks (instead of zeros) for the (i, j) element when $|i - j| > 1$.

2. The 25 elements of a 5×5 matrix A are punched in data cards as fixed-point constants, one to a card. Each number is punched in columns 1–10; each number contains a decimal point; and there is no other data in the cards. Write code to read in the elements of A when the data is in order (a) by rows, and (b) by columns.

3. Same as preceding problem, except that each number is punched in columns 41–50 of its card, and there may be other data in the cards.

4. A job has two data cards containing fields A, B, and C. The locations of the fields and their contents are described below:

Field	Location	Contents
A	cols. 1–10, card 1	floating-point constant, e.g., .2718E1
B	cols. 21–30, card 1	fixed-point constant, e.g., 3.14159
C	cols. 41–45, card 2	integer with leading zeros, e.g., 00005

There is also other data in the cards. Write code to read these three fields and assign their values to the variables A, B, and C. Comment on how leading or trailing blanks in the data fields would be treated by your code.

5. State which of the following statements could not be valid in PL/I:
   (a) PUT LIST (X, Y, SQRT(Z));
   (b) PUT DATA (X, Y, SQRT(Z));
   (c) PUT EDIT (X, Y, SQRT(Z)) ((3)F(10));
   (d) PUT EDIT (5) (F(1));
   (e) GET EDIT ((A(K) DO K = 1 TO 15 WHILE (A(K) > 0))) ((15)F(12,5));
   (f) PUT EDIT (X) (R(FMT));
   (g) GET DATA (A(3));
   (h) GET EDIT ((A(K) DO K = 1 TO N)) ((N)F(5));

7 PROGRAM INTERRUPTS

7.1. INTRODUCTION

Execution of a PL/I program can be interrupted as the result of an error condition or some other more or less infrequent occurrence. Among the numerous possible causes of interrupts are (1) encountering the end of a page while output is being written on a PRINT file, (2) encountering an end-of-file while an input file is being read, (3) occurrence of overflow in a fixed-point arithmetic operation, and (4) occurrence of exponent overflow or underflow in a floating-point arithmetic operation.

PL/I program interrupts may correspond in many cases to actual hardware interrupts in a computer; this might be true of a division-by-zero interrupt, for example. Interrupts that do not correspond to hardware facilities have to be simulated by compiler-generated code. The question of whether or not the effect of an interrupt is achieved by circuitry or by programming need not concern a PL/I user, however; all interrupts seem alike to the programmer. Of course, object-program efficiency may suffer when a PL/I interrupt is simulated by programming because of the additional machine instructions the compiler has to insert in the object program.

Interrupts are a powerful programming tool in PL/I. They provide, for example, a way to recover from error conditions that might otherwise force termination of program execution. In the next few sections we shall discuss what happens when interrupts occur and shall explain how interrupts can be exploited in programming.

7.2. ENABLING AND DISABLING INTERRUPTS

Occurrences that can cause interrupts in PL/I programs are called *conditions*. In PL/I terminology a condition is said to be "raised." For example, when an end-of-file is encountered in reading an input file, the ENDFILE condition is raised for the file. When a condition is raised, an interrupt occurs if the condition is *enabled* and does not occur if the condition is *disabled*. Some conditions are permanently enabled, and others can be enabled or disabled by programming. Of those conditions that can have either status, the condition may be either enabled or disabled initially.

Among the most commonly encountered conditions that can be enabled or disabled are the following, all of which are initially enabled automatically:

(1) ZERODIVIDE (abbr.: ZDIV) is raised when division by zero is attempted in any kind of arithmetic.

(2) UNDERFLOW (abbr.: UFL) is raised when exponent underflow occurs in a floating-point operation.

(3) OVERFLOW (abbr.: OFL) is raised when exponent overflow occurs in a floating-point operation.

(4) FIXEDOVERFLOW (abbr.: FOFL) is raised when the length of the result of a fixed-point operation exceeds (a) 15 in decimal arithmetic, or (b) 31 in binary arithmetic.[1]

The following three conditions are among those that are permanently enabled:

(1) ENDPAGE(file name) is raised when the end of a page is reached in a PRINT file.

(2) ENDFILE(file name) is raised when an end-of-file is encountered in reading an input file.

(3) ERROR is raised for a large number of different error situations, such as taking the square root of a negative number, violating storage protection, using an invalid op-code, and so on.

Several initially disabled conditions that are especially useful for debugging purposes will be discussed in Chapter 11. A number of other significant conditions will also be mentioned in other chapters.

---

[1] These maximum values are implementation dependent. The values given are those for PL/I implementations on the IBM System/360.

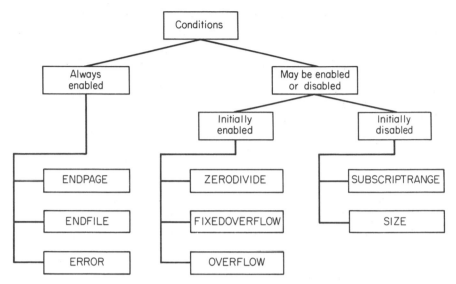

Figure 4. Classification of PL/I conditions with some examples.

In the next section we shall discuss what happens when an interrupt occurs. For the moment let us consider the question of how the enabled-disabled status of a condition can be altered by programming, when alteration is permitted. A *condition prefix* can be used to reverse the status of a condition for the duration of a single statement. Consider, for example, the SUBSCRIPT-RANGE (abbr.: SUBRG) condition, which is raised when a subscript is outside the bounds declared for a variable and which is initially disabled. If we wanted to enable it for the duration of one statement, we could attach a condition prefix to the statement, as in the following example:

$$(SUBRG): X = A(K) + Y*Z;$$

Then an out-of-range subscript would cause an interrupt when the statement was executed. In contrast, consider the UNDERFLOW (abbr.: UFL) condition, which is initially enabled. If we wanted for the duration of one statement to prevent an interrupt for floating-point underflow, we could write[2]

$$(NOUFL): X = A(K) + Y*Z;$$

---

[2]Disabling UNDERFLOW is sometimes advantageous, because it prevents the printing of a standard system message when underflow occurs. A zero is always substituted for a result that underflows, regardless of whether or not UNDERFLOW is enabled.

The key word used in an enabling prefix is the condition name or its abbreviation. The key word in a disabling prefix is the same word preceded by NO. Two or more prefixes can be combined, as in the illustration

```
(NOUFL, SUBRG): X = A(K) + Y*Z;
```

When a statement needs both a condition prefix and a statement label, the prefix must come first, as in the following illustration:

```
(SUBRG): LBL: X = A(K) + Y*Z;
```

It is also possible to enable or disable a condition for more than the duration of just one statement. To do this, one must bracket the group of statements with BEGIN and END statements and apply the condition prefix to the BEGIN statement, as shown below:

```
(SUBRG): BEGIN;
         X = A(K) + Y*Z;
         Z = A(10) + A(K)/2;
         END;
```

The statements between the BEGIN and END statements constitute a BEGIN *block*. Throughout the block, the condition specified in the prefix is either enabled or disabled, as the case may be.

BEGIN blocks can be nested, and in such cases the BEGIN and END statements match up like opening and closing parentheses. For clarity, a label can be given to a BEGIN statement and the same label included in the corresponding END statement, as in this illustration:

```
(SUBRG): LBL: BEGIN;
             . . .
         END LBL;
```

Labeling the BEGIN statement is advisable when a block is long.

We shall say more about BEGIN blocks in Section 8.13.

A condition prefix can also be used before a PROCEDURE statement to enable or disable a condition throughout a procedure. Thus, in order to enable SUBSCRIPTRANGE and disable UNDERFLOW throughout a main program, we could write

```
(SUBRG, NOUFL): GO: PROC OPTIONS (MAIN);
```

7.3. WHEN AN INTERRUPT OCCURS

The actions taken when interrupts occur in a PL/I program can be classified as follows:

(1) *Standard system action.* A standard system action is taken when an interrupt occurs, if the programmer has not provided otherwise. The action taken depends on what PL/I condition causes the interrupt. Most conditions are related to errors, and the standard system action frequently consists of printing a message and raising the ERROR condition, which in turn causes execution to terminate.

(2) *Programmer-defined action.* If a programmer wishes, he can define in his program steps to be taken instead of the standard system action for an interrupt. These steps are specified in an *on-unit*, which is a module of code that the programmer must supply. After an on-unit has been executed as the result of an interrupt, normal program execution can be resumed, if that is desired.

In this section we shall explain how on-units are coded and incorporated in programs. Examples of their use will be given later in this section and in Section 7.5.

An on-unit is always associated with a specific PL/I condition. The on-unit can be thought of as a subprogram to be executed whenever the condition is raised (provided, of course, the condition is enabled). An on-unit for a condition is defined by means of the ON statement, which has the following form:

ON condition-name on-unit;

The simplest on-units are just single statements. For example, to keep count of floating-point underflows, we might write simply

ON UFL N = N + 1;

An on-unit can also be a BEGIN block (see Section 7.2). A BEGIN block must be used whenever more than one statement is needed for the on-unit. For example, to print a message as well as count, we might write[3]

```
ON UFL BEGIN;
N = N + 1;
PUT SKIP LIST ('FLOATING-POINT UNDERFLOW');
END;
```

A BEGIN statement introducing an on-unit cannot be labeled.

---

[3]We have not yet discussed the printing of alphabetic data in PL/I, but an understanding of this is not essential here.

If the end of an on-unit is reached in program execution, one of several things can happen, depending on what condition is associated with the on-unit:

(1) After an on-unit is executed, usually a return is made automatically to the interrupted program at the point immediately following the point of interrupt so that program execution continues normally. No PL/I statement (such as RETURN) is needed to cause this return; it happens automatically when the end of the on-unit is reached.[4] This type of return occurs, for example, after a FIXEDOVERFLOW, ZERO-DIVIDE, UNDERFLOW, OVERFLOW, or ENDPAGE interrupt.

(2) In some cases the step in the interrupted program (that is, the step that caused the interrupt) is retried after an on-unit is executed. For this type of return after an on-unit, it is assumed that the programmer will have corrected in the on-unit the error that caused the interrupt. An example of a condition for which a step is retried after an on-unit is executed is the CONVERSION condition, which is raised for various types of data-conversion errors.

(3) Execution may be terminated when the end of an on-unit is reached. This occurs after an ERROR condition on-unit. The programmer can use the on-unit to diagnose his error, but execution is terminated when the end of the on-unit is reached, just as it would be if there were no on-unit at all.

It is always possible for the programmer to branch out of an on-unit by means of a GO TO so that the end of the on-unit is never reached. In this way the programmer can avoid the action that would occur if the end of the on-unit were actually reached and can instead do whatever he wishes. For example, by writing the statement below, he can branch after getting an end-of-file on SYSIN to a new program phase beginning at LBL:

ON ENDFILE(SYSIN) GO TO LBL;

The ON statement is an executable statement, and its position in a program is therefore important. From the time that it is encountered in the execution of a program, it defines the on-unit that that will be executed when an interrupt occurs for the corresponding condition. A subsequent ON statement for the condition can override this definition and define a new on-unit. A return to the standard system action for an interrupt can be accomplished by using the key word SYSTEM instead of an on-unit in an ON statement. Thus, in

---

[4]In fact, a RETURN statement is not allowed in an on-unit.

order to restore the standard system action for the UNDERFLOW condition, we might write

ON UFL SYSTEM;

We shall say more about enabling interrupts and use of the ON statement in Section 8.10 in connection with the subject of subprograms.

Example: The code given below reads input numbers and prints them one to a line with a page total at the end of each page. An ENDPAGE interrupt occurs at the end of each page, and the ENDPAGE on-unit is used to print the page total, to advance the form to a new page, and to reset the SUM field to zero. When the end-of-file finally is read on SYSIN, the ENDFILE on-unit branches to the final program steps, where a last ENDPAGE interrupt is forced by advancing the form to line 61. This last interrupt provides an opportunity to print the page total for the last page. It may be noted that PUT LINE(61) causes an ENDPAGE interrupt, whereas PUT PAGE does not.

```
/* LIST INPUT NUMBERS WITH PAGE TOTALS */
GO: PROC OPTIONS (MAIN);
        ON ENDFILE(SYSIN) GO TO L2;
        ON ENDPAGE(SYSPRINT) BEGIN;
            PUT SKIP(2) EDIT (SUM) (F(8));
            PUT PAGE;
            SUM = 0;
            END;
        SUM=0;
    L1: GET EDIT (X) (F(4));
        PUT EDIT (X) (COL(1), F(8));
        SUM = SUM + X;
        GO TO L1;
    L2: PUT LINE(61);
        RETURN;
        END GO;
```

7.4. ADDITIONAL FACTS ABOUT ON-UNITS

In this section we summarize briefly some additional facts and rules about on-units.

(1) An ON statement cannot be executed *after* a condition has occurred in order to test for the condition. Consider the code

```
(SUBRG): X = A(K);
        ON SUBRG GO TO LOST;
```

The on-unit in the ON statement would not be executed if the SUBSCRIPTRANGE condition were raised in the preceding statement; the ON statement must come first in order to be effectual. Programmers sometimes mistakenly try to treat an ON like an IF and to put it after a statement to which it is meant to apply.

(2) An on-unit containing more than one statement must be bracketed with BEGIN and END statements. DO and END together cannot be used.

(3) Including the keyword SNAP in an ON statement causes a message to be written automatically on SYSPRINT when an interrupt occurs. For example, we might write

```
ON UFL SNAP N = N + 1;
```

When SNAP is omitted from an ON statement, there is no automatic message.

(4) The SIGNAL statement can be used to force an interrupt. For example, the statement

```
SIGNAL SUBRG;
```

would force a SUBSCRIPTRANGE interrupt. One of the uses of the SIGNAL statement is to simulate error conditions for debugging.

(5) A null or "do nothing" on-unit is sometimes useful. Consider, for example, the ENDPAGE condition, for which the standard system action is to skip the form to the top of the next page. To inhibit this action on SYSPRINT and print right across the crease, we could write

```
ON ENDPAGE(SYSPRINT);
```

A better way to avoid the standard system action for a condition is to disable the condition, if that is possible. ENDPAGE is one condition that cannot be disabled.

(6) Some conditions can be raised by several different types of occurrences. This is true, for example, of the CONVERSION condition, which can be raised because of many different types of input-data errors, among others. The programmer can sometimes identify the type of

error in his program precisely by using the ONCODE built-in function. This function has implementation-dependent numerical values which correspond to various types of errors. The interested reader should consult the documentation for the PL/I system he uses.

(7) A RETURN statement is not allowed in an on-unit. If a programmer wants to terminate program execution with a RETURN after an interrupt occurs, he can use a GO TO in an on-unit to branch to a RETURN outside the on-unit.

Example: To terminate program execution after a certain number of pages, say 100, of output are printed, we might use the code given below. Note that the PUT PAGE command in this code has to be included, because without it we would just print over the crease.

```
DCL PAGECT FIXED BIN INIT (0);
ON ENDPAGE(SYSPRINT) BEGIN;
   PAGECT = PAGECT + 1;
   IF PAGECT > = 100 THEN GO TO HALT;
   PUT PAGE;
   END;
      . . .
HALT: RETURN;
```

(8) By means of the CONDITION condition, programmers can define conditions of their own designs for special uses. The interested reader should consult his PL/I reference manual.

7.5. EXAMPLE

The code shown below illustrates the use of three PL/I conditions: (1) ENDFILE, which is raised when an end-of-file is encountered in reading an input file, (2) SUBSCRIPTRANGE, which is raised when a subscript is used that is outside the bounds declared for a variable, and (3) CONVERSION, which is raised for a variety of errors involving invalid input data (as well as other errors not related to input/output).

The code reads in the nonzero elements of a sparse 5×5 matrix and prints out the entire matrix in a square array. (A *sparse* matrix is one that contains mostly zeros.) The input consists of ≤ 25 cards, each of which contains a pair of subscripts called I and J and the corresponding matrix element A(I, J).

ENDFILE is raised for SYSIN when the end-of-file is read. When this occurs, the last data card has already been processed; so the ENDFILE on-unit merely branches to the final steps of the program, where the matrix is printed.

SUBSCRIPTRANGE (abbr.: SUBRG) is raised if the subscripts of A(I, J) in the GET LIST statement are out of bounds. (This would imply that a data card contained an out-of-bounds value for I or J, possibly because of a keypunch error.) The SUBSCRIPTRANGE on-unit causes the offending subscripts to be printed together with the message "out of range."[5] Then there is a branch to the end of the loop so that the loop can be continued and the next data card read. Note that whereas ENDFILE and CONVERSION are automatically enabled, SUBSCRIPTRANGE has to be enabled by means of a condition prefix.

CONVERSION (abbr.: CONV) is raised if a data field contains an invalid character, such as a letter of the alphabet. The CONVERSION on-unit causes the value of ONSOURCE to be printed and the card containing the invalid data to be skipped. ONSOURCE is a built-in function related to the CONVERSION condition; its value is the contents of the field that caused the condition to be raised.[6] Skipping of the erroneous data card is done by a GET SKIP statement. The SNAP option is used to produce a standard error message whenever a CONVERSION interrupt occurs. Note that after the last input data has been processed, the standard system action for CONVERSION is restored so that a subsequent error of this type cannot cause the on-unit to be executed again.

The ON SUBRG and ON CONV statements are placed inside the DO loop because their on-units contain branches into the loop. Although it would be logical to place these statements ahead of the loop, it would be illegal to do so, because PL/I does not allow branching into the range of a DO loop from outside.

```
/* READ AND PRINT SPARSE MATRIX */
GO: PROC OPTIONS (MAIN);
    DCL A(5, 5) INIT ((25)0);
    ON ENDFILE(SYSIN) GO TO L3;
L1: DO K = 1 TO 25;
    ON SUBRG BEGIN;
        PUT SKIP LIST (I, J, 'OUT OF RANGE');
        GO TO L2;
        END;
    ON CONV SNAP BEGIN;
        PUT SKIP LIST (ONSOURCE);
```

---

[5]We have not yet discussed the printing of alphabetic data in PL/I, but an under standing of this is not essential here.

[6]The value of ONSOURCE is a character string. If it were printed with a PUT EDIT statement, an A-format item would be used. We shall discuss this in detail in Section 9.4.

```
                GET SKIP;
                GO TO L2;
                END;
    (SUBRG):  GET LIST (I, J, A(I, J));
                PUT SKIP LIST (I, J, A(I, J));
        L2:  END L1;
        L3:  ON CONV SYSTEM;
                PUT PAGE EDIT (((A(I, J) DO J = 1 TO 5) DO I = 1 TO 5))
                                              (SKIP, (5)E(14,5));

                RETURN;
                END GO;
```

7.6. PL/I AND FORTRAN

This section is included for the benefit of FORTRAN programmers who wish to draw analogies between PL/I and FORTRAN. There is very little to be said here, since FORTRAN has no interrupt facilities comparable to the PL/I facilities described in this chapter.

(1) Some of the conditions that cause interrupts in PL/I programs, such as floating-point overflow and underflow, can be detected by programming in FORTRAN, even though they do not cause interrupts. For instance, floating-point overflow can be detected by a CALL to the FORTRAN OVERFL subroutine.

(2) Division by zero and fixed-point overflow cause interrupts in PL/I programs, if ZERODIVIDE and FIXEDOVERFLOW are not specifically disabled. On the other hand, division by zero and fixed-point overflow may not be noticed at all in a FORTRAN program unless the programmer makes specific tests for them.

(3) In both PL/I and FORTRAN the programmer can recover control after reading an end-of-file. In PL/I it is done by means of the ENDFILE interrupt; in FORTRAN, by means of the END option of the READ statement (not an interrupt).

EXERCISES

1. One hundred numbers are punched in data cards in a form that can be read with the following code:

```
DCL A(100);
DO K = 1 TO 100;
GET LIST (A(K));
END;
```

With this code, if an alphabetic character should appear in the data, the CONVERSION condition would be raised, and the standard system action would cause termination of execution. Modify and extend this code so that if an alphabetic character appears in the data, the offending field is printed out with a SNAP message and the field is skipped. *Hint*: Use a CONVERSION on-unit and the ONSOURCE built-in function (see Section 7.5).

2. Write code to print a table of reciprocals. Specifically, print N and 1/N for N = 1, 2, 3, . . ., 1000. Have two columns per page, one for N and one for 1/N. Number each page in the upper right-hand corner (1ine 1, about position 110). Use the ENDPAGE condition to detect the end of each page, and do the page numbering in an on-unit. Remember that the form is not ejected automatically when you do not use the standard system action for ENDPAGE.

8 SUBPROGRAMS

8.1. INTRODUCTION

The usefulness of subprograms is a well-recognized fact among experienced programmers. PL/I has facilities for two types of subprograms—*subroutines* and *functions*. A subroutine is invoked by means of a CALL statement, and a function is invoked by use of the function name in an expression. We shall discuss both types of subprograms in this chapter.

Subprograms, like main programs, are *procedures*. They can be classified as *internal procedures* and *external procedures*. An external procedure, as the name implies, is separate from other procedures; it is complete in itself and can be compiled alone. All main programs are external procedures. An internal procedure, on the other hand, is contained in an external procedure and is compiled with it. Moreover, an internal procedure may share some variables with the external procedure that contains it. Although the rules for using internal and external procedures are generally the same, internal procedures involve certain considerations that external procedures do not. We shall confine our attention in this chapter exclusively to the subject of external procedures until Section 8.12, where we shall discuss internal procedures briefly.

8.2. SUBROUTINES

As was mentioned in the preceding section, a subroutine is invoked by means of a CALL statement. The CALL statement specifies the name of the subroutine and usually also an argument list consisting of variables, constants, and expressions. The subroutine name has no special significance and can be chosen in any convenient way.[1]

Example:

$$CALL\ EVAL\ (.\ 567890E4,\ A*B,\ C(3));$$

In certain cases, a dummy variable is automatically created and substituted for an item in an argument list. This occurs, for example, when an argument is a constant or is an expression that must be evaluated before the CALL can take place.

Example: The CALL in the preceding example would have the same effect as the following:

$$DUMMY1 = .\ 567890E4;$$
$$DUMMY2 = A*B;$$
$$CALL\ EVAL\ (DUMMY1,\ DUMMY2,\ C(3));$$

The subroutine itself begins with a PROCEDURE statement labeled with the subroutine name and ends with an END statement containing the same name. A comment can precede the PROCEDURE statement. The PROCE-DURE statement usually also contains a list of parameter variables. The number of arguments in a CALL statement invoking the subroutine and the number of parameters must be equal.

Example:

$$EVAL: PROC\ (X,\ Y,\ Z);$$
$$...$$
$$END\ EVAL;$$

The arguments in a CALL statement match one for one with the parameters in the subroutine's PROCEDURE statement and in effect replace the parameters in the subroutine. In other words, each reference in the subroutine to a parameter variable is treated as if it were a reference to the corresponding argument (or dummy argument).[2] Thus, by references to its parameters, a subroutine can obtain values from the procedure that invoked it and can assign values to variables in that procedure.

---

[1]In PL/I implementations for the IBM System/360, a subroutine name is restricted to at most seven characters in length, if the procedure is an external procedure.

[2]In compiler implementations the addresses of arguments are usually just copied into the subroutine and used as addresses for the parameter variables.

Note that the terms *argument* and *parameter* refer to the same things. What is an argument from the point of view of the invoking procedure is a parameter from the point of view of the subroutine.

A RETURN statement in the subroutine causes control to be returned to the procedure that invoked the subroutine. A subprogram (or, for that matter, a main program) may contain more than one RETURN.

The attributes of arguments used in a CALL statement must be identical to the attributes of the corresponding subroutine parameters. For the most part, the programmer must take care himself to see to it that this is true. The ENTRY attribute, which we shall explain in Section 8.4, can sometimes help in the task of matching attributes.

Now let us consider a more detailed example to illustrate the use of a subroutine.

Example: Suppose that we want to use a subroutine to convert a complex number from the polar form $r\,e^{i\theta}$ to the cartesian form z. (This means that the real part of z is $r \cos \theta$ and the imaginary part is $r \sin \theta$.) Subroutine CART given below uses real R and THETA to compute a complex Z.

```
CART: PROC (R, THETA, Z);
          DCL Z CPLX;
          Z = CPLX(R*COS(THETA), R*SIN(THETA));
          RETURN;
          END CART;
```

(CPLX is a built-in function that forms a complex number $x + iy$ from two real numbers x and y.) In some other procedure, CART could be invoked as shown below:

```
          DCL C CPLX;
          . . .
          CALL CART (.123456E0, AMP, C);
```

8.3. FUNCTIONS

A function subprogram is invoked by inclusion of its name, together with an argument list, in an expression.[3] The function takes on a value in the expression, the value being computed by the subprogram from the data values

---

[3]In PL/I implementations for the IBM System/360, a function name is restricted to at most seven characters in length, if the function is an external procedure.

supplied to it through the argument list. The arguments can be variables, constants, and expressions.

The function subprogram begins with a PROCEDURE statement labeled with the function name and ends with an END statement containing the same name. The PROCEDURE statement also contains a list of parameter variables. As in the case of a subroutine, the number of arguments and the number of parameters must be equal. The arguments match up with function parameters and in effect replace them in the subprogram.

Example: Suppose that a cube-root function named QBRT were to be used in an application. QBRT could be invoked by using it as shown below:

$$X = Y + QBRT(3*Z)/V;$$

The subprogram could begin and end as follows:

QBRT: PROC (X);

. . .

END QBRT;

The value of the argument 3*Z would be used as the value of the parameter X in the function subprogram, and the value of QBRT in the expression Y + QBRT(3*Z)/V would be the cube root of 3*Z.

Like an ordinary element variable, a function has attributes. These attributes must be declared in two places, either explicitly or by default: (1) in the procedure that invokes the function, and (2) in the function subprogram itself. In the absence of specifications to the contrary, these attributes are determined by the same first-letter rule (Section 2.3) used for ordinary variables. To define function attributes explicitly, one must specify them (1) with the RETURNS *attribute* in a DECLARE statement in the invoking procedure, and (2) with the RETURNS *option* in the PROCEDURE statement in the subprogram. The technique for this is illustrated below.

Example: In the preceding procedure, QBRT would have the attributes FLOAT (6) in the invoking procedure, since there is (we assume) no explicit declaration of attributes for the function. QBRT has the same attributes in the subprogram, because no attributes are specified for it in the PROCEDURE statement. If we wanted QBRT to have the attributes FLOAT (16), say, then we would have to do two things: (1) include the following declaration in the invoking procedure:

DCL QBRT RETURNS (FLOAT (16));

and (2) change the PROCEDURE statement to the following:

QBRT: PROC (X) RETURNS (FLOAT (16));

The usual default rules (Section 2.3) apply when not all of the base, scale, and precision attributes are stated. Thus, FLOAT (16) denotes REAL FLOAT DECIMAL (16).

A special form of the RETURN statement is used to cause a return from a function subprogram to the procedure that invoked the function. The keyword RETURN is followed by an expression in parentheses that specifies the function value to be returned to the invoking procedure.

Example:

RETURN(X);
RETURN(3.14);
RETURN(3.14*X);

The expression in parentheses can have any attributes. An automatic conversion will be made so that the function value returned has the attributes specified in the function's PROCEDURE statement or defined by default in the absence of such a specification. It may be noted that the form of the RETURN statement in a subprogram is the one thing that unfailingly differentiates between subroutine and function subprograms.

As in the case of subroutines, function arguments must have the same attributes as the corresponding function parameters. The ENTRY attribute, which we shall discuss in the next section, facilitates the task of making attributes agree.

It is also necessary for the attributes of the function in the invoking procedure to agree with those of the function in the subprogram. It would be an error, for example, for a subprogram to compute a FIXED (15,5) function value when the invoking procedure expected a FLOAT (6) value. There is no automatic conversion to compensate for such a mistake.

Now let us consider some more examples that illustrate in detail how functions are programmed and used.

Example: The function ASIN given below computes arcsin x for $-1 \leq x \leq 1$. Both the function and its parameter have the attributes FLOAT (6) by default. The ERROR condition is raised if an argument outside the range $[-1, 1]$ is encountered. (This is what most of the built-in functions like SQRT and LOG do when an invalid argument is detected.) We shall explain in Section 8.9 the significance of the key word STATIC used in this code. An understanding of this is not essential here.

```
/* ARCSINE FUNCTION */
ASIN: PROC (X);
      DCL PI_OVER_2 INIT(1.5707963) STATIC;
      ABSX = ABS(X);
      IF ABSX > 1 THEN SIGNAL ERROR;
      IF ABSX <= .5 THEN Z = ABSX;
      ELSE Z = SQRT(.5*(1 — ABSX));
      ZSQ = Z*Z;
      R = Z + Z*ZSQ*(.166668 + ZSQ* (.074947 + ZSQ* (.045521 +
          ZSQ* (.023994 + ZSQ*(.042417))));
      IF ABSX > .5 THEN R = PI_OVER_2 — R — R;
      IF X < 0 THEN R = —R;
      RETURN(R);
      END ASIN;
```

Example: Suppose that we want to use a function to convert a complex number from the polar form $re^{i\theta}$ to the cartesian form z. (Compare the example given at the end of the preceding section.) The function subprogram given below uses the real parameters R and THETA to compute a complex function value CART.

```
CART: PROC (R, THETA) RETURNS (CPLX);
      DCL Z CPLX;
      Z = CPLX(R*COS(THETA), R*SIN(THETA));
      RETURN(Z);
      END CART;
```

In a procedure invoking CART, we might have the following:

```
DCL CART RETURNS(CPLX), W CPLX;
...
W = CART(U, V);
```

8.4. ARGUMENT AND PARAMETER ATTRIBUTES

As we have already explained, the attributes of arguments used when a subroutine or function is invoked must agree with those of the corresponding subprogram parameters. It would be an error, for example, to use an argument with the attributes FIXED DECIMAL (5), say, when the corresponding parameter was FLOAT (6). Similarly, it would be an error to use a FLOAT (5) argument when the corresponding parameter was FLOAT (6).[4]

Example: Suppose that a subroutine named EVAL has its parameters declared as shown below:

```
EVAL: PROC (X, N);
      DCL X FLOAT (6), N FIXED (5, 3);
      . . .
      END EVAL;
```

If EVAL were invoked as shown below, there would be two errors:

```
DCL (J, K) FIXED (5, 3);
. . .
CALL EVAL (5.67, J*K);
```

The first error is due to the fact that the argument 5.67 has the attributes FIXED (3, 2), whereas the parameter X is FLOAT (6); this could be corrected by writing the constant as a FLOAT (6) constant, such as 5.67000E0. The second error is due to the fact that J*K is FIXED (11, 6), whereas the parameter N is FIXED (5, 3). This could be corrected by replacing J*K by MULTIPLY(J, K, 5, 3).

The ENTRY attribute provides a way for the programmer to declare the attributes of his subprogram parameters in the procedure that invokes the subprogram. Then, if the attributes of an argument do not agree with those specified for the corresponding parameter, a dummy argument with the correct attributes is created automatically and used instead of the stated argument.

Example: Suppose that the subroutine EVAL discussed in the preceding example were declared and invoked as shown below:

```
DCL (J, K) FIXED (5, 3), EVAL ENTRY (FLOAT (6), FIXED (5, 3));
. . .
CALL EVAL (5.67, J*K);
```

---

[4]Strictly speaking, it is always an error if the precisions of an argument and the corresponding parameter are not identical. In PL/I implementations for the IBM System/360, however, certain programming errors of this type involving floating-point arguments and parameters do not actually cause program failures. If both argument and parameter are treated internally as single-precision floating-point or as double-precision floating-point, then no difficulty arises even though their precisions specified in the program are not equal (see Section 2.14). Thus, it would work to have an argument be FLOAT (5) and the corresponding parameter be FLOAT (6), since both would be treated as single precision internally.

The ENTRY declaration for EVAL specifies the subprogram parameters should have the attributes FLOAT (6) and FIXED (5, 3). Since the arguments used in the CALL do not have these attributes, dummy arguments would be created so that the result would be effectively equivalent to the following:

```
DCL (J, K) FIXED (5, 3), DUMMY1 FLOAT (6), DUMMY2 FIXED (5, 3);
. . .
DUMMY1 = 5.67;
DUMMY2 = J*K;
CALL EVAL (DUMMY1, DUMMY2);
```

The usual default rules (Section 2.3) apply if not all of the base, precision, and scale attributes are specified for a parameter. Thus, FLOAT means REAL FLOAT DECIMAL (6).

Every subprogram parameter must be accounted for when parameter attributes are specified in an ENTRY declaration. A *null specification* indicated by an extra comma should be inserted to indicate the existence of a parameter, if no attribute specification is actually made.

Example:

```
DCL EVAL ENTRY ( , FIXED BIN(15, 6));
```

The ENTRY attribute does not completely solve for the programmer the problem of matching argument and parameter attributes. Correct use of ENTRY assures that an argument value used in a subprogram has the attributes required by the subprogram. On the other hand, it does not assure that a value assigned by the subprogram to one of its parameters (and hence to an argument) has the attributes required in the procedure that invoked the subprogram. The substitution of a dummy argument for an actual argument occurs before a subprogram is invoked. Although it will cause a data conversion of an argument value *before* the CALL takes place, it cannot cause a conversion *after* the return from the subprogram.

Example: Suppose that a subroutine is invoked as follows:

```
DCL EVAL ENTRY (FLOAT, FLOAT);
. . .
CALL EVAL (N, X);
```

Because N has the wrong attributes (FIXED BINARY instead of FLOAT), a dummy argument would be created and the CALL would in effect be treated as follows:

DUMMY = N;

CALL EVAL (DUMMY, X);

Now suppose that the subroutine is as follows:

EVAL: PROC (A, B);

. . .

A = 5;

. . .

END EVAL;

The result would be that a floating-point value would be assigned to DUMMY, not a fixed-point value to N. In fact, the value of N would not be changed at all.

It should be mentioned that the ENTRY and RETURNS attributes are often used together when a function is declared.

Example: Refer to the discussion of the function CART that was described in the last example of the preceding section. The illustration showing how to invoke CART could be improved by including the ENTRY attribute, as shown in the DECLARE statement below:

DCL CART ENTRY (FLOAT, FLOAT) RETURNS (CPLX), W CPLX;

. . .

W = CART (U, V);

8.5. GENERIC FUNCTIONS

Most of the built-in PL/I functions, such as SQRT, FLOAT, etc., are *generic* functions. Such a function is not restricted to arguments with a particular set of attributes, and its own attributes can depend on those of its arguments. For example, SQRT can have an argument with the attributes either FLOAT (6) or FLOAT (16), among others. If the argument is FLOAT (6), then a single-precision square-root routine is invoked; if the argument is FLOAT (16), then a double-precision square-root routine is invoked.[5]

PL/I permits a programmer to define a generic function of his own. The function must be defined to have the GENERIC attribute in a DECLARE state-

---

[5]The remarks in this and the preceding sentence apply to PL/I implementations for the IBM System/360.

ment contained in the procedure invoking the function (not in the subprogram itself). To illustrate this, let us suppose that we want to define a cube-root function QBRT that can have an argument with either the attributes FLOAT (6) and FLOAT (16). We could declare QBRT as follows:

```
DCL QBRT GENERIC (QBRT1 ENTRY (FLOAT(6)) RETURNS (FLOAT(6)),
        QBRT2 ENTRY (FLOAT(16)) RETURNS (FLOAT(16)));
```

The effect of this statement is this: In the procedure containing this declaration, a reference to QBRT is automatically changed into a reference to QBRT1 if the function argument has the attributes FLOAT (6) and into a reference to QBRT2 if the argument has the attributes FLOAT (16). QBRT1 is a function subprogram that returns a result with the attributes FLOAT (6), and QBRT2 is another function subprogram that returns a result with the attributes FLOAT (16). The programmer must supply both of these subprograms.

The generic QBRT function described above would not come close to providing the versatility of the built-in SQRT function. QBRT could not have an argument with attributes other than FLOAT (6) and FLOAT (16). Thus, the expression QBRT (2.45E−1) would be invalid because the argument has the attributes FLOAT (3); fixed-point and complex arguments would also be invalid. The built-in SQRT function, by contrast, can have floating-point arguments of any precision, as well as fixed-point and complex arguments. (Fixed-point arguments are converted to floating-point automatically.) It would require a very elaborate application of the GENERIC attribute to create a QBRT function as versatile as SQRT is.

8.6. RECURSIVE PROCEDURES

If a procedure invokes itself, the procedure is said to be *recursive*. A PL/I function or subroutine can invoke itself if the keyword RECURSIVE is included in the subprogram's PROCEDURE statement. The following example provides an illustration of a recursive function.

Example: The recursive function GAMMA given below evaluates $\Gamma(x)$ for $0 < x \le 57$. For $1 \le x \le 2$ a polynomial approximation to $\Gamma(x)$ is evaluated; otherwise, GAMMA invokes itself in order to exploit the relation $\Gamma(1 + x) = x\Gamma(x)$. If $0 < x < 1$, it invokes itself in order to compute $\Gamma(x) = \Gamma(1 + x)/x$; if $2 < x$, it invokes itself to compute $\Gamma(x) = (x - 1)\Gamma(x - 1)$. An invalid argument causes the ERROR condition to be raised.

```
/* GAMMA FUNCTION */
GAMMA: PROC (X) RECURSIVE;
        IF (X <= 0)|(X > 57) THEN SIGNAL ERROR;
        IF X < 1 THEN RETURN(GAMMA(1 + X)/X);
        IF X > 2 THEN RETURN((X − 1)*GAMMA(X − 1));
        Z = X − 1;
        P = 1 + Z*(−.577102 + Z*(.985854 + Z*(−.876422 + Z*(.832821
            + Z*(−.568473 + Z*(.254821 + Z*(−.051499)))))));
        RETURN(P);
        END GAMMA;
```

8.7. ADDITIONAL FACTS ABOUT SUBPROGRAMS

Some additional facts and rules about subprograms are summarized below:

(1) A function need have no argument whatever. The ENTRY attribute must be specified for such a function in any procedure that invokes the function. (Otherwise, having no argument, the function would look like an ordinary variable.)

Example: The function RANDOM given below uses no arguments. Its value is a random number in the range (0, 1).[6]

```
/* POWER RESIDUE RANDOM NUMBER GENERATOR */
RANDOM: PROC;
            DCL R FIXED BIN (31) INIT(452807053) STATIC;
(NOFOFL):   R = R*452807053;
            RETURN(R*.465661E−9);
            END RANDOM;
```

RANDOM could be invoked as follows:

```
            DCL RANDOM ENTRY;
            . . .
            X = 2*RANDOM − 1;
```

(2) A LABEL variable (Section 3.1) can be used as a subprogram parameter. The LABEL attribute must be specified for the parameter in a DECLARE statement. A LABEL argument is sometimes passed to a

---

[6]This code is machine dependent. It runs on the IBM System/360.

subprogram for use as an error return. The interested reader can refer to his PL/I reference manual for additional information.

Example:

```
SUBR: PROC (X, Y, Z);
      DCL Z LABEL;
      ...
      GO TO Z;
      ...
      END SUBR;
```

(3) An entry name, such as a function name, can be used as a subprogram
argument; the ENTRY attribute must be specified for the corresponding subprogram parameter.

Example: The function GAUSS given below computes an approximate value
for the integral $\int_{-1}^{1} F(x)\, dx$. The parameter F is a function to be used by
GAUSS for integrand evaluation.

```
/* SIX-POINT GAUSSIAN INTEGRATION */
GAUSS: PROC (F);
       DCL F ENTRY, A(3) INIT (.238619, .661209, .932470) STATIC,
           H(3) INIT (.467914, .360762, .171324) STATIC;
       T = 0;
       DO K = 1 TO 3;
       T = T + H(K)*(F(A(K) + F(-A(K))));
       END;
       RETURN(T);
       END GAUSS;
```

GAUSS could be invoked as illustrated below:

```
DCL G ENTRY;
...
Y = GAUSS(G)*Z;
```

Here G would have to be the name of a function subprogram suitable for evaluating the integrand.

(4) In addition to the entry point that is specified as a label for the
PROCEDURE statement of a subprogram, entry points can be specified
by use of the ENTRY statement (not to be confused with the ENTRY
attribute). The interested reader can refer to his PL/I reference
manual for additional information.

Example: Suppose that one subprogram is to be used for calculating either arcsin x or arccos x. Two entry points, ASIN and ACOS, could be defined as indicated below:

ASIN : PROC (X);

. . .

ACOS : ENTRY (X);

. . .

END ASIN;

8.8. ARRAY ARGUMENTS

An array or a cross section of an array can be used as an argument for a PL/I subroutine or function. The programmer must insure that the argument in the invoking procedure and the corresponding parameter in the subprogram have the same dimensions. The simplest way to achieve this is to declare the argument in the invoking program and the corresponding paramenter in the subprogram with identical dimension attributes.

Example: Suppose that we want to use a subroutine to multiply two 5×5 matrices. The following subroutine multiplies A by B and assigns the result to C:

```
MULT: PROC (A, B, C);
      DCL A(5, 5), B(5, 5), C(5, 5);
LP:   DO I = 1 TO 5;
      DO J = 1 TO 5;
      C(I, J) = SUM(A(I, *)*B(*, J));
      END LP;
      RETURN;
      END MULT;
```

(The built-in function SUM was discussed in Section 5.3.) In another procedure we might invoke MULT in the following way in order to multiply P times Q and assign the result to R:

```
DCL P(5, 5), Q(5, 5), R(5, 5);
. . .
CALL MULT (P, Q, R);
```

A second way to make sure that an array argument and its corresponding subprogram parameter have the same dimension attributes is to include the bounds as arguments in the CALL statement.

Example: The array parameters in subroutine MULT could be declared as shown on the next page:

```
MULT: PROC (A, B, C, N);
       DCL A(N, N), B(N, N), C(N, N);
       . . .
       END MULT;
```

The value of N could then be included as an argument in the CALL invoking MULT, as illustrated below:

```
DCL P(5, 5), Q(5, 5), R(5, 5);
. . .
K = 5;
CALL MULT (P, Q, R, K);
```

A third and still better way to make sure that an array argument and its corresponding subprogram parameter have the same dimension attributes is to use asterisks in specifying the dimensions of the subprogram array parameter. The asterisks indicate that the dimension specifications for the parameter are to be copied automatically from those of the corresponding argument whenever the subprogram is invoked. We shall illustrate the use of this technique after we have discussed functions with array arguments.

As was stated in Section 5.6, if we use a built-in function like SQRT or ABS with an array argument, the result is another array obtained by applying the function to the array elementwise. Thus, we can get the square root of each element of an array A by writing SQRT(A). A programmer-coded function is never treated this way. When any function that is not a built-in function is used with an array as an argument, the result is not an array but just a single scalar value. The array argument is passed to the function subprogram all at once rather than an element at a time. Thus, if we code a cube-root function called QBRT, we cannot write QBRT(A) in order to get the cube root of each element of an array A. There is no way in PL/I for a programmer to code a function subprogram with an array value.

It should be recalled that not every built-in function yields an array result when used with an array argument. An example is the SUM function, which takes an array for its argument and whose value is the sum of the array elements. The only built-in functions like this, however, are those that are specifically for array manipulations, such as SUM and PROD.

The next example illustrates both the use of a function with an array argument and the asterisk notation mentioned earlier.

Example: Suppose that we want to use a function to compute the Euclidean norm of a matrix. (The Euclidean norm of a matrix is the square root of the

sum of the squares of the matrix elements.) The function NORM computes the
Euclidean norm of a matrix A of arbitrary size:

```
NORM: PROC (A) RETURNS (FLOAT);
       DCL A(*, *);
       RETURN(SQRT(SUM(A**2)));
       END NORM;
```

In another procedure the following code might be used to compute the norms
of two matrices X and Y:

```
DCL X(5, 5), Y(4, 6), NORM RETURNS (FLOAT);
...
XN = NORM(X);
YN = NORM(Y);
```

Note, incidentally, that we could not rescale X to have norm one by writing X =
X/NORM(X). NORM(X) would be calculated 25 times and would change its value
repeatedly (see Section 5.5).

In a subprogram one often needs to know the bounds of the dimensions of
an array parameter. When the dimension is specified by an asterisk, its bounds
can be found by means of the LBOUND and HBOUND built-in functions. If
the upper bound of the second dimension of an array A were equal to five, for
example, then the value of HBOUND(A, 2) would be five.

Example: Suppose that we want to use a function to compute the row norm of
a matrix. (The row norm of a matrix is the maximum absolute row sum.)
Function ROW given below computes this norm for a matrix of arbitrary size.

```
ROW: PROC(A);
       DCL A(*, *);
       T = 0;
LP:    DO K = LBOUND(A, 1) TO HBOUND(A, 1);
       T = MAX(T, SUM(ABS(A(K, *))));
       END LP;
       RETURN(T);
       END ROW;
```

(MAX is a built-in function whose value is the maximum of its individual arguments.)

A restriction on the use of array arguments is that an array DEFINED on
another array by means of iSUB's (Section 5.3) cannot be used as an argument.
(The elements of such an array might not occupy consecutive storage locations.)

8.9. STORAGE ALLOCATION

A PL/I variable can have any one of four *storage-class attributes*: AUTOMATIC (abbr.: AUTO), STATIC, CONTROLLED (abbr.: CTL), and BASED. These attributes are specified in DECLARE statements. Except for EXTERNAL variables, which we shall discuss in Section 8.11, variables are AUTOMATIC by default, in the absence of explicit storage-class declarations.[7]

Example:

DCL X FLOAT (16) STATIC, Y(5, 5) CTL;

As we shall explain, the storage class of a variable determines how storage is allocated to the variable during program execution.

BASED storage will not be considered in this section. We shall take it up in Chapter 10 as part of our study of list processing in PL/I.

We have already discussed the use of CONTROLLED storage in connection with the subject of dynamic storage allocation for arrays (Section 5.4). As the reader should recall from that discussion, storage is allocated to a CONTROLLED variable when an ALLOCATE statement naming the variable is encountered during program execution, and the storage is released when a FREE statement is executed. It should be added now on this subject that CONTROLLED storage allocated in a subprogram is *not* released automatically when a return from the subprogram to the procedure that invoked it occurs. If a programmer allocates CONTROLLED storage during execution of a subprogram, then he must release it himself by means of a FREE statement, if he wants it released.

An AUTOMATIC variable is allocated storage when the procedure that contains the variable is entered. The storage is released when the procedure returns control to the procedure that invoked it. For an AUTOMATIC variable in the main procedure of a job, this means that storage is allocated when object program execution begins and is retained until the run terminates. For an AUTOMATIC variable in a subprogram, it means that storage is allocated when the subprogram is invoked and is released when the subprogram makes a return to the procedure that invoked it. In between times that a subprogram is invoked, an AUTOMATIC variable in the subprogram has no storage allocated to it. It follows from this that a value cannot be retained by an AUTOMATIC variable in a subprogram in between invocations of the subprogram.

A STATIC variable in either the main procedure or in a subprogram is allocated storage when the object program loads, and it retains that storage un-

---

[7]EXTERNAL variables are STATIC by default.

til the run terminates. Thus, unlike an AUTOMATIC variable, a STATIC variable in a subprogram can retain a value in between times that the subprogram is invoked.

Automatic storage and controlled storage have the advantage over static storage that they make more efficient use of a program's available storage resources. Storage used in a subprogram can be released and used again elsewhere during a job. Static storage, on the other hand, has the advantage that it is allocated only once, instead of repeatedly, and that there is therefore less overhead involved in its use. A programmer has to decide for himself which storage class is best for each of his variables.

As we explained in Sections 2.7 and 5.2, the INITIAL attribute can be used to initialize a variable to a particular value. Initialization actually occurs when storage is allocated to the variable. This means that a STATIC variable is initialized just once, when the object program is loaded. On the other hand, an AUTOMATIC or CONTROLLED variable is initialized each time storage is allocated to the variable. Thus, for example, an AUTOMATIC variable in a subprogram could be initialized over and over again, once for each time the subprogram was invoked. If, for the sake of efficiency, the programmer wanted to avoid wasteful reinitializations, he could declare the variable STATIC. It was for this reason that the variable PI_OVER_2 was made STATIC in the ASIN example at the end of Section 8.3.

We summarize below some additional rules concerning storage-class attributes.

(1) An array with adjustable dimensions cannot be STATIC.

(2) A subprogram parameter for which no storage-class attribute is declared can be associated with an argument of any storage class. The only storage-class attribute that can be declared for a parameter is CONTROLLED, and in this case the corresponding argument must always also be CONTROLLED. There are difficulties involved with using CONTROLLED parameters; the interested reader should consult his PL/I reference manual.

(3) When a RECURSIVE procedure invokes itself, the current value of an AUTOMATIC or CONTROLLED variable is saved in a push-down stack. This is not true of a STATIC variable, however, and the current value of such a variable could be destroyed when a procedure invokes itself. Therefore, static storage must be used carefully in RECURSIVE procedures.

(4) A storage-class attribute cannot be declared for a DEFINED variable, either in a main program or in a subprogram.

8.10. INTERRUPTS IN SUBPROGRAMS

In a subprogram the enabled-disabled status of a condition is not affected by the status of the condition in a procedure that invokes the subprogram. In other words, the scope of a condition prefix used in one procedure does not include subprograms invoked by the procedure.[8]

The scope of an ON statement, on the other hand, does extend into subprograms. In the absence of specifications to the contrary, the on-unit that is executed when a condition is raised in a subprogram is the same on-unit that would have been executed if the condition had been raised in the procedure that invoked the subprogram. (The "on-unit" might be just the standard system action.)

If a subprogram needs an on-unit that is different from the one in effect in the procedure that invoked it, an ON statement can be used in the subprogram to suspend the old on-unit and define a new one for the condition in question. The scope of such an ON statement includes the subprogram and any subprograms it might invoke in turn but does not include the procedure that invoked the subprogram. When an ON statement in a subprogram overrides the on-unit in effect in the invoking procedure, a record of the old on-unit is saved in a push-down stack so that the old on-unit can be reinstated later. The old on-unit is reinstated when one of two things happens: (1) the subprogram returns control to the procedure that invoked it; (2) a statement of the form

REVERT condition name;

is executed. (What REVERT does is to reinstate the on-unit that is at the top of the push-down stack.)

The "stacking" of on-units does not occur when two ON statements for a condition are used just within one procedure (see Section 7.3). In that situation the newly defined on-unit merely supersedes the old one, and the old is forgotten. Stacking occurs when a subprogram suspends the interrupt arrangements in effect in the procedure that invoked it.

8.11. EXTERNAL VARIABLES

As we have already explained, data values can be communicated between two procedures through an argument list. Another way for procedures to communicate is with EXTERNAL variables. An EXTERNAL variable is one that is declared to have the EXTERNAL (abbr.: EXT) attribute.[9]

---

[8]This is true only for subprograms that are external procedures. The rule for internal procedures is different. We shall discuss it in Section 8. 12.

[9]In PL/I implementations for the IBM System/360, EXTERNAL variables cannot have names more than seven characters in length.

Example:

```
DCL (X, Y) EXT, Z FLOAT (16) EXT;
```

If a variable is declared to be EXTERNAL in two procedures, such as a main program and a subprogram, then a value assigned to the variable in either procedure is available automatically for use in the other. The variable is, in effect, shared between the two procedures. Since the matching is done by name, the variable must have the same name in both procedures. The variable must also be declared with identical attributes in both procedures, because no automatic data conversions are performed when data is passed from one procedure to the other.

> **Example:** Suppose that we want to use a subroutine to convert a complex number from the polar form $re^{i\theta}$ to the cartesian form z. (See the discussion for subroutine CART in Section 8.2.) In the version of CART given below, R, THETA, and Z are EXTERNAL variables instead of parameters.

```
CART: PROC;
      DCL Z CPLX EXT, (R, THETA) EXT;
      Z = CPLX(R*COS(THETA), R*SIN(THETA));
      RETURN;
      END CART;
```

This subroutine could be invoked as shown below:

```
DCL (R, THETA) EXT, Z CPLX EXT;
. . .
R = 567E−2;
THETA = .5;
CALL CART;
```

After the CALL, Z would have the required value.

The following additional rules also relate to the use of EXTERNAL variables:

(1) An EXTERNAL variable can be STATIC or CONTROLLED, but not AUTOMATIC. In the absence of specifications to the contrary, an EXTERNAL variable is assumed to be STATIC. (Compare Section 8.9.)

(2) The INITIAL attribute can be used to initialize the value of an EXTERNAL variable, but the INITIAL attribute and initial value must be declared in every DECLARE statement in which the EXTERNAL variable is declared.

(3) A DEFINED variable cannot be EXTERNAL, although its base variable can be.

8.12. INTERNAL PROCEDURES

As we explained in Section 8.1, PL/I subprograms are of two kinds: external procedures and internal procedures. In our treatment of the subject of subprograms so far, we have restricted ourselves to external procedures only. We shall now discuss briefly the use of internal procedures.

Internal procedures have all the general characteristics of external procedures and are used in the same ways as external procedures. They can be functions or subroutines. Also, they have parameters and are invoked just as external procedures are. What is distinctive about an internal procedure is that it is nested in another procedure, which may be either another subprogram or the main procedure. Two such procedures are closely related and cannot be compiled separately. (The reader should remember that an external procedure is always capable of independent compilation.)

The reason why PL/I allows one procedure to be nested within another is that the two procedures can then share in the use of certain variables. An external procedure, it should be recalled, has two ways of communicating with a procedure that invokes it: (1) through an argument list, and (2) through EXTERNAL variables. Besides these two ways, an internal procedure can communicate with the procedure that contains it merely by referencing variables used in the containing procedure. Variables in the containing procedure are said to be *known* to the internal procedure. The internal procedure can also employ variables known only to itself. Specifically, its own parameters and any variables declared within it are known only to itself and not to the outer procedure; and a variable declared in an internal procedure can have without confusion the same name as another variable used in the containing procedure. A statement label used in an internal procedure is also known only in that procedure.

Let us consider an illustration of how an internal procedure can be used. Suppose that in the main procedure of a job we have a matrix M that must be set equal to the identity matrix from time to time. We can relegate to an internal subroutine the task of setting M equal to the identity.

```
GO: PROC OPTIONS (MAIN);
    DCL M(5, 5) FLOAT;
    CALL IDEN;
    . . .
    CALL IDEN;
    . . .
```

```
                    RETURN;
          IDEN: PROC;
                DCL I;
                M = 0;
          LP: DO I = 1 TO 5;
                M(I, I) = 1;
                END LP;
                RETURN;
                END IDEN;
                END GO;
```

Note that IDEN is nested within the main procedure and is therefore an internal procedure. M is known to IDEN, since it is not a parameter in IDEN and is not declared in IDEN; on the other hand, the variable I in the subroutine is not known outside IDEN, because it is declared. If another I should be used in the main procedure outside of IDEN, the two I's would be treated as distinct variables.

The position of an internal procedure within the procedure that contains it has no special significance. Thus, subroutine IDEN in the foregoing illustration could just as well have been first within the main procedure.

In an internal procedure, the enabled-disabled status of a condition is affected by its status in a procedure containing the internal procedure. In particular, if one procedure contains another, the scope of a condition prefix attached to the outer PROCEDURE statement includes all of the internal procedure. The scope of a condition prefix attached to the inner PROCEDURE statement includes only the internal procedure. In the case of an external procedure, it will be recalled (Section 8.10), the enabled-disabled status of a condition depends exclusively on the external procedure and is not affected by other procedures.

It is instructive to reflect on what one would have to do to change an external procedure into an internal one, or vice versa. Suppose, for simplicity, that the main procedure of a job invokes an external procedure and that there are no other procedures involved. The external procedure could be made into an internal one as follows: (1) Nest the subprogram in the main procedure. (2) List in DECLARE statements in the subprogram every subprogram variable for which there is another variable with the same name in the main procedure. (3) Attach a suitable condition prefix to the subprogram PROCEDURE statement, if the enabled-disabled status of a condition would now be reversed because of a prefix used in the main procedure.

Suppose, on the other hand, that the main procedure invokes an internal procedure and that there are no other procedures involved. The internal procedure could be made into an external one as follows: (1) Remove the subprogram from the main procedure so that it stands alone. (2) Declare as an

EXTERNAL variable (Section 8.11) in both the main procedure and the sub-program every variable used in both procedures. (3) Attach a suitable condition prefix to the subprogram PROCEDURE statement, if the enabled-disabled status of a condition formerly defined by a prefix in the main procedure would now be reversed.

It might be thought that, when a subprogram is nested within another procedure and the two procedures are compiled together, it would not be necessary to make the attributes of arguments and parameters be identical. After all, automatic data conversions could in principle be supplied by the compiler. They are *not* supplied, however. When a programmer codes an internal procedure, he must take the same care in matching argument and parameter attributes that he would take if he were coding an external procedure.

The advantage that an internal procedure has over an external one is its ability to share variables with a procedure that contains it. Because of this very fact, however, internal procedures present a pitfall that external procedures do not. The trap is that a programmer might use a variable in an internal procedure, thinking that the variable is known only to that procedure, whereas actually the variable had a wider scope. This could happen if the variable were not named in a DECLARE statement in the internal procedure. The effect of this might be that there would be only one variable in a program where the programmer thought there were two and that a data value would be destroyed unintentionally. The programmer can avoid this trap by declaring in the internal procedure every variable that need not be known outside that procedure.

We have not discussed in this section all the rules involved with using internal procedures. Certain complications can arise when procedures are nested to depths greater than one, and there are restrictions on the conditions under which one internal procedure can reference another one. The interested reader should refer to his PL/I reference manual.

8.13. BEGIN BLOCKS

BEGIN blocks were mentioned briefly in Sections 7.2 and 7.3 in connection with the subjects of condition prefixes and on-units. It is appropriate to discuss them now in more detail.

A BEGIN block is a set of statements bracketed by BEGIN and END statements. For the sake of clarity, it is usually desirable to label the BEGIN statement and to name the same label in the corresponding END statement.[10]

---

[10]When a BEGIN block is used as an on-unit, however, the BEGIN statement cannot be labeled.

Example:

```
LB: BEGIN;
    ...
    END LB;
```

The BEGIN block is the second of two *block types* in PL/I. The other is the *procedure block*, which we have already discussed without calling it by the name "block." Every main procedure and every subroutine or function procedure is a procedure block. As we shall explain, BEGIN blocks have many properties in common with procedures so far as storage allocation and scope of names are concerned. (To be accurate, we really should say that many properties of procedures are actually properties of blocks generally.) The fact that BEGIN blocks and procedure blocks are so much alike suggests that BEGIN blocks should be thought of as just in-line subprograms.

The effect of including a DECLARE statement within a BEGIN block is analogous to the effect of including one within an internal procedure. If a variable is declared inside a BEGIN block, then the variable is known only inside the block. Furthermore, if the variable is AUTOMATIC, storage is allocated for it only when the block is entered, and the storage is released when control passes out of the block. Thus, a BEGIN block provides a means of obtaining dynamic storage allocation. Consider the following illustration;

```
       M, N = 5;
LBL: BEGIN;
     DCL A(M, N);
     ...
     END LBL;
```

The variable A declared within the block is known only inside the block. If there were also a variable A used outside the block, the two A's would be distinct variables. Storage for the array A is not allocated until the block is entered, and the storage is released when control passes from the block. (Control could pass out of the block either as the result of flowing through the END or as the result of a GO TO branching out of the block.)

It should be recalled that one can get dynamic storage allocation in PL/I without using BEGIN blocks. Thus, variable A in the preceding illustration could have been declared to be CONTROLLED and storage allocated to it by means of an ALLOCATE statement (see Section 5.4).

Use of a BEGIN block can also affect a program in other ways. For example, the scope of an ON statement used inside a BEGIN block does not extend beyond the block. We shall not discuss other such properties of BEGIN blocks; the interested reader should consult his PL/I reference manual.

8.14. PL/I AND FORTRAN

The following remarks are intended for FORTRAN programmers who want to draw analogies between PL/I and FORTRAN.

(1) Both PL/I and FORTRAN have subroutine and function subprograms.

(2) In PL/I terminology FORTRAN subprograms are all external procedures.

(3) What are called "parameters" in PL/I are called "dummy arguments" in FORTRAN. In PL/I terminology "dummy argument" refers not to an argument at all but rather to an argument that is substituted for an argument specified in an argument list.

(4) Matching of argument and parameter attributes is mandatory in both PL/I and FORTRAN. The task is somewhat more difficult in PL/I, because there are more data types and more precisions to contend with.

(5) The PL/I ENTRY attribute is analogous in some respects to the FORTRAN EXTERNAL type declaration.

(6) The work of the PL/I RETURNS attribute is performed in FORTRAN by type declaration statements, such as DOUBLE PRECISION and INTEGER.

(7) FORTRAN has no facilities analogous to PL/I generic functions. In FORTRAN it is necessary to write SQRT to get a single-precision square root and to write DSQRT to get a double-precision one; in PL/I SQRT serves for both purposes.

(8) FORTRAN has no facilities for recursion analogous to those discussed in Section 8.6.

(9) Although a FORTRAN function can have an array argument, it cannot have an array value. Built-in PL/I functions can have array values, though programmer-coded ones cannot.

(10) There is nothing in FORTRAN analogous to the asterisk notation for dimensions in a PL/I subprogram. Variable dimensions can be used in a FORTRAN subprogram, but the dimensions have to be passed as arguments.

(11) In PL/I terminology all FORTRAN storage is static. FORTRAN has no facilites analogous to PL/I automatic and controlled storage.

(12) PL/I EXTERNAL variables are analogous to FORTRAN COMMON variables. PL/I EXTERNAL variables are matched by name, however, whereas FORTRAN COMMON variables are matched by position.

(13) FORTRAN arithmetic statement functions are somewhat like PL/I internal procedures, but not as versatile. The simplest way to translate a FORTRAN arithmetic statement function into PL/I is to use a function subprogram coded as an internal procedure.

(14) FORTRAN has no facility analogous to the PL/I BEGIN block.

(15) In FORTRAN terminology PL/I arguments are referenced "by location," rather than "by value." There is no facility in PL/I for referencing an argument by value. It may be mentioned, however, that in PL/I a dummy argument is created whenever an argument in a CALL statement is enclosed in parentheses, as in CALL SUB (X, (Y)). The effect of this is at least similar to the effect of referencing an argument by value.

EXERCISES

1. Code a function that takes a one-dimensional floating-point array as its argument and whose value is the absolute-largest number in the array.

2. Code a function that takes a square, double-precision floating-point matrix as its argument and whose value is the (double-precision) trace of the matrix. (The trace of a square matrix is the sum of its diagonal elements.) Make a test to verify that the array is actually square, and raise the ERROR condition if it is not.

3. Code a subroutine that converts a complex number z into polar form $re^{i\theta}$. The input to the subroutine should be a COMPLEX variable Z, and the output should be REAL variables R and THETA. *Hint:* If $z = re^{i\theta}$, then $r = |z|$ and

$$\theta = \arctan \frac{x}{y}$$

where x denotes the real part of z and y denotes the imaginary part.

4. A function routine for evaluating arcsin x for $|x| \leq 1$ can be designed as follows: If $|x| \leq \frac{1}{2}$, return the value of $P(x)$, where $P(x)$ denotes a polynomial approximation to arcsin x for $|x| \leq \frac{1}{2}$. If $\frac{1}{2} < |x| \leq 1$, return the value of (sign x) $(\frac{1}{2}\pi - 2$ arcsin $(\frac{1}{2}(1 - |x|)))$. Code such a routine using the recursive capability of PL/I. [Note that if $\frac{1}{2} < |x| \leq 1$, then $|\frac{1}{2}(1 - |x|)| \leq \frac{1}{2}$.] A suitable $P(x)$ can be obtained from the arcsine routine given in an example in Section 8.3.

9 CHARACTER STRINGS AND BIT STRINGS

9.1. INTRODUCTION

PL/I provides facilities for handling two types of nonnumeric data: character strings and bit strings. A character string is a sequence of arbitrary characters treated as a single item of data, whereas a bit string is a sequence of zeros and ones treated as a single item of data. Both kinds of strings can be manipulated in various ways. We shall discuss character strings first and shall devote most of this chapter to them, returning to bit strings in Section 9.14.

9.2. CHARACTER-STRING CONSTANTS

A character-string consists of characters enclosed in single quotation marks. A blank inside quotes is significant and is treated as part of the string. We shall use the symbol b throughout this chapter to denote a blank character.

Examples:

'ABC', 'AbZ', '12345', '*bV54', 'bbb'

Characters not in the PL/I character set (Section 1.2) can be included in character-string constants, provided they are valid in the computer being used. If a single quotation mark is to be used as part of a character-string constant (rather than as a delimiter), it must be written as two consecutive single quotation marks.

It is sometimes necessary in string manipulation to use the *null string*, which is a string containing no characters. The constant for the null string is `''` (two single quotation marks).

An unsigned integer constant can be used as a *repetition factor* in a character-string constant to indicate that the characters in quotation marks are to be repeated a certain number of times.

Examples:

(5)'*' is equivalent to '*****'.
(4)'AB' is equivalent to 'ABABABAB'.

9.3. CHARACTER-STRING VARIABLES

A character-string variable can be declared in either of two ways. The first way is to specify the CHARACTER (abbr.: CHAR) attribute for the variable in a DECLARE statement. The declaration must include a length specification stating the number of characters that the string will contain. The length specification appears in parentheses after the keyword CHARACTER (or its abbreviation).

Example: The statement

DCL A CHAR (5), K CHAR (4);

defines A and K to be character-string variables with lengths five and four, respectively.

An array of character strings can be declared by specifying a dimension attribute immediately after the name of the array in a DECLARE.

Example: The statement

DCL A(5) CHAR (3);

defines an array A consisting of five strings, each three characters long. The fourth element is A(4), for example.

The second way to declare a character-string variable is to specify the PICTURE (abbr.: PIC) attribute for the variable in a DECLARE statement. The picture is a series of picture specification characters enclosed in single quotation marks and specifying position by position what types of characters the string may contain. The specification characters that can be used in the picture of a character-string variable are A, 9, and X:

(1) A indicates that the corresponding position in the string may contain any alphabetic character or a blank.[1]

(2) 9 indicates that the corresponding position in the string may contain any digit (0 through 9) or a blank.

(3) X indicates that the corresponding position in the string may contain any character.

Each picture used to define a character-string variable must contain at least one A or X, and no picture characters other than A, 9, and X can be used.

Example: The statement

DCL A PIC'A9X';

defines a character-string variable A with a length of three. The first character can be any alphabetic character or a blank; the second, any digit or a blank; and the third, any character at all.

When a character-string variable has been declared by means of a picture, the CONVERSION condition is raised whenever there one attempts to assign to the variable a character string that does not look the way the picture says it should.

Note that, it a picture contains only X's, the PICTURE attribute is equivalent to the CHARACTER attribute. For instance, PIC'XXX' is equivalent to CHAR (3).

A character-string variable can be initialized by means of the INITIAL attribute. The constant used to specify an initial value is normally a character-string constant with the same length as the variable. If the length of the constant exceeds the variable, the constant is truncated on the right. If the length of the constant is less than the length of the variable, the constant is padded on the right with blanks.

Example: The statement

DCL A CHAR (4) INIT ('1234'), B CHAR (5) INIT ('b');

causes A to be assigned the value '1234' and B to be assigned the value 'bbbbb' when storage is allocated to the variables.

Storage-class attributes (Section 8.9) can be specified for character-string variables, just as for arithmetic variables and with the same significance; the

---

[1]The "alphabetic" characters are the 26 letters of the alphabet, together with the characters $, #, and @.

default is AUTOMATIC. For a CONTROLLED variable, length can be specified by an asterisk when the variable is declared; then the actual length can be indicated later when storage for the variable is allocated by means of an ALLOCATE statement. This is analogous to the process for defining the dimensions of a CONTROLLED array (Section 5.4).

Example:

```
DCL A CHAR (*) CTL;
...
ALLOCATE A CHAR (5000);
...
FREE A;
```

9.4. INPUT/OUTPUT OF CHARACTER STRINGS

Character-string data can be processed by all three of the stream input/ output methods that were described in Chapter 6: list-directed, data-directed, and edit-directed input/output.

For both the list-directed and data-directed methods, input/output of character-string data is handled according to the same general rules used for arithmetic data. The only difference is in the use of character-string variables and constants instead of arithmetic variables and constants.

Example: Let A and B be two character-string variables of lengths five and four respectively. Suppose that we want to read in the string 'ABC12' and assign it to B. With list-directed input, we might have

```
DCL A CHAR (5), B CHAR (4);
GET LIST (A, B);
```

The data in the input stream could be

'ABC12', '*b55'

With data-directed input, we could have

```
DCL A CHAR (5), B CHAR (4);
GET DATA (A, B);
```

In this case the data in the input stream could be

A = 'ABC12', B = '*b55';

In should be noted that a character-string input value must be enclosed in single quotation marks if it is to be read in by means of either a GET LIST or a GET DATA statement. Likewise, if a character string is written out by means of a PUT DATA statement, the value that is written out is enclosed in quotes automatically. This is also true when a character string is written out by means of a PUT LIST statement on a file that is not a PRINT file (Section 6.10). On the other hand, if a string is written out on a PRINT file (such as SYSPRINT) by means of a PUT LIST statement, the output value is not enclosed in quotation marks. Omitting the quotation marks improves the readability of the printed matter.

Two data-format items (Section 6.6) can be used to process character-string data in edit-directed input/output. The first is the A-format item, which is written in the form A(n), where n specifies the number of characters to be read in or to be written out. The characters processed can be any characters that are valid in the computer being used. For input, no quotation marks are required in the data field, since the length of the string is specified in the format. If quotation marks do appear in an input field, they are treated as part of the string. Likewise, no quotation marks are supplied automatically on output.

> **Example:** Consider again the problem that was discussed in the preceding example, where we wanted to read in values for variables A and B. With edit-directed input, we could have the following:

> DCL A CHAR (5), B CHAR (4);
> GET EDIT (A, B) (A(5), A(4));

The data in the input stream could then be

ABC12*b55

When an A-format item is used for output, the length specification can be omitted so that the item has form A instead of A(n). In such a case the value of n is automatically construed to be the length of the character string being written out; this is illustrated below. In this example note the use of a character-string constant in the PUT EDIT output list. This is a convenient technique for labeling output.

> **Example:** To print on a new page the value of an arithmetic variable named PI, we might write

> PUT PAGE EDIT ('PIb=', PI) (A, F(5,2));

Since the length of the string 'PIb=' is four, the A-format item is treated as if it were A(4). If PI has the value 3.14, the output will be as follows:

Plb=b3.14

The second data-format item that can be used to process character-string data is a character-string P format (Section 6.8). This is a P format containing the picture characters A, X, and 9, which have the same significance in this context that they have in a PICTURE declaration (Section 9.3); that is, they specify what types of characters are allowed in the data. At least one A or X must be used in any character-string P format, and no picture characters other than A, X, and 9 can be used.[2] The value of this type of format is that it permits one to check a character string for validity during input or output, something that is not possible with an A format. The CONVERSION condition is raised if one attempts to process under a P format a character string that does not look the way the picture says it should.

Example:

GET EDIT (A, B) (P'AAA99', P'X999');

A general rule about processing character strings is that a string can be truncated on the right or padded with blanks on the right if this is necessary to make the string fit somewhere. This is a basic principle that applies to input/output as well as elsewhere. Suppose, for example, that a string of length p is written out under the format A(q). If $p > q$, the string is truncated on the right; if $p < q$, the string is padded with blanks on the right. It is not considered an error for a string to be truncated or padded, and no error condition results.

9.5. BASIC CHARACTER-STRING OPERATIONS

Values can be assigned to character-string variables by means of ordinary assignment statements. If a string is too long for the variable to which it is assigned, the string is truncated on the right. If the string is too short, it is padded on the right with blanks.

Example: Consider the following code:

```
DCL A CHAR (3), B CHAR (4), C CHAR (5);
B = 'WXYZ';
A = B;
C = B;
```

---

[2]A P format is a character-string format if it contains at least one A or X. Otherwise, it is a numeric-character format (Section 6.8). Note that a 9 specifies a digit or a blank in a character-string format, but only a digit in a numeric-character format.

After this code is executed, B has the value 'WXYZ'; A, the value 'WXY'; and C, the value 'WXYZb'.

When a value is assigned to a fixed-point variable, the SIZE condition is raised if a significant digit has to be truncated on the left-hand end of a number (Section 2.9). It might be thought that truncation of a character string would also cause some error condition to be raised, but this is not the case. Neither truncation nor padding of a string is considered to be an error in PL/I.

If a character-string variable is declared by means of a picture (Section 9.3), then the CONVERSION condition will be raised whenever there is assigned to the variable a string that does not look the way the picture says it should.

Two strings can be *concatenated*, or chained together, by means of the concatenation operator ||.

Example: Consider the code

```
DCL A CHAR (2) INIT ('XY'), B CHAR (4);
B = A || 'Z*';
```

After this code is executed, B has the value 'XYZ*'.

9.6. CONDITIONAL EXPRESSIONS INVOLVING CHARACTER STRINGS

In Chapter 3 we explained how conditional expressions could be formed through use of comparison operators (see Section 3.2) and logical operators (see Section 3.4). At that time we considered only the use of arithmetic data. Character-string variables, constants, and expressions can also be used, however, to form conditional expressions. The chief use of such conditional expressions is in IF clauses.

Example: Assume that A and B are character-string variables, each of length five.

```
IF A = B THEN GO TO L7;
IF A = 'bbbbb' THEN RETURN;
IF (A<B) | (B = '*****') THEN B = A;
IF (A || B) = '1234567890' THEN A = 'ZYXWV';
```

If a comparison involves two strings of unequal length, the shorter string is padded on the right with blanks before the comparison is made. Thus, the condition 'AB' = 'ABb' is true, even though the two character strings are of different lengths.

The collating sequence used for greater-than, less-than comparisons depends on the internal representation of data in the computer used and is therefore machine dependent.[3] Thus, for example, the conditional 'G' > '7' might be true in one computer and false in another.

It is recommended that programmers use parentheses in conditional expressions in order to make the sequence of operations explicit. Thus, (A || B) = C is preferable to A || B = C, even though the two expressions have the same interpretation.[4] Use of parentheses to indicate the order of operations is not strictly necessary if a programmer knows the rules for priority of operations, but it is safer and clearer. We shall discuss the priority rules in Section 9.18.

It is permissible to compare character-string data with arithmetic data in a conditional expression. In such a case the character string is automatically converted to an arithmetic value for the test. If the string cannot be converted to a valid arithmetic value, the CONVERSION condition is raised. The programmer is advised, however, not to mix data types in a comparison operation. The string-to-arithmetic conversion that it causes to occur is wasteful in any case, and it may cause a CONVERSION error if the string data can be alphabetic.

9.7. BUILT-IN FUNCTIONS FOR STRING MANIPULATION

PL/I provides several built-in functions that facilitate string operations. We shall describe some of the most important ones below briefly.

(1) Probably the most useful string-handling function is SUBSTR, which extracts a substring from a given string. A reference to SUBSTR has the following form:

SUBSTR(string, substring starting position, substring length)

The function value is the substring defined by the function arguments. The third argument can be omitted, in which case the substring is understood to extend all the way through the end of the given string. If the arguments are such that the "substring" extends beyond the limits of the original string, the STRINGRANGE (abbr.: STRG) condition is raised; this condition is initially disabled. Some addition remarks on the SUBSTR function are given later in this section.

---

[3]See Section 1.2 for the collating sequence used in the IBM System/360.

[4]In the original PL/I language, the expression A || B = C was interpreted as A || (B = C) rather than (A || B) = C. The rules on priority of operations were subsequently changed. The fact that it is not obvious just what the priority rules should be is an argument for using parentheses frequently.

Example:

```
DCL X CHAR (5) INIT ('12345'), Y CHAR (3);
Y = SUBSTR(X, 2, 3);
```

After this code is executed, Y has the value '234'. If the second sratement were

```
(STRG): Y = SUBSTR(X, 4, 3);
```

then the STRINGRANGE condition would be raised and an interrupt would occur, since the specified substring is supposed to include positions 4-6 of X, whereas X has only five positions.

(2) The LENGTH functon finds the length of a string. A reference to the function has the following form:

LENGTH(string)

The function value is the length of the specified string. LENGTH is especially useful in work with variable-length strings (Section 9.8) and subprograms (Section 9.11).

(3) The INDEX function searches a given string for the starting position of a specified substring. A reference to the function has the following form:

INDEX(string to be searched, string to be searched for)

The function value is zero if the string searched for does not exist as a substring of the string searched; otherwise, its value is the position of the first character of the substring. If the substring appears more than once in the given string, the substring identified is the leftmost one, since the search is from left to right.

Example:

```
DCL Z CHAR (8) INIT ('ABCb*XBC'), Y CHAR (1);
K = INDEX(Z, 'BC');
L = INDEX(Z, 'b');
Y = SUBSTR(Z, INDEX(Z, '*') + 1, 1);
```

After this code is executed, the value of K is two, and the value of L is four. Also, Y has the value 'X', which is the first character after '*'.

(4) The VERIFY function searches a given string to verify that every character in the string is represented among the characters in a second string called a *verification string*. A reference to the function has the following form:

VERIFY(string to be verified, verification string)

If every character in the string to be verified is a character in the verification string, then the function value is zero; otherwise, the function value is the position in the string to be verified of the first character (from the left) not represented in the verification string.

Example:

```
DCL A CHAR (5) INIT ('123.4');
IF VERIFY(A, '0123456789') ¬= 0 THEN PUT LIST ('NONNUMERIC');
```

This code causes the string A to be searched for a character that is not a digit. When the code is executed, the value of VERIFY is four, since the fourth position of A is the first nondigital position.

Note that in certain uses VERIFY reverses the role of INDEX. Thus, the value of INDEX(C, 'b') is the position of the first blank in C, whereas the value of VERIFY(C, 'b') is the position of the first non-blank character in C.

(5) The TRANSLATE function causes substitutions to be made systematically for specified characters in a given string. A reference to the function has the following form:

TRANSLATE (string to be translated, replacement string, position string)

The value of TRANSLATE is a new string identical to the first argument except for substitutions made as follows: Any character in the string to be translated that also appears in the *position string* is replaced by the corresponding character in the *replacement string*. The characters in the replacement string and position string correspond by position; the replacement string is padded with blanks if it is shorter than the position string. The translated string (that is, the function value) has the same length as the given string.

Example:

```
                DCL A CHAR (5) INIT ('AbC.5');
                A = TRANSLATE(A, '0Q', 'b6');
```

This use of TRANSLATE causes any 'b' in A to be replaced by 'O' and any '6' to be replaced by 'Q'. After the code is executed, the value of A is 'A0C. 5'.

In addition to being a function, SUBSTR is also a *pseudovariable*, which means that it can appear on the left side of an assignment statement. In this usage the substring defined by SUBSTR is *assigned* a value without any other change in the string containing it.

Example:

```
DCL X CHAR (5) INIT ('12345');
SUBSTR(X, 3, 2) = 'PQ';
```

After this code is executed, X has the value '12PQ5'.

The next example demonstrates an application of the SUBSTR pseudovariable.

Example: The code given below is a complete program for reading cards and printing them with slashed zeros. The technique used to slash zeros in a print line is to overprint the line with a second line containing only blanks and slashes, the slashes being in those positions that contained zeros in the original line.

```
/* LIST DECK 80-80 WITH SLASHED ZEROS */
GO : PROC OPTIONS (MAIN);
        DCL (LINE, MASK) CHAR (80);
        ON ENDFILE(SYSIN) GO TO L4;
L1 : DO M = 1 BY 1;
        GET EDIT (LINE) (A(80));
        PUT EDIT (LINE) (COL(1), A);
        MASK = '   ';
L2 : DO N = 1 BY 1;
        K = INDEX (LINE, '0');
        IF K = 0 THEN GO TO L3;
        SUBSTR(LINE, K, 1) = '   ';
        SUBSTR(MASK, K, 1) = '/';
        END L2;
L3 : PUT SKIP(0) EDIT (MASK) (A);
        END L1;
L4 : RETURN;
        END GO;
```

9.8. VARYING CHARACTER-STRING VARIABLES

The character-string variables that we have considered until now have all been fixed-length ones, but a character-string variable can also have variable length. To define such a variable, one must specify the VARYING (abbr.: VAR) attribute along with the CHARACTER attribute when declaring the variable. A length specification must still be provided as well, but this is interpreted as a maximum length for the variable rather than as a fixed length. A VARYING string cannot be declared by means of the PICTURE attribute.

Example:

DCL X CHAR (100) VAR;

This declaration defines X to be a variable-length character-string variable whose maximum length is 100.

As was explained in Section 9.5, an ordinary character-string variable is padded out with blanks on the right when a short string is assigned to it. The chief characteristic of a VARYING character-string variable is that it is not padded with blanks in such a case. Instead, the VARYING variable takes both the value and length of the string assigned to it.

The current length of a VARYING string can always be determined by means of the built-in LENGTH function (Section 9.7).

Example:

```
DCL A CHAR (8) VAR, B CHAR (9), C CHAR (3) INIT ('123');
A = C;
A = A || 'Y' || C;
B = A;
K = LENGTH(A);
```

After the first assignment statement is executed A has the value '123' and length 3; after the second assignment statement, the value '123Y123' and length 7. B has the value '123Y123bb' and K has the value 7.

The principle that a VARYING variable takes its length from the string assigned to it also applies when a value for the variable is read in by means of a GET statement.

Example: Consider the following code:

```
DCL X CHAR (8) VAR;
GET LIST (X);
```

Suppose that the data in the input stream is

'1234'

After the code is executed, A has the value '1234' and length four.

Two other facts about VARYING character-string variables are these: (1) The elements of a VARYING character-string array do not have to be equal in length; any element can have any length ≤ the maximum, regardless of what the lengths of the other elements in the array may be. (2) The result of concatenating a VARYING string with any other string (fixed-length or VARYING) is a VARYING string.

9.9. DEFINED VARIABLES

One character-string variable can be declared to share storage with another character-string variable by means of the DEFINED (abbr.: DEF) attribute (Sections 2.8 and 5.3). In the absence of specifications to the contrary, the first character of the DEFINED string is assumed to correspond to the first character of the base substrings.

Example:

```
DCL A CHAR (5), B CHAR (4) DEF A;
```

The four positions of B are the same as the first four positions of A.

The storage required for a DEFINED variable must not fall outside the storage limits of its base variable.

A DEFINED variable can be offset with respect to its base variable by use of the POSITION (abbr.: POS) attribute. This attribute permits the programmer to specify the position in the base string to which the first character of the DEFINED string corresponds.

Example:

```
DCL A CHAR (5), B CHAR (3) DEF A POS (2);
```

The three positions of B are the same as positions 2–4 of A.

The POSITION attribute provides a method by which the programmer can process substrings without using the built-in function SUBSTR.

Example: The built-in function DATE, which takes no arguments, has for its value a character string of length six *'yymmdd'*, where *yy* is the year, *mm* is the month, and *dd* is the day of the month. Suppose that we want to express the date in the form *mm/dd/yy* for printing purposes. We could do this as follows:

```
DCL A CHAR (6), B CHAR (8);
A = DATE;
B = SUBSTR(A, 3, 2) || '/' || SUBSTR(A, 5, 2) || '/' || SUBSTR(A, 1, 2);
```

Alternatively, we could write the following:

```
DCL A CHAR (6), MONTH CHAR (2) DEF A POS (3), DAY CHAR (2)
            DEF A POS (5), YEAR CHAR (2) DEF A;
A = DATE;
B = MONTH || '/' || DAY || '/' || YEAR;
```

Example: Consider the following declaration:

```
DCL ALPHABET CHAR (26) INIT ('ABCDEFGHIJKLMNOPQRSTUVWXYZ'),
            LETTER(26) CHAR (1) DEF ALPHABET;
```

LETTER is an array variable such that the value of LETTER(N) is the Nth letter of the alphabet.

A storage-class attribute (such as STATIC) cannot be declared for a DEFINED variable, and neither a DEFINED variable nor its base variable can be VARYING.

9.10. EXAMPLE

The coding example given below illustrates many of the techniques discussed so far in this chapter. The code is a complete program for enciphering a text by the Vigenère scheme. In this method the text to be enciphered is matched letter by letter with a key. If the letter in the key is the ith letter of the alphabet and the letter in the text is the jth letter, then the corresponding cipher letter is taken to be the nth letter of the alphabet, where $n = 1 +$ mod $(i + j - 2, 26)$. The key is formed by repeating a prescribed key word a sufficient number of times. For purposes, both the key word and the text are assumed to contain only alphabetic charaters, with all blanks squeezed out. A simple illustration of the method is shown below:

```
key     computercomputercomputercomputercomputercomputerco
text    nowisthetimeforallgoodmentocometotheaidoftheircountry
cipher  pcixmmlvvwytzhvrnzsdiwqvpharifikqhttubhfhhttckgfwbfgs
```

In the following code, MOD is a built-in PL/I function whose value is the remainder when its first argument is divided by its second argument.

```
/* ENCIPHERING BY VIGENERE SCHEME */
GO: PROC OPTIONS (MAIN);
    DCL ALPHABET CHAR(26) INIT ('ABCDEFGHIJKLMNOPQRSTUVWXYZ'),
        LETTER(26) CHAR (1) DEF ALPHABET, KEYWORD CHAR (20) VAR,
        (KEY, CIPHER) CHAR (1000) VAR INIT (' '), TEXT CHAR (1000) VAR;
    GET LIST (KEYWORD, TEXT);
L1: DO WHILE (LENGTH(KEY) < LENGTH(TEXT));
    KEY = KEY || KEYWORD;
    END L1;
L2: DO K = 1 TO LENGTH(TEXT);
L3: DO I = 1 TO 26 WHILE (SUBSTR(TEXT, K, 1)¬ = LETTER(I));
    END L3;
L4: DO J = 1 TO 26 WHILE (SUBSTR(KEY, K, 1)¬ = LETTER(J));
    END L4;
    CIPHER = CIPHER || LETTER(MOD(I + J − 2, 26) + 1);
    END L2;
    PUT LIST (CIPHER);
    RETURN;
    END GO;
```

9.11. SUBPROGRAMS

Character strings can be used as subprogram arguments, parameters, and function values. The rules about matching attributes (Sections 8.2 through 8.4) apply when character-string data is used, just as they do when arithmetic data is used.

Consider the matter of agreement of attributes between an argument and the corresponding subprogram parameter. If the parameter is declared in the subprogram to be CHAR (5), say, then the argument in the invoking procedure must also be CHAR (5). The ENTRY attribute (Section 8.4) can be used in the invoking procedure, if desired, to cause a dummy argument with the correct attributes to be created automatically and substituted for an argument that does not have the attributes of the corresponding parameter. This technique is illustrated below.

Example: The function NCHAR given below searches a string of length ten from right to left to find the first position that does not contain a specified character. The function value is zero if every position in the string contains the character; otherwise, its value is the position (counting from the left) of the first character found in the search to be different from the specified character. (Note that this position is identified by counting from the *left*, although the search is from the *right*.)

```
/* FIND FIRST 'NONCHARACTER', SEARCHING FROM RIGHT.*/
NCHAR: PROC (STR, CHR);
          DCL STR CHAR (10), CHR CHAR (1);
LOOP:     DO K = 10 TO 1 BY –1;
          IF SUBSTR(STR, K, 1) ¬= CHR THEN RETURN(K);
          END LOOP;
          RETURN(0);
          END NCHAR;
```

This function could be invoked as illustrated below:

$$N = NCHAR('NEWbYORKbb', 'b');$$

In this case the value of NCHAR (and hence also the value of N) would be eight. Since STR and CHR are declared with lengths 10 and 1, respectively, it would be an error to use arguments with other lengths when one is invoking NCHAR. The following DECLARE statement could be used, however, in the invoking procedure:

$$DCL\ NCHAR\ ENTRY\ (CHAR\ (10),\ CHAR\ (1));$$

Then, if an argument for NCHAR were used without the correct attributes, a dummy argument with the correct ones would be substituted for it. Thus, the statement

$$N = NCHAR('NEWbYORK', 'b');$$

would be equivalent in effect to the following:

```
DCL DUMMY CHAR (10);
DUMMY = 'NEWbYORK';
N = NCHAR(DUMMY, 'b');
```

It is permitted in a subprogram to declare the length of a character-string parameter with an asterisk. This is analogous to specifying the dimensions of an array with asterisks (Section 8.8). The length of the parameter is automatically construed to be the length of the argument when the subprogram is invoked. If the parameter length is needed for use in the subprogram, it can be found by means of the LENGTH built-in function. Use of the asterisk notation often avoids the need for an ENTRY declaration, since it means that an argument does not have to have a specific length.

Example: The subprogram below is the function NCHAR from the preceding example, modified so that the length of the first parameter is specified with an asterisk.

```
/* FIND FIRST "NONCHARACTER", SEARCHING FROM RIGHT. */
NCHAR: PROC (STR, CHR);
        DCL STR CHAR (*), CHR CHAR (1);
LOOP:   DO K = LENGTH(STR) TO 1 BY -1;
        IF SUBSTR (STR, K, 1) ¬= CHR THEN RETURN(K);
        END LOOP;
        RETURN(0);
        END NCHAR;
```

For a function to have a character-string value, the function attributes must be declared (1) with the RETURNS attribute in a DECLARE statement in the invoking procedure (Section 8.3), and (2) with the RETURNS option in the subprogram's PROCEDURE statement.

> **Example:** Suppose that the function NCHAR discussed above were changed so that the function value were the first character that was not a specified character (rather than the position of that character). In the invoking procedure, we would have the following:

```
DCL NCHAR RETURNS (CHAR (1));
```

> The PROCEDURE statement in the subprogram would be as follows:

```
NCHAR: PROC (STG, CHR) RETURNS (CHAR (1));
```

A function can also have a VARYING character-string value, as is illustrated in the next example. This example, incidentally, shows how one can exploit the LENGTH function in a subprogram.

> **Example:** The function REVERSE given below takes a character-string argument and reverses the order of the characters in the string. The function value is the reordered string. REVERSE must be VARYING, since the length of its argument, and hence its own length, are arbitrary. The maximum length of REVERSE is assumed to be 10.

```
/* REVERSE THE CHARACTERS IN A CHARACTER STRING */
REVERSE: PROC (X) RETURNS (CHAR (10) VAR);
        DCL X CHAR (*), Y(LENGTH(X)) CHAR (1) DEF X,
            T CHAR (LENGTH(X)) VAR INIT (' ');
        DO K=LENGTH(X) TO 1 BY -1;
        T = T || Y(K);
        END;
        RETURN(T);
        END REVERSE;
```

This function could be invoked as illustrated below:

```
DCL REVERSE RETURNS (CHAR (10) VAR), Y CHAR (5), Z CHAR (6);
Y = REVERSE('ABCDE');
Z = REVERSE('ABCDEF');
```

In this case Y would have the value 'EDCBA', and Z would have the value 'FEDCBA'.

Subprogram arguments and parameters can also be VARYING. The only requirement is that an argument and its corresponding parameter must be either both VARYING or both not VARYING.

9.12. GET STRING, PUT STRING

A GET statement in PL/I can "read" input from a character string, as well as from an external source. Similarly, a PUT statement can "write" on a character string. In such cases, there is no true input or output, only internal data movement and editing. The programmer specifies these operations by using GET and PUT statements that contain the key word STRING together with a specification in parentheses of the string to be read from or written on.

Example: Consider the following code:

```
DCL X CHAR (10), Y CHAR (2), N FIXED DEC;
X = 'ABCDEbb5FG';
GET STRING(X) EDIT (Y, N) (X(3), A(2), F(3));
```

After this code is executed, Y has the value 'DE', and N has the value five.

Although the input/output can be data-directed, list-directed, or edit-directed, the edit-directed type is the most useful of these three types, because of the editing facilities it provides.

GET STRING and PUT STRING statements differ in certain respects from ordinary GET and PUT statements. First, the PAGE, LINE, and SKIP options have no meaning and are invalid; likewise, the PAGE, LINE, SKIP, and COLUMN format items are invalid. Thus, the statement

```
PUT PAGE STRING(X) EDIT (C) (SKIP, A(5));
```

is invalid because of the PAGE option and the SKIP format item it contains. Second, a string processed by a GET STRING of PUT STRING statement is always read or written beginning with its first position. Input or output does not resume where it left off previously, but instead always starts at the beginning of the string.

Probably the most useful property of the GET STRING statement is that it makes it possible for one to read data under more than one format or with a choice of several formats.

Example: Suppose that a data card contains a ten-column field punched with a floating-point number in which the exponent is indicated with a D rather than with an E. For example, the data field might contain bbb2.45D-6. (FORTRAN D-format data is like this.) This field cannot be read under an E-format item in PL/I. In the code below, the ten-column field is read in as a character string, the D is found and changed to E, and then the corrected field is "read" again under an E-format item by means of a GET STRING statement.

```
DCL C CHAR (10);
GET EDIT (C) (A(10));
SUBSTR(C, INDEX(C, 'D'), 1) ='E';
GET STRING(C) EDIT(X) (E(10,5));
```

9.13. NUMERIC-CHARACTER VARIABLES

So far in this book, we have considered two of the four types of problem data that can be used in a PL/I program: coded-arithmetic data[5] and character-string data. A third type of problem data is bit-string data, which we shall discuss later in this chapter. The fourth and last problem data type is numeric-character data, which we shall discuss below.

A numeric-character data item is a fixed-point or floating-point decimal number stored in character-string form. Besides digits, the character-string representation of the number may include certain special characters, such as a decimal point, a plus sign or minus sign, a dollar mark, and commas. A numeric-character variable is declared by means of the PICTURE (abbr.: PIC) attribute. The PICTURE consists of a series of picture specification characters enclosed in single quotation marks and describing the character-string representation of the field position by position.

Example:

DCL M PIC'999V99', X PIC'SZ,ZZZV.99';

The specification characters that can be used in a picture defining a numeric-character variable are the same as those described in our discussion of P-format items in Section 6.8, and they have the same meanings. For example, a 9 defines a digit position; a comma specifies a position where a comma is to

---

[5]"Coded-arithmetic data" is the name given to all the familiar arithmetic data types, such as FIXED BINARY, FLOAT DECIMAL, and so forth.

be inserted; and an S defines a position where a plus or minus sign is stored. The reader should recall from our discussion of P-format items that the V indicates where the decimal point is *understood* to be for arithmetic purposes, whereas the period defines a position where a (nonfunctional) decimal point is actually inserted. (Since it is not functional, the period is usually omitted from a PICTURE unless the field is being printed.) Other picture specification characters provide for zero suppression, slash insertion, "overpunched" signs, floating-point exponents, and many other things. We shall not go into a detailed explanation of these; the interested reader should consult his PL/I reference manual.

A numeric-character variable has *two* values: an arithmetic value and a character-string value. Which one is used depends on context, as we shall explain below. The arithmetic value is the obvious numerical value and is the value most often used. The character-string value is a character string containing the characters actually stored in the field—not only the digits but also any nonnumeric characters edited into the field because of the picture.

Example: Consider the following code:

```
DCL X PIC'S9,999V.99', Y PIC'Z9V99';
X = 1234.56;
Y = 1.23;
```

After this code is executed, the arithmetic value of X is 1234.56, and the character-string value is '+1,234.56'. The arithmetic value of Y is 1.23, and the character-string value is 'b123'.

The character-string value of a numeric-character variable is used in the following situations:

(1) When the variable appears in a character-string expression.

(2) When the variable is assigned to a character-string variable.

(3) When the variable is printed with data-directed or list-directed output.

In all other cases, the arithmetic value of the numeric-character variable is used. As the reader can see, there is very little risk of confusing the two values of a numeric-character variable. The arithmetic value is used in arithmetic contexts, and the character-string value is used in character-string contexts.

Example: Consider the following code:

```
DCL X PIC'S9,999V.99', Y CHAR (9), Z CHAR (10), N FIXED (6, 2);
X = -1234.56;
Y = X;
Z = X || '*';
N = X + 2;
```

After this code is executed, the value of Y is '-1,234.56'; of Z, '-1,234.56*'; and of N, -1232.56.

Some additional points concerning numeric-character data are briefly summarized below:

(1) Although numeric-character variables have both arithmetic and character-string values, they can be assigned only arithmetic values (or values that can be converted to arithmetic values). If a character-string value is assigned to a numeric-character variable, the string must be converted to an arithmetic value before the assignment can take place.

(2) Numeric-character data is always decimal, never binary.[6]

(3) A PICTURE defining a numeric-character variable cannot contain either an A or an X picture specification character.

(4) There are no numeric-character constants. The appropriate constants to use in conjunction with numeric-character variables are the ordinary decimal arithmetic constants.

(5) Numeric-character variables provide an exception to the rule that a variable cannot be DEFINED over a base variable if the two variables have different attributes. A CHARACTER variable can be DEFINED over a numeric-character base.

(6) A numeric-character variable cannot have a negative arithmetic value unless its PICTURE contains a character specifying the presence of a sign (such as an S or a minus sign).

Because of their hybrid nature, numeric-character variables are often useful when one must work with arithmetic data and character-string data simultaneously. As we shall explain in Section 9.17, numeric-character data have an advantage over coded-arithmetic data in the way they are converted to character-string form. Unless there is a clear need for a numeric-character variable, however, it is usually better to use a FIXED DECIMAL or FLOAT DECIMAL variable for the sake of efficiency.

This is a convenient point for summarizing the uses of the PICTURE attribute in PL/I. PICTURE can be used in a DECLARE statement for either of two purposes:

(1) To declare a character-string variable (Section 9.2). The picture can contain only the characters A, X, and 9 and must contain at least one A or X. Such a picture is called a *character-string picture*.

---

[6]Binary numeric-character data is defined in the PL/I language. At this time, however, it is not implemented in the F-level PL/I compiler for the IBM System/360.

(2) To declare a numeric-character variable. The picture cannot contain an A or an X but may contain any others in a large set of picture specification characters, such as Z, 9, S, and /. Such a picture is called a *numeric-character picture*.

These two uses of PICTURE should not be confused; they are two different things. It should be noted that the 9 picture specification character, which is the only character that can be used for both purposes (1) and (2), indicates a digit or a blank in (1) but only a digit in (2).

Both types of pictures have corresponding P-format items for use in edit-directed input/output. See Sections 6.8 and 9.4.

> **Example:** The code shown below is a complete program that reproduces a card deck and labels it in columns 73-80. The (arbitrarily chosen) characters 'POLY' are punched as a label in columns 73-76, and sequence numbers beginning with 0000 are punched in columns 77-80. The variable N is declared as a numeric-character variable because it is used both arithmetically and as string data. Note that leading zeros are not suppressed in the sequence numbers. This code, incidentally, illustrates the fact that a numeric-character variable can be used as the control variable in a DO loop.[7]

```
/* REPRODUCE, LABEL, AND SEQUENCE A CARD DECK */
GO: PROC OPTIONS (MAIN);
        DCL N PIC '9999', CARD CHAR (80), COLS73__80 CHAR (8) DEF
            CARD POS (73), PUNCH OUTPUT FILE;
        ON ENDFILE(SYSIN) GO TO L2;
        OPEN FILE(PUNCH) LINESIZE(80);
L1:  DO N = 0 BY 1;
        GET EDIT (CARD) (A(80));
        COLS73__80 = 'POLY' || N;
        PUT FILE(PUNCH) EDIT (CARD) (A(80));
        END L1;
L2:  RETURN;
        END GO;
```

9.14. BIT STRINGS

The second type of string data that can be used in a PL/I program is the bit string. A bit string is a string of zeros and ones treated as a single item of data. Many of the rules for workings with bit strings are similar to these for

---

[7]On the IBM System/360 this code will reproduce object decks as well as source decks.

working with character strings, and we shall not discuss them in great detail. Some uses of bit strings in logical operations will be considered in the next section.

A bit-string variable can be declared by specifying the BIT attribute and the length of the string in a DECLARE statement.

Example: The statement

    DCL T BIT(15);

defines a bit-string variable T whose length is 15 bits.

A bit-string constant consists of a sequence of zeros and ones enclosed in single quotes and followed by the letter B. A repetitive specification like that used for character-string constants (Section 9.2) is also permitted with bit-string constants.

Example:

    '11011000'B, (32)'0'B, (5)'01'B

The null bit string is denoted by ''B.

Bit strings can be manipulated much like character strings. They can be concatenated, for example, and the SUBSTR function can be used to extract substrings from them. Like character strings, bit strings are truncated or padded on the right when it is necessary to adjust their length for any reason. They are padded with zeros rather than blanks, however, when padding is needed. (A blank is invalid in a bit string.)

Input/output of bit strings can be performed with either list-directed, data-directed, or edit-directed stream input/output operations. The techniques are again analogous to those used for character-string data. In the case of edit-directed input/output, the B-format item is used to specify bit positions; it is analogous to the A-format item used for character-string data.

One elementary but often useful application of bit strings involves the UNSPEC built-in function. This function takes one argument and has for its value a bit string representing the way the argument is stored internally in the machine.[8] The length of the bit string is variable and depends on the attributes of the argument. UNSPEC can also be used as a pseudovariable when one

---

[8]Since the internal representation of data values is implementation dependent, UNSPEC values are also implementation dependent.

wants to assign a value to a variable by specifying in bit-string form the internal representation desired. Such coding is sometimes used in numerical analysis.

Example: Consider the following code:

```
DCL T BIT (32);
X = 1;
T = UNSPEC(X);
UNSPEC(Y) = '01000001001100000000000000000'B;
```

After this code is executed,[9] the value of T is '010000010001000000000000000000' B, and the value of Y (in decimal notation) is 3.

The following example illustrates how bit-string data can be used in a program.

Example: The code given below is a function subprogram for converting a bit-string parameter value into a hexadecimal number expressed as a character string. The length of the bit-string parameter A is assumed to be a multiple of four. The function value HEX is a VARYING character string whose length works out to be one-fourth of the length of A. Using concatenation, the code builds the hexadecimal representation digit by digit. At each step it extracts a four-bit substring of A, converts the substring into a four-bit fixed-binary number DIGIT, and determines the corresponding hexadecimal digit to be concatenated to the character string. The conversion of string data to arithmetic data is a technique that we have not mentioned previously. In this code, a four-bit string is converted into a four-bit binary number in the obvious way. (Thus, '1100'B would be converted to 1100B, which is the binary representation for 12.) We shall discuss the subject of conversions between string data and arithmetic data in more detail in Section 9.17.

```
/* CONVERT BIT STRING TO HEX CHARACTER STRING */
HEX: PROC (A) RETURNS (CHAR (16) VAR);
        DCL A BIT (*), HEXREP CHAR (16) VAR INIT (''), HEX_DIGITS CHAR (16)
            INIT ('0123456789ABCDEF') STATIC, TABLE (0:15) CHAR (1) DEF
            HEX_DIGITS, DIGIT FIXED BIN (4);
LP:   DO K = 1 TO LENGTH(A)/4;
        DIGIT = SUBSTR(A, 4*K−3, 4);
        HEXREP = HEXREP||TABLE(DIGIT);
        END LP;
        RETURN(HEXREP);
        END HEX;
```

---

[9]These results are correct for PL/I implementations on the IBM System/360.

This function might be used as shown below in order to print out in hexadecimal form the internal representation of a floating-point variable X whose internal representation is known to be 32 bits long.

```
DCL HEX RETURNS (CHAR (16) VAR);
...
PUT LIST (HEX(UNSPEC(X)));
```

If the internal binary representation of X were, say,

01000001010100000000000000000000,

then the value printed would be 41500000.

9.15. BIT-STRING OPERATORS

As we mentioned in the preceding section, bit strings can be concatenated; that is, they can be combined by use of the concatenation operator ||. Bit-string expressions can also be formed by use of the following logical operators:

Operator	Meaning
¬	not
&	and
|	or

The "not" operator is a prefix operator that causes the bits of a string to be reversed so that zero becomes one and one becomes zero. Thus, if A is a bit string, then ¬A is a bit string of the same length as A whose bits are obtained by reversing those of A. The "and" and "or" operators are infix operators. Consider a bit-string expression A(op)B, where A and B are bit strings and (op) is either the "and" or the "or" operator. Then A(op)B is also a bit string and is formed in the following way. If one of the two strings A and B is shorter than the other, the shorter one is padded on the right with zeros. The two strings are then matched bit for bit according to the rules shown below in order to form the bits of A(op)B.

$$(0 \,\&\, 0) = 0 \qquad\qquad (0 \mid 0) = 0$$
$$(1 \,\&\, 0) = (0 \,\&\, 1) = 0 \qquad (1 \mid 0) = (0 \mid 1) = 1$$
$$(1 \,\&\, 1) = 1 \qquad\qquad (1 \mid 1) = 1$$

(The reader will probably recognize these two operations as those of Boolean algebra.) As a result of the way A(op)B is formed, its length is the larger of the lengths of A and B.

Example:

$$\neg((\text{'01101'B} \And \text{'111'B}) \mid \text{'00100'B}) = \neg(\text{'01100'B} \mid \text{'00100'B})$$
$$= \neg \text{'01100'B} = \text{'10011'B}$$

In bit-string expressions the order in which operations are to be performed can always be specified unambiguously by means of parentheses. We shall explain in Section 9.18 the priority rules that apply when parentheses are omitted.

In previous chapters we have had occasion to mention conditional expressions several times. Their use was discussed in connection with IF statements (Section 3.2), with WHILE clauses in DO statements (Section 4.4), and with iteration factors in formats for edit-directed input/output (Section 6.7). Conditional expressions are relevant to our study of bit-string operations in this section because a conditional expression in PL/I is treated by the compiler as a bit string of length one. The bit-string value is '0'B if the condition is false and is '1'B if the condition is true. Thus, a logical expression like

$$((-1 <= K) \mid (K <= 5)) \And (J >= 6)$$

which might appear in an IF or WHILE clause, is really just a bit-string expression of the form (A | B) & C, where A, B, and C are bit strings of length one. For most purposes, it is not necessary to think of conditional expressions as bit strings, but the fact that they are bit strings is sometimes significant and should be kept in mind.

Example: The code below assigns an identity matrix to the $n \times n$ matrix A:

```
LP: DO I = 1 TO N;
    DO J = 1 TO N;
    A(I, J) = (I = J);
    END LP;
```

The conditional expression I = J has the value 1'B' when I and J are equal and the value '0'B otherwise. This bit-string value must be converted into an arithmetic value in order to be assigned to the arithmetic variable A(I, J). This conversion is done in the obvious way, with '0'B converting to zero and '1'B converting to one. (In effect, the I = J in this code is the Kronecker delta.)

As we have said, a programmer usually does not need to recall the fact that a conditional expression is a bit string. The fact is important, however, when the programmer wishes to use a function value as the conditional expression in a IF or WHILE clause. In such cases the function value should have a bit-string value with length one.

Example: The function NUM given below is a function for testing a character-string parameter X to determine whether or not the string contains only numeric characters (0-9). The function value NUM is a bit string of length one. If any position of X contains a character other than a digit, then the value of NUM is '0'B. If every position contains a digit, then the value of NUM is '1'B.

```
NUM:  PROC (X) RETURNS (BIT (1));
      DCL X CHAR (*);
      IF VERIFY(X, '0123456789') ¬= 0 THEN RETURN('0'B);
      RETURN('1'B);
      END NUM;
```

NUM could be invoked as illustrated below, where strings A and B are tested for nonnumeric characters:

```
DCL A CHAR (5), B CHAR (7), NUM RETURNS (BIT (1));
...
IF NUM(A) THEN PUT LIST ('A IS NUMERIC');
IF ¬NUM(B) THEN PUT LIST ('B IS NONNUMERIC');
```

The reason for designing NUM to have a bit-string value is to allow it to be invoked in this way.

9.16. EXAMPLE

The code given below is a complete program for compressing a PL/I source program by suppressing superfluous blanks. Although the application is an elementary one, the code provides an opportunity to exploit many of the string-processing techniques that have been discussed in this chapter.

As many as 100 PL/I source program cards can be read in as data. Columns 2–72 from these data cards are concatenated to form a long character string named CODE, which is the source program text to be compressed. CODE is examined character by character for blanks, and another long character string named COMPRESS is formed which is the same as CODE but with extra blanks suppressed. As characters are copied from CODE to COMPRESS, a substring of blank characters is compressed to a single blank unless the string is part of a character-string constant. The code keeps track of such constants by means of a bit-string switch named QUOTE, whose value is '1'B when the character currently being processed in CODE is part of a character-string constant and whose value is '0'B otherwise. The compressed PL/I source program is finally punched out in a new card deck.

```
/* COMPRESS A PL/I SOURCE PROGRAM BY SUPPRESSING SPACES */
GO:  PROC OPTIONS (MAIN);
     DCL QUOTE BIT (1) INIT ('0'B), TEMP CHAR (71), (CODE, COMPRESS)
         CHAR (7100) VAR INIT (' '), (T1, T2) CHAR (1), PUNCH OUTPUT FILE;
     ON ENDFILE(SYSIN) GO TO L2;
L1:  DO K = 1 TO 100;
```

```
        GET EDIT (TEMP) (COL(2), A(71));
        CODE=CODE||TEMP;
        END L1;
L2:     DO K = 1 TO LENGTH(CODE)—1;
        T1 = SUBSTR(CODE, K, 1);
        T2 = SUBSTR(CODE, K+1, 1);
        IF T1 = '''' THEN QUOTE = ¬QUOTE;
        IF ¬((T1 = ' ') & (T2 = ' ') & (¬QUOTE)) THEN COMPRESS
           = COMPRESS||T1;
        END L2;
        IF T2 ¬= ' ' THEN COMPRESS = COMPRESS||T2;
        OPEN FILE(PUNCH) LINESIZE(80);
        L = LENGTH(COMPRESS);
        NCARDS = (70 + L)/71;
L3:     DO K = 1 TO NCARDS—1;
        PUT FILE(PUNCH) EDIT (SUBSTR(COMPRESS, 71*K—70, 71)) (COL (2), A);
        END L3;
        PUT FILE(PUNCH) EDIT (SUBSTR(COMPRESS, 71*(NCARDS—1) + 1,
           L—71*(NCARDS—1))) (COL(2), A);
        RETURN;
        END GO;
```

The result of using this program to compress the subprogram on page 152 is something like this:

```
/* FIND FIRST "NONCHARACTER", SEARCHING FROM RIGHT. */ NCHAR: PROC
(STR, CHR); DCL STR CHAR (*), CHR CHAR (1); LOOP: DO K = LENGTH(STR)
TO 1 BY —1; IF SUBSTR(STR, K, 1) ¬= CHR THEN RETURN(K); END LOOP;
RETURN(0); END NCHAR;
```

9.17. DATA CONVERSIONS

PL/I permits any kind of problem data to be converted to any other kind for which the conversion is meaningful. Conversions between arithmetic data types, such as from fixed decimal to fixed binary, are commonplace. Thus, if we write the statement K = .1, where K is a fixed-binary variable, then we force the fixed-decimal constant .1 to be converted to fixed binary. The rules used by PL/I to perform such arithmetic data conversions were discussed in Chapter 2.

In this section we shall discuss the rules for data conversions when string data is involved. This will include conversions between (1) bit-string and character-string data, (2) bit-string and arithmetic data, and (3) character-string and arithmetic data.[10] Since the conversion rules are rather numerous, we shall not go into great detail in these explanations; we shall merely describe generally how conversions are implemented and shall point out some programming pitfalls.

There are numerous situations in which automatic conversions to or from string data can occur. Two of the most common are the following:

(1) If the data value on the right of the equals sign in an assignment statement has attributes different from those of the variable on the left, then there is a data conversion before the assignment takes place. For example, if we write the assignment statement N = '15', where N is fixed decimal, the character string '15' must be converted to fixed decimal. Similarly, if we write B = 5, where B is a bit string variable, the decimal constant 5 must be converted to a bit string.

(2) If a data value is used in an operation suitable only for another type of data, then there is a data conversion before the operation is performed. For example, if we write 'AB' || 5, then the decimal constant 5 must be converted into a character string, since only strings can be concatenated. Similarly, if we write the expression '15' + 7, the character string '15' must be converted into a decimal number before the addition can be performed.

A programmer can force the conversion of arithmetic data to string data in any context by using the built-in functions BIT and CHARACTER (abbr.: CHAR), each of which causes an arithmetic argument to be converted to the corresponding string type. Similarly, the built-in functions BIN and DEC (Section 2.15) can be used to cause string data to be converted to arithmetic data. A conversion can also occur because of an ENTRY attribute, a RETURN statement in a function subprogram, certain input/output operations, and for various other reasons.

We now consider three categories of data conversions involving string data. Since the conversion rules discussed below are not explained in detail, the interested reader must investigate specific questions by referring to his PL/I reference manual.

(1) *Between bit string and character string.* A bit string is converted into a character string by making each zero bit into a character zero and

---

[10]By "arithmetic data" we mean what is called "coded-arithmetic data" in strict PL/I terminology (see Section 9.13). This includes all the familiar PL/I data types used in arithmetic work, such as FIXED BINARY and FLOAT DECIMAL, but excludes numeric-character data.

each one bit into a character one. The length of the character string is the same as the length of the bit string. A character string is converted into a bit string by the reverse of this process. An attempt to convert a character string into a bit string when the character string contains characters other than zeros and ones causes the CONVERSION condition to be raised.

Example:

$$\text{'101'B || 'XYZ' = '101' || 'XYZ' = '101XYZ'}$$
$$\neg \text{'0110' = } \neg \text{'0110'B = '1001'B}$$

(2) *Between arithmetic and bit string.* An arithmetic value is converted into a bit string by converting its absolute value into an unsigned binary number and truncating the result to an integer. The bit string length is the number of bits in the integer, and this depends on the attributes of the original data value. A bit string is converted into an arithmetic value by treating its bits as an unsigned binary integer. The arithmetic value is therefore a fixed-binary number whose precision is the length of the bit string.

Example:

$$5 \text{ || '010'B = '0101'B || '010'B = '0101010'B}$$
$$7 + \text{'101'B} = 7 + 101\text{B} = 111\text{B} + 101\text{B} = 1100\text{B}$$

(3) *Between arithmetic and character string.* An arithmetic value is converted to a character string by expressing it in the form of a decimal constant and forming a character string from the characters in this decimal representation. The string length depends on the number of positions needed for this decimal representation. In any case, the length is *more* than the (decimal) precision of the number, since there is always a sign position (minus or blank). There may also be a decimal point and a floating-point exponent. A character string is converted to an arithmetic value by treating the characters in the string as an arithmetic constant (possibly signed). If the string characters do not represent a valid PL/I constant, then the CONVERSION condition is raised.

Example:

$$5 \text{ || 'ABC' = 'bbb5' || 'ABC' = 'bbb5ABC'}$$
$$1.234 + \text{'5'} = 1.234 + 5 = 6.234$$

As the reader probably noticed in these examples, it is not always obvious what the length of the string will be when an arithmetic value is converted into a string. In such a conversion, the length of the resulting string is almost never equal to the precision of the original arithmetic data, a fact that causes trouble over and over again for some programmers.[11] Making a false assumption that they are equal is a pitfall that has to be watched for continually. Consider the following example:

```
DCL B BIT (1), C CHAR (1);
B = 1;
C = 2;
```

The programmer might assume that B would take the value '1'B and that C would take the value '2'. What actually happens is this: The decimal constant 1 is first converted to the four-bit binary number 0001B (on the basis of the rules given in Section 2.12), which in turn becomes the bit string '0001'B. This string is truncated to '0'B, and this is the value assigned to B. The decimal constant 2 is converted into the character string 'bbb2'. (PL/I includes the three extra positions to provide for (1) a sign, (2) a decimal point, and (3) a zero to the left of the decimal point of a pure fraction, in case any of these should be needed.) This string is then truncated to 'b', and this value is assigned to C.

The conversions discussed in the preceding paragraph resulted from assigning arithmetic values to string variables. It might be thought that in such a conversion the length of the target variable (the variable on the left of the assignment statement) would be taken into account when the data value on the right side of the assignment statement is converted to a string. Thus, for example, it might be thought that the constant 2 in the statement C = 2 would be converted to a string of length one (rather than four) because C is of length one. In PL/I it is a general rule, however, that neither the precision of an arithmetic target variable nor the length of a string target variable is considered when a data value on the right of an assignment statement is subjected to a conversion. The precision or length is adjusted *after* the conversion. There is only one exception to this rule: In a purely arithmetic conversion involving a change of base, the number on the right of an assignment statement is converted directly to the precision of the target variable. Thus, if we write K = .1, where K is FIXED BIN (31, 31), the decimal constant .1 is converted directly

---

[11]In particular, when a FIXED DECIMAL or FIXED BINARY data value is converted to a character string, the resulting string length is *never* equal to the precision of the arithmetic data. The reader should consult his PL/I reference manual for the exact rules.

to a 31-bit binary number. If we write K = .1, however, where K is CHAR(2), then the constant .1 is converted to 'b0.1' and this string is truncated to 'b0' before assignment to K.

It is appropriate to mention here that when a numeric-character data item is converted to a character string there is no pitfall concerning the form and length of the resulting string. (See the explanation of "character-string value" of a numeric-character variable that was given in Section 9.13.) Consider the following illustration:

```
DCL (C, D) CHAR (2), M FIXED DEC (1,1), N PIC'V.9';
M, N = .1;
C = M;
D = N;
```

In the C assignment the value of M is converted to 'b0.1', which is then truncated on the right, so that C is assigned the value 'b0'. On the other hand, D is assigned the value '.1', which is the character-string value of the numeric-character variable N.

In view of the complications that can arise in certain conversions involving string data, programmers are advised to avoid unnecessary conversions involving such data. The fact that conversions are made automatically does not imply that they can be used indifferently.

9.18. PRIORITY OF OPERATORS

All the operators that can be used to form expressions in a PL/I program have now been discussed. We encountered the arithmetic operators ($+ - * /$ $**$) in Section 2.13, the comparison operators ($< \neg< <= = \neg> >= \neg=$) in Section 3.2, and the logical operators ($\neg$ & |) in Section 3.4. In this chapter we have discussed the concatenation operator (||) and the bit-string operators ($\neg$ & |). Since logical expressions in PL/I are treated as bit-string expressions, the logical operators and the bit-string operators are, of course, the same. Now that we have all these operators at our disposal, we can discuss the general rules for priority of operators.

Heretofore (as in Section 9.15) we have usually said merely that by means of parentheses one can specify unambiguously the order in which operations are performed in a complex expression. The rules for priority of operators that we shall now explain specify how an expression is to be interpreted when the order of operations is not indicated by parentheses.

The various operators can all be classified in seven priority levels, as shown:

Priority level 1 (highest)   **, prefix $+$, prefix $-$, $\neg$

                     2   *, /

                     3   infix $+$, infix $-$

                     4 ||

                     5          $< \ \neg< \ <= \ = \ \neg= \ >= \ > \ \neg>$

                     6   &

             7 (lowest) |

when operators with different priority levels appear together in an expression, the operation with the highest priority takes place first. If two or more operators of priority level 1 appear in an expression, the order of priority of those operators is from right to left within the expression. For operators of priority levels other than level 1, if two or more operators of the same level appear in an expression, the order of priority of those operators is from left to right in the expression.

Example:

Expression	Equivalent Form
A & B | C	(A & B) | C
A $<=$ B & C	(A $<=$ B) & C
A $=$ B $=$ C	A $=$ (B $=$ C)
$\neg$ A & B	($\neg$A) & B
A $+$ 3 & B || C	(A $+$ 3) & (B || C)
A & B | C || D	(A & B) | (C || D)
A | B & C || D	A | (B & (C || D))
$\neg$A $+$ B	($\neg$A) $+$ B
$\neg$A**B/2	($\neg$(A**B))/2

9.19. PL/I AND FORTRAN

The following remarks are intended for FORTRAN programmers who want to draw analogies between PL/I and FORTRAN.

(1) PL/I character-string data is analogous to FORTRAN Hollerith data. There is almost no comparison, however, between the capabilities of the two languages for manipulating this type of data, because FORTRAN has almost none of the string-handling facilities of PL/I.

(2) In their role in logical expressions, PL/I bit-string are analogous to FORTRAN logical data. Thus, the PL/I bit-string operators $\neg$, &, and | correspond to the FORTRAN logical operators .NOT., .AND., and

.OR.. Likewise, the bit-string constants '0'B and '1'B correspond to the FORTRAN logical constants .TRUE. and .FALSE.. FORTRAN has no other data type analogous to bit-string data.[12]

(3) PL/I makes an automatic data conversion from any problem data type to any other when context requires it, whereas FORTRAN does not. In particular, FORTRAN does not allow conversions between logical data and other data types.

(4) The rules for priority of operations in PL/I and FORTRAN are compatible with one exception: The "not" operators in the two languages occupy different places in their respective operator hierarchies. Thus, .NOT. A .EQ. B in FORTRAN means .NOT.(A .EQ. B), whereas $\neg$ A = B in PL/I means ($\neg$A) = B.

EXERCISES

1. Suppose that a variable is to be used to store a seven-position telephone number. Describe briefly what kind of data values could be assigned to the variable without causing an error if the variable were declared with the attributes (a) CHAR (7), (b) PIC 'AA99999', (c) PIC 'XXXXXXX', (b) PIC '9999999', (e) FIXED (7).

2. Code a function to test a charater-string argument to find out whether or not all the characters in the string are letters of the alphabet (A-Z). Let the argument be a fixed-length string of length ≤ 25. Let the function value be a bit string of length one whose value is '1'B if the string is alphabetic and is '0'B if not. Illustrate how your function could be invoked.

3. Code a function to convert a character-string argument representing a hexadecimal number into a bit string. (This just reverses the task of the function HEX described in the last example of Section 9.14.) Let the argument be a fixed-length character string of length ≤ 16. Let the function value be a VARYING bit string. Illustrate how your function could be invoked.

4. What is the value of
   (a) SUBSTR(SUBSTR('1234567890', 4), 2, 3)?
   (b) INDEX(SUBSTR('1234567890', 4), '8')?

5. Parenthesize the following expressions to show what the priority of operations is.
   (a) $\neg$ A∗B < 0 | C = 5   (b) 0 < A < 1
   (c) $\neg$ A∗∗B   (d) A | B || C & D

---

[12]Some FORTRAN systems used several years ago included Boolean operations that were similar to PL/I bit-string operations.

6. Consider the code given below. What will be printed and where?

```
DCL PI FIXED DEC (5,2);
PI = 3.14159;
PUT LINE(30) EDIT ('PI =', PI) (A, F(5,2));
```

7. What will be the value of D after the following code is executed?

```
DCL A CHAR (10) INIT ('ABCDE12345'), B CHAR (5) DEF A POS (6), C CHAR (25),
    D FIXED (1);
PUT STRING(C) EDIT (B) (A(5));
GET STRING(C) EDIT (D) (X(2), F(1));
```

8. Redo the code given at the end of Section 9.7, using the TRANSLATE function instead of the SUBSTR pseudovariable to construct the MASK field.

10 BASED STORAGE AND LIST PROCESSING

10.1. BASED AND POINTER VARIABLES

In this chapter we introduce the subject of *based storage*. This is the last of the four PL/I storage classes: static, automatic, controlled, and based. Like automatic and controlled storage, based storage may be allocated dynamically during program execution. As with controlled storage, the programmer controls the allocation of based storage by means of ALLOCATE and FREE statements.

Based storage is a powerful tool in PL/I and has many important uses, notably for list processing. We shall discuss some of the principles of list processing beginning in the next section. Locate-mode input/output for RECORD files is another application, but one we shall not discuss here.

Use of based storage involves use of BASED and POINTER variables. These are variables that are declared to have the BASED and POINTER (abbr.: PTR) attributes, respectively.

Example:

```
DCL X BASED, P PTR;
```

Often a POINTER variable is associated with a BASED variable by naming the POINTER in the declaration of the BASED variable, as illustrated below. In such a case it is not necessary to declare the POINTER explicitly, since it is

171

a POINTER because of context.[1] We shall explain later the significance of the BASED-POINTER association.

Example:

DCL X BASED (P);

Here X is BASED and P is its associated POINTER. P does not have to be declared explicitly.

All the PL/I variables that we have studied until now have had this property: They have storage assigned specifically to them during execution. If program execution halted abruptly, any variable that could be referenced at the time of the halt would have a memory address where its data value was stored. Knowing just the name of the variable, we could (at least theoretically) find its address and thus also its current value. This is, of course, exactly what programmers do when they study memory dumps.

The unique property of BASED variables is that they do *not* have specific storage locations. They can, in effect, be anywhere. If we wanted to know what the value of a BASED variable named X was at the time of a halt, we could not find it without having extra information. Just the name X would not be enough; we would also have to be told specifically to what address to refer. The effect of this fact in PL/I programming is that we cannot reference a BASED variable unless we also supply its address.

That is what POINTER variables are for. The value of a POINTER is an absolute core-storage address. When a BASED variable is referenced in a PL/I program, it is always *qualified* by a POINTER, whose value is the address of the BASED variable. To find the value of a BASED variable X after a halt occurred, what we would have to know would be the value of the POINTER whose value was the address of X.

Pointer qualification of a BASED variable may be either *explicit* or *implicit*. We consider explicit qualification first.

Explicit qualification is specified by means of the arrow notation illustrated below:[2]

P—>X

P is assumed to be a POINTER variable and X to be a BASED variable. The

---

[1] At this time, a BASED variable in the F-level PL/I implementation for the IBM System/360 *must* have an associated POINTER.

[2] The arrow —> used to denote pointer qualification is a composite symbol made by combining a minus sign and a greater-than symbol.

expression P—>X means "the variable X whose address is given by P."

Example:

> DCL X BASED, Y BASED, P PTR, Q PTR;
>
> . . .
>
> P—>X = Q—>Y + 3.14;

In this example P and Q are assumed to have (address) values; we shall explain later how they get their values. The assignment statement causes the data stored in the address specified by Q to be added to 3.14 and the result to be stored in the address specified by P.

A BASED variable can always be explicitly qualified by any POINTER variable. It *must* be explicitly qualified if no POINTER was associated with it when the BASED attribute was declared.

Now let us consider implicit qualification. If a BASED variable was declared with an associated POINTER, then the BASED variable may be referenced without use of the arrow notation. In such a case, it is automatically qualified with its associated POINTER and is said to be *implicitly qualified*.

Example:

> DCL X BASED (P), Y BASED (Q);
>
> . . .
>
> X = Y + 3.14;

This assignment statement is equivalent to P—>X = Q—>Y + 3.14, since X and Y are implicitly qualified by their associated POINTER variables.

It is an error to reference a BASED variable without explicit qualification if the BASED variable has no associated POINTER.

The reader must understand that the relation between a BASED variable and a POINTER used to qualify it (implicitly or explicitly) is nothing more than this: The POINTER value is used as the storage address of the BASED variable. Any POINTER can be used, correctly or incorrectly, to qualify any BASED variable. The absence of restraints allows the programmer great scope for manipulation of storage but also requires him to keep the pointers from getting mixed up. It is up to the programmer to see to it that the right POINTER is used with the right BASED variable.

Now let us consider the two questions of how storage is allocated for BASED variables and how POINTER variables get their values.

The programmer can allocate based storage by means of the following form of the ALLOCATE statement:

ALLOCATE based variable SET (pointer variable);

The statement causes (1) storage to be allocated to the BASED variable, and (2) the address of that storage to be assigned to the POINTER variable. If the BASED variable has an associated POINTER, then the SET clause can be omitted. In this case the address of the storage allocated to the BASED variable is assigned to the associated POINTER.

Example:

```
DCL X BASED (P), N FIXEΓ (3,2) BASED (Q), R PTR;
ALLOCATE X;
X = 0;
ALLOCATE N SET (R);
R—>N = X;
```

The statement ALLOCATE X is equivalent to ALLOCATE X SET (P), since P is associated with X. It causes storage to be allocated for X and the address of that storage to be assigned to P. Similarly, the second ALLOCATE statement causes storage to be allocated for N and the address of that storage to be assigned to R. The POINTER variable Q, which is associated with N in the DECLARE, is not assigned any value. It would be an error to refer to N (that is, to Q—>N) before Q is assigned a value.

The programmer releases based storage by means of a statement of the form

FREE based variable;

This statement causes the storage occupied by the specified BASED variable to be released for possible reuse later.

Example:

```
FREE Q—>N;
FREE X;
```

As usual, a BASED variable not explicitly qualified is implicitly qualified with the POINTER specified when the variable was declared.

We have mentioned one way in which a value can be assigned to a POINTER variable, namely, by use of the ALLOCATE statement. A second way is to assign to one POINTER the value of another.

POINTER variables can also be tested for equality or inequality in an IF statement or in the WHILE clause of a DO statement.

Example:

```
DCL (P, Q) PTR;
...
IF P = Q THEN ...
...
DO WHILE (P ¬= Q);
...
```

Storage can be allocated to a BASED variable over and over again, so that several *generations* of the variable come into existence. By means of pointer manipulations, all of these generations can be available for use at one time. This fact is what makes list-processing applications feasible in PL/I and is the main reason for the usefulness of based storage. Consider the following code:

```
DCL X BASED (P), (Q, R) PTR;
ALLOCATE X;
ALLOCATE X SET (Q);
ALLOCATE X SET (R);
```

After this code is executed, there are three generations of X, the first addressed by POINTER P, the second by Q, and the third by R. A reference to X (that is, to P—>X) is to the first generation, Q—>X to the second, and R—>X to the third. If we wanted to release the storage of the second generation, say, we could write

```
FREE Q—>X;
```

It should be recalled that repeated ALLOCATE statements can also be used to create several generations of a CONTROLLED variable. Only the most recent generation, however, would be available at any time.

Now let us consider a simple example that illustrates some of the principles discussed so far.

Example: Suppose that it is desired to read in and store a deck of ≤ 1000 data cards. A simple code for doing this *without* based storage is the following:

```
        DCL CARD(1000) CHAR(80);
        ON ENDFILE(SYSIN) GO TO JMP;
        GET EDIT ((CARD(K) DO K = 1 TO 1000)) (A(80));
JMP:
```

In this program, storage has to be allocated for 1000 cards, even though the actual number read may turn out to be substantially less than 1000. Now consider the following code, which uses based storage to avoid allocating storage unnecessarily:[3]

```
        DCL CARD CHAR (80) BASED, P(1000) PTR;
        ON ENDFILE(SYSIN) GO TO L2;
L1:     DO K = 1 TO 1000;
        ALLOCATE CARD SET (P(K));
        GET EDIT (P(K)—>CARD) (A(80));
        END L1;
L2:     FREE P(K)—>CARD;
```

The method used in this code is this: Each time a card is to be read in, storage is allocated to the BASED variable CARD and the input is read into this storage. Addresses of the cards are retained in a POINTER array P in such a way that P(K) points at the Kth card. The FREE statement releases the (unused) storage already allocated for an input card when the end-of-file was encountered. The important thing to note is that, after the code is executed, there are as many generations of CARD as there were data cards and no more than that.

10.2. BUILDING LISTS

In this section we shall explain further how BASED and POINTER variables can be used in list-processing work. As we mentioned in the preceding section, this is one of the most important uses of based storage in PL/I.

A *list* in programming is a sequence of variables (or generations of one variable) linked together by pointers. In what is probably the simplest case, a list is organized as follows: (1) A specific "anchor" pointer points to the first item in the list. (2) The first list item contains a pointer linking it to the second item; the second item contains a pointer linking it to the third item; and so on. (3) The last list item also contains a pointer with a special value indicating that there are no more items in the list. In PL/I programming, structure variables (Section 5.9) turn out to be particularly useful in forming lists, because a structure can contain a POINTER as a subfield in addition to other subfields. We can use repeated generations of a BASED structure variable as items

---

[3]At this time, a qualifying pointer cannot be subscripted in the F-level PL/I implementation for the IBM System/360. See also the footnote on p. 172.

in a list and use a POINTER subfield in the structure to link one list item to another.

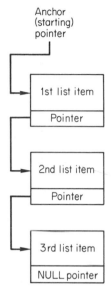

Figure 5. Representation of a list terminated by the NULL pointer value.

The main rules for using a BASED structure are summarized below:

(1) The BASED attribute should be declared only for the major-level structure variable. Minor-level variables are then automatically BASED, too, with the same implicit POINTER as that declared for the major-level variable.

(2) ALLOCATE and FREE statements can refer only to the major-level variable.

(3) A POINTER identifying a particular generation of a major-level variable also identifies the minor-level variables in that generation. Suppose, for example, that A is a major-level structure variable and that B is a minor-level variable in A. Then, if P—>A refers to a particular generation of A, it follows that P—>B refers to the variable B in that generation of A. Whenever a minor-level variable is referenced without explicit POINTER qualification, it is implicitly qualified by the POINTER named in the declaration of the BASED attribute for the major-level variable.

Example:

```
DCL 1 A BASED (P),
      2 B CHAR (3),
      2 C PTR,
      Q PTR;
ALLOCATE A;
ALLOCATE A SET (Q);
B = 'XYZ';
C = Q;
Q—>B = '***';
```

Here the first generation of A is P—>A and the second generation is Q—>A. The POINTER C in the first generation (in other words, P—>C) is made to point to the second generation (in other words, to Q—>A). The statement B = 'XYZ' is equivalent to P—>B = 'XYZ' because B is implicitly qualified by P. The statement Q—>B = '***' illustrates how to reference a minor-level variable in the second generation of A. It would be an error in this code to say ALLOCATE B, because B is a minor-level variable.

In the next example we shall use repeated generations of BASED structure variable to form a list. From this simple example, the reader should be able to see the basic scheme for constructing a list.

It is necessary to mention here the built-in function NULL, which is used in this example. NULL is a built-in function that takes no arguments. Its value is the *null pointer value*, which is a special pointer value different from any core-storage address. The NULL function value is commonly assigned to the last pointer in a list as an end-of-list indicator. That is how it is used in the example.

Example: Consider once again the problem of reading in and storing a deck of ≤ 1000 cards (see the example at the end of the preceding section). The code shown below does this by forming the cards into a list chained together by pointers. Each time a card is read in, storage is allocated to the BASED structure variable STORAGE_AREA, which contains two subfields named CARD and CHAIN. CARD holds a card image, and CHAIN is a POINTER linking one generation of STORAGE_AREA to the next. For the generation of STORAGE_AREA in which the last data card is stored, the value of CHAIN is assigned the value NULL as a flag to indicate the end of the list.

```
DCL 1 STORAGE_AREA BASED (P),
      2 CARD CHAR (80),
      2 CHAIN PTR,
      (Q, START) PTR;
    ON ENDFILE(SYSIN) GO TO L2;
L1: DO K = 1 TO 1000;
    ALLOCATE STORAGE_AREA;
```

```
        GET EDIT (CARD) (A(80));
        IF K = 1 THEN START = P;  ELSE Q—>CHAIN = P;
        Q = P;
        END L1;
  L2:   Q—>CHAIN = NULL;
        FREE STORAGE__AREA;
```

"Leafing through" the list created by this code is easy. Suppose, for example, that we wanted to print out the cards. This could be done as follows:

```
        P = START;
  L3:   DO WHILE (P ¬= NULL);
        PUT EDIT (CARD) (COL(1), A(80));
        P = CHAIN;
        END L3;
```

10.3. EXAMPLE

One application of list-processing methods is in the storage and manipulation of sparse matrices. (A *sparse* matrix is one with a small proportion of nonzero elements.) Using an array to store a sparse matrix would be wasteful of storage, since most of the storage locations in the array would merely contain zeros. More economical use of storage is obtained by storing the nonzero matrix elements in a list.

One way to do this for an n-square matrix is to form a list in which each list item contains (1) a nonzero matrix element, (2) a sequence number specifying the position of the element in the matrix, and (3) a pointer linking the item to the next list item. The sequence number in this scheme is the number of the element when the matrix elements are numbered row by row sequentially from 1 to n^2 as shown below for the $n = 3$:

$$
\begin{array}{ccc}
1 & 2 & 3 \\
4 & 5 & 6 \\
7 & 8 & 9
\end{array}
$$

The sequence number k for the (i, j) element can be calculated by means of the formula $k = n(i - 1) + j$.

In the code shown below we read in and store a sparse matrix in such a list. Each data card contains a nonzero matrix element together with its row number and column number. The starting address of the list is assigned to the POINTER variable START, and the end of the list is flagged by means of a NULL pointer in the last list item.

After this matrix has been stored, its Euclidean norm is calculated. (The

Euclidean norm of a matrix is the square root of the squares of the matrix elements.) This provides a simple illustration of how a matrix stored in list form might be referenced. Less trivial matrix calculations would require, of course, much more extensive coding.

In this example the order of the matrix is assumed to be 100.

```
/* STORE SPARSE MATRIX IN LIST AND COMPUTE NORM */
GO: PROC OPTIONS (MAIN);
     DCL 1 ELEMENT BASED (P),
           2 A,
           2 K,
           2 CHAIN PTR,
          (START, OLDP) PTR;
        ON ENDFILE(SYSIN) GO TO L2;
/* READ AND STORE MATRIX ELEMENTS IN LIST */
L1:  DO M = 1 TO 10000;
     GET EDIT (I, J, X) (COL(1), (2)F(5), F(10));
     ALLOCATE ELEMENT;
     K = 100*(I — 1) + J;
     A = X;
     IF M = 1 THEN START = P;  ELSE OLDP—>CHAIN = P;
     OLDP = P;
     END L1;
L2:  OLDP—>CHAIN = NULL;
/* COMPUTE EUCLIDEAN NORM */
     SUM = 0;
     P = START;
L3:  DO WHILE (P ¬= NULL);
     SUM = SUM + A*A;
     P = CHAIN;
     END L3;
     ENORM = SQRT(SUM);
     PUT DATA (ENORM);
     RETURN;
     END GO;
```

10.4. AREA AND OFFSET VARIABLES

The programmer can exercise certain controls over the allocation of based storage by use of AREA variables, which denote *areas* (or regions) of core storage from which based storage can be allocated. An AREA variable is defined by specifying the AREA attribute for the variable in a DECLARE statement.

This attribute should include a specification in parentheses of the size of the core-storage area to be associated with the variable:[4]

Example:

DCL R AREA (2500);

The programmer can use the following form of the ALLOCATE statement in order to cause storage to be allocated from a particular area to a BASED variable rather than merely from the general pool of available core storage.

ALLOCATE based variable SET (pointer variable) IN (area variable);

As before, the SET clause can be omitted. The corresponding form of the FREE statement is

FREE based variable IN (area variable);

If an IN clause is used in the ALLOCATE statement for a BASED variable, then it must also be used in any FREE statement releasing the storage.

Example:

DCL R AREA (2500), X BASED (Q);
ALLOCATE X IN (R);
. . .
FREE X IN (R);

AREA variables have several uses. One use is to limit the storage that can be allocated to a list. If storage space in an area is allocated to list items until the area overflows, then the AREA condition is raised. We shall illustrate the use of this fact in an example later.

A second use is to make it possible for one to free the storage used for an entire list without having to free list items one at a time. If a list is stored in an area, then the entire list can be freed by means of an area-assignment statement of the form

area variable = EMPTY;

EMPTY is a built-in function which takes no arguments and whose value is an "empty" area, that is, an area all of whose space is available for allocation. Assigning EMPTY to an AREA variable causes all storage in the area to be released and made available for reuse.

A third use of AREA variables is to facilitate copying lists in storage. This can be done with the aid of an area assignment statement of the form:

---

[4]The method of measuring area size is implementation dependent. In IBM System/ 360 PL/I implementations, size is measured in bytes; if no size is specified in the declaration of an area variable, the size is assumed to be 1000 bytes. The maximum number of bytes allowed is 32,767.

area variable = area variable;

Such an assignment causes storage formerly allocated in the target area to be released and the entire contents of the first area to be assigned to the target area. Thus a list stored in one area can be duplicated in another area by means of a single area-assignment statement.

The possibility of copying the contents of one area into another gives rise to the use of OFFSET variables. This is the second of the two types of *locator*[5] variables in PL/I, of which the other is the POINTER variable. An OFFSET variable is defined by specifying the OFFSET attribute for the variable in a DECLARE statement. The name of an AREA variable with which the OFFSET variable is associated is specified in parentheses as part of the declaration.

Example:

DCL POOL AREA (2500), Q OFFSET (POOL);

An OFFSET variable is like a POINTER variable in that its value specifies the address of a variable. The difference is that an OFFSET variable locates the variable by its position relative to the start of an area (the area named in the OFFSET declaration), whereas a POINTER variable locates the variable by its absolute core-storage address.

OFFSET variables can be used in the same ways as POINTER variables. Thus an OFFSET variable can be used as a qualifier and can be specified in the SET clause of an ALLOCATE statement.[6] Either type of locator variable can be assigned the value of another locator variable of either type; an automatic conversion takes place whenever necessary. Thus, for example, a statement of the following form is permissible:

offset variable = pointer variable;

If a list is to be copied from one area to another by means of an area assignment statement, the list items must be located by means of OFFSET rather than POINTER variables. POINTER values locating items in the "from" area would not locate the items in the target area, since POINTER values are absolute addresses. On the other hand, OFFSET variables could be used to locate items in both areas, since they identify locations relative to area starting points rather than by absolute addresses.

By means of RECORD-type input/output, an area can be written on an external storage device and subsequently reread, even in a later computer run. Thus a list, provided it is stored in an area, can be written out and reread. This

---

[5]Unlike the words *pointer* and *offset*, the word *locator* is not a PL/I keyword.

[6]At this time, neither of these uses of an OFFSET is permitted in the F-level PL/I implementation for the IBM System/360.

process also requires use of offsets rather than pointers, since the absolute storage addresses of data may change when the data is written out and then read back.

The reader should refer to his PL/I reference manual for further information about how to use AREA and OFFSET variables.

10.5. ADDITIONAL RULES ABOUT BASED AND LOCATOR VARIABLES

In this section we shall summarize briefly some additional facts and rules about BASED and locator (POINTER and OFFSET) variables.

(1) A BASED variable cannot have the EXTERNAL or VARYING attributes, nor can it be used as the base for a DEFINED variable. A POINTER qualifying a BASED variable can, however, be EXTERNAL.

(2) A BASED variable can be initialized by means of the INITIAL attribute, provided the variable is allocated storage by use of the ALLOCATE statement. (Otherwise there would be no opportunity to perform the initialization.)

(3) A BASED variable can be referenced even though it has not been allocated storage by means of the ALLOCATE statement.

(4) ADDR is a built-in function taking a variable for its argument. The function value is the absolute core-storage address of the start of its argument. ADDR is often used in the process of "equivalencing" two variables so that they share storage. ADDR can also be used as an explicit qualifier, as in the expression ADDR(A)—>B.[7]

Example:

```
DCL A(25,25), B(25,25) FIXED BIN (31) BASED (P);
P = ADDR(A);
```

Here P is assigned the address of the starting point of the array A, and any references to A and B are therefore to the same storage.

(5) The dimensions of a BASED array cannot be defined by an asterisk in a DECLARE statement and then specified later in an ALLOCATE array (see Section 5.4). On the other hand, one can obtain adjustable dimensions for a BASED array by specifying variables for the array

---

[7]At this time, a function cannot be used as a qualifier in the F-level PL/I implementation for the IBM System/360.

bounds.[8] Then, provided the BASED array is not allocated storage by means of an ALLOCATE statement, the bounds of the array are recalculated each time the array is referenced. These calculations are always performed with current values for the variables involved. Similar treatment is given to the length of a BASED string variable.

Example:

<pre>
DCL A(N,N) BASED (P), B(100,100);
P = ADDR(B);
</pre>

In this code, whenever an element of A is referenced, the current value of N is used to determine the dimensions of A, and this value of N can be changed at any time.

(6) The allocation of based storage is not affected by the block structure of PL/I programs. Thus, for example, storage allocated in a subprogram is *not* released automatically when control returns from the subprogram to the procedure that invoked it.

(7) A BASED variable cannot be read in or written out by means of a data-directed input/output command.

(8) Multiple allocations and multiple freeings of storage can be performed in one ALLOCATE or one FREE statement.

Example:

<pre>
ALLOCATE X, Y SET (Q), Z SET (P) IN (R);
FREE X, Q—>Y, Z IN (R);
</pre>

(9) Locator variables cannot be used in arithmetic operations. The only operators that can be used with locator data are the comparison operators $=$ and $\neg=$.

(10) Locator variables cannot be read in or written out by STREAM input/output.

(11) A locator variable can itself be BASED, and both BASED and locator variables can be subscripted. Thus, expressions like $P—>Q—>X$, $P(K)—>X$, and $P—>X(K)$ are valid.[9]

(12) A locator variable can be initialized, but only by the INITIAL CALL

---

[8]At this time, this usage is not permitted in the F-level PL/I implementation for the IBM System/360.

[9]At this time, a qualifier can be neither BASED nor subscripted in the F-level PL/I implementation for the IBM System/360.

method, which we have not discussed. In particular, the following declaration is *invalid*:

DCL P PTR INIT (NULL);

(13) No conversions are permitted between locator data and other data types. Conversions from OFFSET to POINTER and from POINTER to OFFSET are valid, however.

(14) A variable is a POINTER by context (and thus does not have to be declared explicitly) if (1) it is named in the declaration of the BASED attribute for some variable, (2) it is named in the SET clause of an ALLOCATE statement, or (3) it is used as an explicit qualifier with the arrow notation.

(15) An expression in the arrow notation is an inseparable entity. Thus, 3*P—>X can only mean 3*(P—>X). Note that an expression like P—>3*X is invalid, because 3*X cannot be BASED.

(16) POINTER, OFFSET, and AREA variables can all be used as subprogram arguments and parameters, and they can be returned as function values. As usual, it is necessary for the programmer to pay attention to the matching of attributes.

(17) A BASED variable can be used as an argument for a subprogram, but a subprogram parameter cannot be BASED. If a subprogram parameter has no storage class attribute declared for it, however, an argument associated with the parameter can be BASED.

(18) There are no operators that can be used with AREA variables and no conversions that can be performed on them.

10.6. EXAMPLE

The code given below, although it is for a trivial application, illustrates many of the techniques for handling BASED variables that we have discussed in this chapter. It should repay the effort required for the reader to study and understand it.

Data cards are read and stored until an end-of-file is encountered. Each card contains a field named A in columns 1–5 and a field named B in columns 6–10. As cards are read in, they are chained together in a list so that their order in the list is ascending sequence for field A. Likewise, they are chained together in another list in ascending sequence for field B. (There is only one card image in storage for each data card, but the one set of card images is organized in two lists.) Finally, the cards are printed out in both A-sequence and B-sequence.

The cards are stored in an area named WORK_SPACE, which is large enough to hold 100 cards. If the area overflows, the AREA condition is raised and a message is written. One generation of the structure **BLOCK** is used to store a card and two pointers, one pointer for each list. For reasons of programming convenience, a card is not stored in the first generation of BLOCK. The end-of-list indicator for each list is the null pointer value.

Note in this example the use of (1) contextual pointer declaration, (2) multiple allocations with one ALLOCATE, (3) the IN clauses in the ALLOCATE and FREE statements, and (4) the ON AREA statement.

```
/* BUILD TWO LISTS FROM CARD INPUT DATA */
GO:  PROC OPTIONS (MAIN);
     DCL 1 BLOCK BASED (P),
            2 CARD CHAR (80),
            2 APTR PTR,
            2 BPTR PTR,
            WORK_SPACE AREA  (8976);
     ON AREA BEGIN;
          PUT PAGE EDIT ('WORK_SPACE EXHAUSTED') (A);
          GO TO RET; END;
     ALLOCATE BLOCK IN (WORK_SPACE);
     ASTART, BSTART = P;  APTR, BPTR = NULL;
     ON ENDFILE(SYSIN) GO TO EOF;
L1:  ALLOCATE BLOCK SET (Q) IN (WORK_SPACE);
     GET EDIT (Q—>CARD) (A(80));

/* LINK CARD IN A—CHAIN */
     P = ASTART;
A1:  DO WHILE (APTR ¬= NULL);
     R = APTR;
     IF SUBSTR(Q—>CARD, 1, 5) <= SUBSTR(R—>CARD, 1, 5)
                                     THEN GO TO A2;
     P = APTR;
     END A1;
A2:  Q—>APTR = APTR;  APTR = Q;

/* LINK CARD IN B—CHAIN */
     P = BSTART;
B1:  DO WHILE (BPTR ¬= NULL);
     R = BPTR;
     IF SUBSTR(Q—>CARD, 6, 5) <= SUBSTR(R—>CARD, 6, 5)
                                     THEN GO TO B2;
     P = BPTR;
     END B1;
B2:  Q—>BPTR = BPTR;  BPTR = Q;
```

```
      GO TO L1;
/* AFTER ENDFILE PRINT CARDS IN BOTH SEQUENCES */
EOF:  FREE Q—>BLOCK IN (WORK__SPACE);
      PUT PAGE EDIT ('CHAIN A', 'CHAIN B') (A, COL(66), A);
      P = ASTART—>APTR;  Q = BSTART—>BPTR;
L2:   DO WHILE (P ¬= NULL);
      PUT EDIT (P—>CARD, Q—>CARD) (COL(1), A(40), COL(66), A(40));
      P = P—>APTR; Q = Q—>BPTR;
      END L2;
RET:  RETURN;
      END GO;
```

10.7. STORAGE CLASSES

With the discussion of BASED variables in this chapter, we have now completed our study of the four PL/I storage classes: automatic, static, controlled, and based. It is convenient to summarize here some points on the subject of storage classes.

In the absence of a specifically declared storage-class attribute, a variable is treated as AUTOMATIC, with one exception: If a variable is declared EXTERNAL, then it is STATIC by default.

From our discussion in Section 8.9, the reader will recall that storage for an AUTOMATIC variable is allocated upon entry into the procedure or BEGIN block in which the variable is known and that the storage is released upon exit from that procedure or BEGIN block. Storage for a STATIC variable, on the other hand, is allocated when the program loads and is not released until program execution terminates. We discussed in Section 8.9 some of the considerations that affect a choice between these two storage classes.

Storage for both CONTROLLED and BASED variables is explicitly allocated and released by the programmer through use of the ALLOCATE and FREE statements. Entering or leaving procedure and BEGIN blocks has no effect on the allocation or freeing of storage for such variables. Although these two storage classes are similar in some respects, there is also a fundamental difference between them. Successive generations of a CONTROLLED variable are stored in a push-down stack, and only the most recent generation of the variable is available for use. On the other hand, successive generations of a BASED variable are not stacked, and any of them can be referenced at any time by manipulating pointers properly. This difference between controlled and based storage is what usually decides the choice between the two classes for programming purposes.

We summarize below some of the main rules concerning storage-class attributes:

(1) An EXTERNAL variable can be CONTROLLED or STATIC, but not AUTOMATIC or BASED.

(2) A storage-class attribute can be declared for a major structure variable but not for variables contained in a structure. If the major structure variable has a storage-class attribute, then all variables contained in it have the same attribute automatically.

(3) A major stucture variable that is BASED or CONTROLLED can be referenced in ALLOCATE and FREE statements, but variables contained in a BASED or CONTROLLED structure cannot.

(4) A storage-class attribute cannot be declared for a DEFINED variable. The base variable for a DEFINED variable can be STATIC, AUTOMATIC, or CONTROLLED, but not BASED.

(5) The only storage-class attribute that can be declared for a subprogram parameter is CONTROLLED. If no such attribute is declared, then an argument corresponding to the parameter can be of any storage class. If a parameter is CONTROLLED, however, then an associated argument must also be CONTROLLED.

(6) Arrays with adjustable dimensions and strings with adjustable lengths cannot be STATIC.

(7) Asterisks can be used to declare the dimensions of a CONTROLLED array or the length of a CONTROLLED string but cannot be used in declarations of BASED arrays or strings. The bounds of a BASED array or the length of a BASED string can, however, be variable. If the BASED array or string is not allocated storage by means of an ALLOCATE statement, the current value is always used for a variable bound or variable length (see Section 10.5, paragraph (5)).

(8) The INITIAL attribute can be used to initialize an AUTOMATIC, STATIC, or CONTROLLED variable. It can also be used to initialize a BASED variable, provided the variable is allocated storage with an ALLOCATE.

(9) A string variable cannot be both VARYING and BASED. Note, however, that the length of a fixed-length string can be a variable in certain circumstances. See (7) above.

EXERCISES

1. What will be the value of Z after the following code is executed?

```
DCL Y BASED (P);
X = 5;
P = ADDR(X);
Z = Y**2;
```

2. What is the value of C after the following code is executed?

```
DCL 1 A BASED (P), 2 B FIXED (1), 2 Q PTR, R PTR, C FIXED (1);
ALLOCATE A;
B = 1;
ALLOCATE A SET (R);
R−>B = 2;
Q = R;
P = P−>Q;
C = B;
```

3. What is the value of Y after the following code is executed?

```
DCL (A, B) AREA (100) BASED (P), X BASED (Q), R OFFSET (A),
    T OFFSET (B), Q PTR;
ALLOCATE A, B;
ALLOCATE X IN (A);
R = Q;
X = 5;
ALLOCATE X IN (B);
X = 6;
B = A;
P = T;
Y = X;
```

4. Assume that a sparse matrix is stored in a list as illustrated in Section 10.3, with the elements in row-major order. Write code to compute the row norm of the matrix. (The row norm of a matrix is the maximum of the absolute row sums. See the last example in Section 8.8.)

5. Assume that a sparse matrix is stored in a list as in the example of Section 10.3, with the elements in row-major order. Design and code a function-type subprogram named ROW that can be used to find the starting address of a specified row in the matrix. The function value ROW should be a POINTER whose value is the desired address. Code the function for use as an external procedure.

11 DEBUGGING

11.1. INTRODUCTION

We shall try to provide in this chapter some helpful information for programmers on the subject of debugging. In Sections 11.2 through 11.6 we shall discuss some PL/I language facilities that can be used to speed up debugging. In Section 11.7 we shall suggest some techniques for debugging list-processing programs. Finally, in Sections 11.8 and 11.9 we shall point out some of the pitfalls that seem frequently to cause trouble for programmers working with PL/I for the first time.

11.2. LANGUAGE OPTIONS

In some circumstances the programmer can exercise PL/I language options that will aid his debugging. We shall discuss two of these: (1) the COPY option of the GET statement and (2) the SNAP option of the ON statement.

(1) COPY. This keyword can be included in the data-directed, list-directed, and edit-directed forms of the GET statement. The keyword can be placed at the end of a GET statement, just before the semicolon. This is not the only permissible position for the keyword, but it is advantageous because it allows the word to be easily removed later, when debugging is finished.

Example:

```
GET EDIT (A, B) (F(6), E(13,5)) COPY;
GET SKIP DATA (X, N, Y) COPY;
GET FILE(AUXFILE) LIST ((A(K) DO K = 1 TO N)) COPY;
```

The COPY option causes the input data being read in by the GET statement to be printed automatically on the file SYSPRINT. The data is not reformatted but is printed just as it appeared in the input stream or, in other words, just as it was "seen" by the PL/I input-processing routine.

When it is suspected that input data is not being processed as intended in a program, the COPY option is a useful diagnostic aid. It shows the programmer what input data is being processed by a GET statement (in contrast to what the programmer *thinks* is being processed).

(2) SNAP. This keyword can be used in an ON statement after the condition name.

Example:

```
ON FOFL SNAP COUNT = COUNT + 1;
ON UFL SNAP BEGIN; ... END;
```

The SNAP option causes a message to be written whenever the on-unit defined by the ON statement is executed.

SNAP is useful to a programmer who wants prnited evidence that an on-unit is being executed. It would always be possible, of course, to get a printed message by including a PUT statement in the on-unit, but SNAP is easier to use.

11.3. SUBSCRIPTRANGE AND STRINGRANGE CONDITIONS

PL/I has two conditions that can be used to detect during program execution a data reference in a region of core storage outside the region actually allocated for the data in question. These conditions are SUBSCRIPTRANGE and STRINGRANGE.

(1) SUBSCRIPTRANGE (abbr.: SUBRG) is raised when a subscript is used whose value is outside the bounds specified in the declaration of the subscripted variable. The condition is initially disabled and so must

be enabled by means of a condition prefix if it is to be used. The standard system action for a SUBSCRIPTRANGE interrupt is to print a message and terminate execution by raising the ERROR condition. If SUBSCRIPTRANGE is not enabled, an out-of-range subscript is not detected.

Example:

```
          DCL A(99);
          DO K = 1 TO 100;
(SUBRG): A(K) = 0;
          END;
```

A SUBSCRIPTRANGE interrupt will occur on the last time through the loop, since A(100) does not exist.

(2) STRINGRANGE (abbr.: STRG) is raised when a string defined by the SUBSTR built-in function or pseudovariable (Section 9.7) is not a substring of the string named in its arguments (the first argument). This condition is also initially disabled. The standard system action for a STRINGRANGE interrupt is to "trim" the "substring" so that it really is a substring and then to continue execution. If the programmer wants a message or wants to terminate execution, he must write a suitable ON statement. If STRINGRANGE is not enabled, an invalid substring reference is not detected.

Example:

```
          DCL C CHAR (25);
          ON STRG SNAP SIGNAL ERROR;
(STRG): SUBSTR(C,20,10) = 'b';
```

STRINGRANGE will be raised in the statement because the substring is supposed to include positions 20–29 of string C, while C has only 25 positions. A SNAP message will be printed, and the ERROR condition will be raised so that execution will terminate.

The simplest way to use one of these conditions for debugging is to enable it throughout a procedure by means of a condition prefix attached to the PROCEDURE statement. Thus, we could have

```
(SUBRG):
GO: PROC OPTIONS (MAIN);
    . . .
END GO;
```

After a program is debugged, it is desirable to disable SUBSCRIPTRANGE and STRINGRANGE, since the extra tests that have to be incorporated in the PL/I object code add extra execution time to a job.

11.4. SIZE CONDITION

A PL/I condition that should be used more often in program testing is the SIZE condition. This condition is raised when high-order digits (that is, digits on the left) are lost in the assignment of a value to a fixed-point variable. SIZE is initially disabled and so must be enabled by means of a condition prefix if it is to be used. The standard system action is to print a message and to terminate execution by raising the ERROR condition.

Example: Consider the following code:

```
        DCL M FIXED DEC (5);
    (SIZE): M = 123456;
```

The assignment statement would cause the SIZE condition to be raised, because the target field M does not have a sufficient number of digits to the left of the decimal point to hold the value assigned to it.

The SIZE condition can be raised as the result of an input/output operation, as well as because of an assignment statement, if the operation causes high-order digits to be lost.

Example: Consider the following code:

```
        DCL M FIXED DEC (5);
        M = 12345;
    (SIZE): PUT EDIT (M) (F(3));
```

Here the value 12345 cannot be printed in a field having only three digits to the left of the decimal point, and the SIZE condition would be raised.

It is important for the reader to distinguish clearly between FIXEDOVER-FLOW and SIZE errors. Many beginning PL/I programmers confuse SIZE errors with FIXEDOVERFLOW errors and do not appreciate the need for enabling SIZE. (FIXEDOVERFLOW is initially enabled, whereas SIZE is not.)

The FIXEDOVERFLOW condition is raised when the result of a fixed-point arithmetic operation exceeds (a) 15 digits in decimal arithmetic or (b) 31 digits in binary arithmetic.[1] FIXEDOVERFLOW is not raised merely because

---

[1]These maximum values are implementation dependent. The values given are those for PL/I implementations on the IBM System/360.

the result of a fixed-point operation exceeds the declared precision of the variable to which the result is assigned. That is where SIZE comes in.

Example: Consider the following code:

```
DCL N FIXED DEC (5);
N = 99999;
N = N + 1;
```

It might be thought that FIXEDOVERFLOW would be raised as a result of the statement, but this is not the case. Although the value assigned to N would be wrong, there would be no message, and program execution would continue. The error actually involved here is not a FIXEDOVERFLOW error at all, but a SIZE error. If the last statement were changed to

```
(SIZE): N = N + 1;
```

then there would be an error message and execution would terminate.

When testing a program involving fixed-point arithmetic, the programmer should enable SIZE throughout the program.

11.5. FINISH CONDITION

FINISH is another PL/I condition that can be used by the programmer for debugging purposes. It is raised after an error has been encountered that will lead to termination of execution, but before the program is actually terminated. More specifically, it is raised as part of the standard system action for the ERROR condition, which is itself raised on account of an execution error. FINISH is also raised by any statement that can cause termination of program execution, such as a RETURN statement in the main procedure.

The significance of the FINISH condition for debugging purposes is the programmer can use a FINISH on-unit to regain control after a job-terminating error has been encountered. He can, for example, use the on-unit to print out debugging information that he may need in order to diagnose the bug. If the programmer does not branch out of a FINISH on-unit, or, in other words, if he allows the end of the on-unit to be reached, then the job finally terminates as it would have if there had been no on-unit.

Example: In the following code an error will occur when SQRT(X) is evaluated, since X is a REAL variable with a negative value. This type of error causes job termination. Before the job terminates, the FINISH on-unit is executed, which causes the offending value of X to be printed.

```
ON FINISH PUT DATA (X);
X = −2;
Y = SQRT(X);
```

It is sometimes helpful to print out in a FINISH on-unit the value of the built-in function ONCODE by writing PUT LIST (ONCODE) or some similar statement. The value of ONCODE is an implementation-dependent number that identifies within limits the cause of a job-terminating error.

The programmer should note there is danger of an endless loop when he uses a FINISH on-unit to regain control after an error has occurred. A second error, it must be remembered, will cause the FINISH condition to be raised a second time. If the programmer does not want his FINISH on-unit to be executed a second time, he should restore the standard system action for the FINISH condition by executing the statement ON FINISH SYSTEM. Probably the best place to put the statement is first in the FINISH on-unit itself, as illustrated below:

```
ON FINISH BEGIN;
    ON FINISH SYSTEM;
    GO TO L1;
    END;
```

11.6. CHECK CONDITION

One of the most powerful debugging tools available to the PL/I programmer is the CHECK condition. To use this condition, one must list one or more variables in a CHECK condition prefix as illustrated in the example below. Unlike condition prefixes for most other PL/I conditions, CHECK condition prefixes can be applied only to PROCEDURE and BEGIN statements. (This means that the scope of a CHECK is always an entire procedure or BEGIN block.)

Example:

```
(CHECK(A)): GO: PROC OPTIONS (MAIN);
(CHECK(A, B, C): F: PROC (X);
(CHECK(X, N)): BEGIN;
```

When a variable has been listed in a CHECK prefix, the CHECK condition is raised every time a value is assigned to the variable. The standard system action is to print out the new value in data-directed output format and then continue execution. Thus, for example, if the prefix CHECK(X) were used, the standard action would have the same effect as inserting the statement PUT DATA (X) just after those places where a value is or might be assigned to X.

CHECK is raised not only when a checked variable is the target in an assignment statement but also when a value is read in by means of a GET statement and assigned to the variable. CHECK is not raised, on the other hand, when a checked variable is merely *used* in a calculation, nor is it raised if the value of a checked variable is altered indirectly. Thus, if a checked variable were the base for some DEFINED variable, CHECK would not be raised when a value was assigned to the DEFINED variable. The reader can consult his PL/I reference manual for a precise statement of the circumstances in which the condition is raised.

Checking cannot be specified for (1) subprogram parameters, (2) BASED variables, and (3) DEFINED variables. (The base variable for a DEFINED variable, can be checked, however.)

An array variable can be specified for checking by naming it in a CHECK prefix, but the array name must be unsubscripted. In such a case the CHECK condition is raised whenever a value is assigned to any element of the array.

As for any PL/I condition, the programmer can write an on-unit to be executed when a CHECK interrupt occurs. The form of an ON CHECK statement is the following:

ON CHECK(one or more variables) on-unit;

The listed variables must be among those that the programmer specified for checking by listing them in a CHECK prefix. The on-unit is executed if the CHECK condition is raised for one of the listed variables. After an interrupt, if control reaches the end of the on-unit, control returns automatically to the next instruction in the interrupted program.

Several ON CHECK statements can be used in a single program so that different on-units are executed when the CHECK condition is raised for different variables. The advantage to using an ON CHECK statement in a program is that it makes it possible for the programmer to get debugging output selectively. He can test for certain situations when a CHECK interrupt occurs and produce printed output only when he wishes, rather than every time an interrupt occurs.

The names of problem-data variables are not the only items that can be listed in a CHECK condition prefix. Thus, a statement label can also be included, among other things. When a statement label is specified for checking, the CHECK condition is raised just before the labeled statement is executed. The standard system action is to print out the label and continue execution. Specifying a statement label for checking is a convenient program checkout technique with which to verify that a particular path in a program is tested. We shall not explain here any of the other uses of the CHECK condition; the reader should consult his PL/I reference manual.

> **Example:** The code given below was used as an example in Section 5.8. We have specified the array variable U, the element variable MAX, and the statement label LB have been specified for checking by listing them in a CHECK prefix attached to the PROCEDURE statement. Two ON CHECK statements have also been included, one for each variable, and the on-units are coded so that debugging output will be printed only if certain (arbitrarily chosen) tests are satisfied.

```
/* COMPUTE  DOMINANT  EIGENVALUE  OF  POSITIVE  MATRIX  BY  POWER
   METHOD. */
(CHECK(MAX, U, LB)):
GO: PROC OPTIONS (MAIN);
       DCL (A(*, *), U(*), V(*), OLDU(*)) CTL, MAX FLOAT, EPSILON INIT (1E−5);
       ON CHECK(MAX) BEGIN; IF (MAX < 0) | (MAX > SQRT(SUM(A**2))) THEN
           PUT SKIP DATA (MAX, U, V); END;
       ON CHECK(U) BEGIN; IF U(2) ¬>0 THEN PUT SKIP DATA (U); END;
       N = 3;
       ALLOCATE A(N,N) INIT (5, 4, 3, 1, 2, 7, 8, 6, 1), U(N), V(N), OLDU(N);
       U = 1;
L1:    DO K = 1 TO 20;
       MAX = 0;
L2:    DO I = 1 TO N;
       V(I) = SUM(A(I, *)*U);
       IF V(I) > MAX THEN MAX = V(I);
       END L2;
LB:    OLDU = U;
       U = V/MAX;
       IF ALL(ABS((U − OLDU)/U) < EPSILON) THEN GO TO L3;
       END L1;
L3:    PUT SKIP DATA (K, MAX, U);
       RETURN;
       END GO;
```

11.7. DEBUGGING LIST-PROCESSING PROGRAMS

The debugging of list-processing programs, such as those in Sections 10.3 and 10.6, seems to be more difficult for many PL/I programmers than debugging generally. Probably the main reason for this is the likelihood of jumbling the pointers that link list items together. When pointers are wrong, list items may be "lost" in core storage so that the pointers and other data cannot even be recovered and examined. A second difficulty is that pointer values cannot be printed out in STREAM output, a fact that complicates the analysis of pointer errors.

A technique to avoid "losing" list items because of pointer errors is to store the addresses of list items in a pointer array in the order in which the list items are created. The pointers in this array are just for debugging and are in addition to the pointers which are actually part of the list items and which link the items together in some sequence. If the pointers linking list items get jumbled, items can still be found by means of the pointer array. The data contents of the list items, including pointers, can then be examined.

The problem of how to print a pointer P for debugging purposes can be solved by printing DEC(UNSPEC(P)), which is the internal (probably binary) representation of P converted to decimal. Although the value printed is just a core storage address whose absolute value has no particular significance to the programmer, it does identify a list item uniquely, and this is usually sufficient for debugging.

Another suggestion that may sometimes help to prevent bugs is not to use implicit pointer qualification. In a program with complicated pointer manipulations, it prevents confusion if one uses explicit pointer qualification for every reference to a BASED variable.

Some of the techniques just discussed are illustrated in the following example.

Example: The code given below is a truncated version of the sparse matrix code used as an example in Section 10.3. Additional statements have been inserted in order to store the addresses of list items in a POINTER array named NAT__SEQ. After the list has been constructed, it is dumped with the aid of the POINTER array. For each list item the code prints (1) the matrix element, (2) the sequence number of the element, (3) the address of the list item, and (4) the address of the next item in the list. The two addresses are printed by the DEC-UNSPEC technique mentioned earlier.

```
/* STORE SPARSE MATRIX IN LIST AND COMPUTE NORM */
GO: PROC OPTIONS (MAIN);
    DCL 1 ELEMENT BASED (P),
          2 A,
          2 K,
          2 CHAIN PTR,
        (START, OLDP) PTR;
    DCL NAT__SEQ(100) PTR;                          /* DEBUGGING */
    ON ENDFILE(SYSIN) GO TO L2;
```

```
/* READ AND STORE MATRIX ELEMENTS IN LIST */
L1:   DO M = 1 TO 10000;
      GET EDIT (I, J, X) (COL(1), (2)F(5), F(10));
      ALLOCATE ELEMENT;
      NAT__SEQ(M) = P;
      K = 100*(I−1) + J;                          /* DEBUGGING */
      A = X;
      IF M = 1 THEN START = P;  ELSE OLDP−>CHAIN = P;
      OLDP = P;
      END L1;
L2:   OLDP−>CHAIN = NULL;

/* DUMP LIST BY MEANS OF POINTER ARRAY FOR DEBUGGING */
L4:   DO L = 1 TO M−1;
      P = NAT__SEQ(L);
      PUT SKIP LIST (A, K, DEC(UNSPEC(ADDR(ELEMENT))),
                          DEC(UNSPEC(CHAIN)));
      END L4;
      RETURN;
      END GO;
```

The output of this code for a run on the IBM System/360 with a small quantity of test data was as shown below. The negative "address" is the NULL pointer. Note how the organization of the list in storage can be reconstructed from the information in this printout.

1.50000E+01	3	454488	454472
1.00000E+00	102	454472	454456
1.00000E+01	103	454456	454440
4.00000E+00	205	454440	454424
5.00000E+00	301	454424	454408
9.00000E+00	404	454408	−16777216

11.8. VARIOUS PITFALLS

In this section we shall mention a few pitfalls that are likely to trouble PL/I programmers. We are not concerned here with programming errors that lead to compiler diagnostics, since programmers can hardly overlook those. More hazardous traps are ones in which a programmer can write code that does not do what he wants but is nevertheless valid PL/I code and does not cause compiler diagnostics. A list of such traps could be extended indefinitely. In the next section we shall also mention some points that FORTRAN programmers just learning PL/I particularly have to keep in mind.

(1) Many errors result from insufficient attention to the PL/I fixed-point precision rules (Section 2.13). Some of the pitfalls in this area were discussed in Section 2.16. Even the most harmless-looking calculations can cause trouble, as the following example illustrates:

```
DCL K FIXED BIN (15), N FIXED DEC (5);
N = 10;
DO K = 1 TO N/2;
  . . .
END;
```

Here the DO loop is not executed. The expression N/2, which has (decimal) precision (15,10), has to be converted to binary, because K is binary. A decimal field with precision (15,10) converts to a binary field with precision (31,34), which cannot contain a value as large as 5 (see the rules in Section 2.13). The DO statement is, therefore, in effect treated as DO K = 1 TO 0, and the loop is skipped.

Simple practices that one can follow in order to avoid troubles over precision rules are (a) to avoid mixed binary and decimal fixed-point arithmetic, (b) to enable the SIZE condition during program testing, (c) to check carefully the precisions of complicated fixed-point expressions, especially when they contain divisions, and (d) to make frequent use of built-in functions that allow control over precision, such as BIN and DIVIDE.

(2) It must be remembered that, when a decimal arithmetic value is converted to a character string, the length of the string is *never* equal to the precision of the decimal field. This fact can be a problem any time that arithmetic operations have to be performed on a character-string field. Consider this illustration:

```
DCL C CHAR (1);
C = '1';
C = C + 1;
```

After this code is executed, C has the value 'b', not '2'. The expression C + 1 in the last statement has the attributes FIXED DEC (2) and the value 2. This value converts to the string 'bbbb2', which is truncated on the right to 'b' for assignment to C. (Incidentally, changing the last statement to C = C + '1' would not alter this.)

When character data and arithmetic data must be used together in an operation, the type of problem just described can often be avoided if one uses a numeric-character variable rather than a character-string variable. Thus, in the example, if C were declared PIC'9' rather than CHAR (1), then the value of C would be correct after the code was executed (see Sections 9.13 and 9.17).

(3) As we explained in Chapter 8, the attributes of subprogram arguments and parameters must agree. Mismatching of attributes causes no compiler diagnostics and may not cause a breakdown during program execution.[2] It may merely cause answers to be wrong. A high percentage of errors involving mismatching of attributes can be avoided by regular use of the ENTRY attribute, which was explained in Section 8.4.

(4) There are at least two situations in which the PL/I programmer may fall into the trap of writing A = B = C when he really should use other code: (a) The correct statement for assigning the value of C to both A and B is

$$A, B = C;$$

Used as an assignment statement, A = B = C is interpreted as A = (B = C), where B = C is a comparison expression with a bit-string value. (b) The correct IF-statement test for equality of A, B, and C is

$$IF (A = B) \& (B = C) THEN \ldots$$

The clause IF A = B = C is interpreted as IF (A = B) = C, where A = B is a comparison expression with a bit-string value, and the test is on whether or not C has this value.

(5) When initializing an array by means of the INITIAL attribute, the programmer must remember that, in order to initialize every element, he must specify initial values for *all* the elements. Thus, the following statement does *not* initialize every element of array A to zero:

$$DCL A(10) INIT (0);$$

The effect of the statement is merely to initialize A(1) to zero and to leave the other elements with undefined values (see Section 5.2). What is required in

---

[2]On the IBM System/360, mismatching of attributes is the most common cause of a "data interrupt" error (not to be confused with a CONVERSION error). If a subprogram parameter is declared to be decimal, while the corresponding argument is not decimal, a data interrupt during program execution is likely, because the nondecimal data will probably not happen to have the special format required for use of the computer's decimal arithmetic. Only if the parameter is decimal is the mismatching of attributes likely to be detected in this way, however. The ERROR condition is raised when a data interrupt occurs in a PL/I program.

order to initialize every element to zero is the statement

$$\text{DCL A(10) INIT ((10)0);}$$

11.9. PL/I AND FORTRAN

In this section we shall list some points that FORTRAN programmers should keep in mind when they begin to use PL/I. As in the preceding section, we are particularly concerned with preventing the type of coding error that does not cause a compiler diagnostic because the code has some valid, though unintended, interpretation in PL/I.

(1) In the reading of card input, the PL/I GET statement, unlike the FORTRAN READ statement, does not automatically cause a new input card to be read (see the discussion on the stream concept in Section 6.3). The following form of the GET statement can be used when it is desired to start with a new card on each GET:

$$\text{GET EDIT (. . .) (COL(1), . . .);}$$

Note that the following type of statement would not in general be suitable for this same purpose:

$$\text{GET EDIT (. . .) (SKIP, . . .);}$$

If this statement were used as the first GET statement in a program, the first data card would be completely skipped.

(2) In PL/I edit-directed input/output, a SKIP item at the end of a format is not processed unless the format has to be rescanned. Thus, the SKIP in the GET statement below would be ineffectual:

$$\text{GET EDIT (X) (F(10,5), SKIP);}$$

This situation is unlike that in FORTRAN, where a slash at the end of a format is processed even if there is no rescan. One way to force a skip is to use a separate GET or PUT statement for the purpose, as illustrated below:

$$\text{GET EDIT (X) (F(10,5));}$$
$$\text{GET SKIP;}$$

(3) Fixed-point arithmetic in PL/I is *not* integer arithmetic, as it is in FORTRAN. Integer arithmetic can be obtained in PL/I merely by taking the TRUNC function of every fixed-point quotient. This function truncates the

fractional part of its argument. (Addition, subtraction, or multiplication of integers produces integral results; only division of integers can produce non-integral results.) It may also be noted that the quotient of two binary fixed-point variables each of precision (31,0) is also of precision (31,0). Because of this, fixed-point arithmetic exclusively involving binary fixed-point variables of precision (31,0) is integer arithmetic. An analogous remark applies for decimal fixed-point variables of precision (15,0).

(4) The FORTRAN DO statement

$$DO\ 5\ K = 1,\ 25$$

specifies that a loop is to be executed 25 times, with K running from 1 to 25 by steps of 1. The PL/I counterpart to this is *not*

$$DO\ K = 1,\ 25;$$

but rather

$$DO\ K = 1\ TO\ 25;$$

The PL/I statement DO K = 1, 25 specifies that the loop is to be executed twice, once with K = 1 and once with K = 25.

(5) The PL/I ON statement has no retroactive effect. Thus, for example, an ON ZERODIVIDE statement must be executed *before* a zerodivide error occurs, if the ON statement is to have any effect. This is different from the situation in FORTRAN, where a divide-check error can be detected *after* it occurs by means of the DVCHK subroutine.

(6) Although the FORTRAN and PL/I MOD functions are similar, they do not produce the same result if the first argument is negative. Thus, the FORTRAN value for MOD(−5, 2) would be −1, whereas the PL/I value would be +1.

EXERCISES

For each of the following codes, state what value is obtained for X. If for some reason X will not be assigned a value, explain what happens.

1. DCL (A, B) CHAR (1);
   A = '1';
   B = 1;
   IF A = B THEN X = 5;
   ELSE X = 6;

2. DCL A CHAR (1) INIT ('P');
   IF A = 1 THEN X = 5;
   ELSE X = 6;

3. A, B = 3;
   IF A = B = 1 THEN X = 5;
   ELSE X = 6;

4. X = 5;
   Y = 1/0;
   ON ZDIV X = 6;

5. X = 25 + 1/7;

6. X = 5;
   DO K = 1 WHILE (X < 7);
   X = X + 1;
   END;

7. X = 2/3.14159265358979;

8. Assume for this problem that the machine representation for .1 in floating-point form equals $1 - \epsilon$, where ϵ is a small positive number, such as, say, $\epsilon = .000001$.
   DO X = 0 BY .1 WHILE (X < 1);
   END;

9. IF .1 < BIN(.07,31,31) THEN X = 5;
   ELSE X = 6;

12 FORMAC

12.1. INTRODUCTION

FORMAC is a programming language used to specify *algebraic* and *analytic* operations. It is to be distinguished from languages like PL/I, FORTRAN, and ALGOL, which have facilities for *arithmetic* operations but not for algebraic and analytic ones. FORMAC or some similar language, of which there are several, should be in the repertory of every scientific programmer. The range of FORMAC applications is surprisingly wide.

In the brief space of one chapter we are not able to describe all of the FORMAC facilities or to illustrate more than a few of the language's uses. The reader who studies this chapter carefully, however, should be able to pursue the subject on his own without difficulty.

The FORMAC system that we shall discuss in this chapter is a system for the IBM System/360 that operates in conjunction with PL/I.[1] A FORMAC program contains two kinds of statements: PL/I statements and FORMAC statements. The FORMAC compiler or "preprocessor," as it is properly called, leaves alone the PL/I statements and converts the FORMAC statements into calls to subprograms that can perform the FORMAC manipulations. The output of this

[1]The FORMAC program and reference manual are available from the IBM Program Library. The program is classified as a Type III program, which means that, unlike the PL/I compiler for the IBM System/360, it is not a programming product of the IBM Corporation. The FORMAC reference manual is *PL/I-Formac Interpreter*, by R. Tobey, *et al.* (IBM Federal Systems Division, 1967). An obsolescent FORMAC system for the IBM 7090/7094 has the same relation to FORTRAN that the current system has to PL/I.

preprocessor is a PL/I source program suitable for compilation by the F-level PL/I compiler. Since any PL/I statement can be used in a FORMAC program, a FORMAC user has at his disposal all the resources of PL/I plus FORMAC's special facilities for performing algebraic and analytic operations.

A FORMAC source program has the same general format as an ordinary PL/I program. Statements end with semicolons and can be punched anywhere in columns 2–72. Blanks have no special significance. Like a PL/I main program, a FORMAC main program begins with a PROCEDURE OPTIONS (MAIN) statement and ends with an END statement. The first statement after the PROCEDURE statement must be

FORMAC_OPTIONS;

In our examples we shall frequently include the following statement:

OPTSET (LINELENGTH=72);

This defines the length of a print line produced by FORMAC to be 72 characters, which is a convenient size for reproduction. In the absence of such a statement, line length is 120 characters. The OPTSET statement (option-set) is one that we shall mention several times in this chapter in connection with other FORMAC language options.

Subsequent sections of this chapter will contain several examples of complete FORMAC progams.

12.2. FORMAC FUNDAMENTALS

FORMAC, like PL/I, has an assignment statement, which has the following general form:

LET (variable = expression);

This statement causes an algebraic expression to be assigned as the value of a variable.

Example:

LET (A = B + C);
LET (X = 2 + Y/3);
LET (Z = 1/2 + SIN(X)**2);

The FORMAC arithmetic operators are the same as those in PL/I, and the priority rules concerning their order of application are the same (Section 2.10).

The variables, constants, and functions used in FORMAC LET statements are different from those in PL/I and are subject to different rules. We shall discuss the variables and constants below and shall take up functions in later sections. Some basic rules concerning FORMAC variables are the following:

(1) Any name that would be a valid name for a PL/I variable is a valid name for a FORMAC variable, provided that (a) the name does not contain more than eight characters, and (b) the underscore is not used.

(2) FORMAC variables have no attributes, such as FIXED and FLOAT, and the first letter of a variable's name has no special significance.

(3) A FORMAC variable can have the same name as a PL/I variable used in the same program, and there is neither relation nor confusion between the two.

(4) A FORMAC variable can be subscripted with up to four subscripts.

(5) A FORMAC variable never has to be declared (in fact, cannot be declared), even if it is subscripted.

FORMAC constants are of two types, floating-point constants and rational constants:

(1) A constant written with a decimal point or an exponent, such as 3.14 or 314E-2, is a floating-point constant.[2] The maximum number of digits allowed in such a constant (not counting the exponent) is nine.

(2) A constant written as an integer or as a ratio of two integers, such as 5 or 2/3, is rational constant. There is no limit to the number of digits that can be used in such a constant.

Arithmetic operations involving only rational numbers are performed *exactly* in rational arithmetic with unlimited precision, and results are always reduced to lowest terms. A calculation involving a floating-point number is performed in double-precision floating-point arithmetic. Rational numbers are not converted to floating-point unless mixed with floating-point in an arithmetic calculation. Floating-point numbers are never converted to rational form.

A FORMAC variable may have for its value (1) a numeric value, either floating-point or rational, or (2) a symbolic algebraic expression. It may also have no value at all, in which case it is said to be an *atomic* variable.

---

[2]All floating-point values are stored internally in double-precision format. Note that a constant like 3.14, which would be fixed-point in PL/I, is floating-point in FORMAC. The FORMAC rule for classifying constants is more like the FORTRAN rule than like the PL/I rule.

Example:

> LET (A = 5);
> LET (B = 3.14);
> LET (C = (X + Y)∗∗2);

Here A has a rational value; B, a floating-point value; and C has for its value the symbolic algebraic expression $(X + Y)^2$. The variables X and Y (which we assume to be not previously defined) have no values and therefore are atomic variables.

When a previously defined variable appears in an expression on the right-hand side of the equals sign in a LET statement, the value of the variable is automatically substituted for it when the LET statement is executed. Certain commonplace expressions that arise are simplified automatically. For example, (X∗∗2)∗∗(1/2) is always simplified to X. (A complete list of simplifying transformations is given in the FORMAC manual.) On the other hand, products are not multiplied out automatically in order to remove parentheses. We shall explain later in this section and also in Section 12.4 some ways in which the programmer can control the simplification of expressions.

Example:

> LET (A = B + C);
> LET (D = Z∗∗(1/2));
> LET (Y = A∗X + D∗∗2);

After this code is executed, the value of Y is the expression $(B + C) X + Z$. Note that the parentheses are not removed automatically.

Retroactive substitutions never occur automatically.

Example:

> LET (A = B + C);
> LET (B = 2);

After this code is executed, the value of A is still B + C and not 2 + C, as might be thought. If the statement LET (A = A) were executed, the value of A would still be B + C.

As we shall explain in Section 12.4, there is a way to force a substitution, but it is not automatic.

The value of a FORMAC variable can be redefined repeatedly by means of LET statements. A variable that has been assigned a value can also be restored to atomic status by means of the ATOMIZE statement, which has the following form:

ATOMIZE (variable);

Example:

LET (A = 5);
LET (B = A);
ATOMIZE (A);
LET (B = B + A);

After this code is executed, B has the value A + 5, and A is an atomic variable.

As we mentioned earlier, products are not normally multiplied out in order to remove parentheses. Thus expressions like $(X + Y)**5$ and $(A + B)*(C + D)$ would not be multiplied out. The programmer can, however, cause such products to be multiplied out automatically by executing the following statement, which turns on the EXPAND option:[3]

OPTSET (EXPND);

Subsequent return to the no-expansion rule can be accomplished by turning off the EXPAND option through execution of the statement OPTSET(NOEXPND).

Printing of the values of FORMAC variables on SYSPRINT can be accomplished by use of the PRINT__OUT statement, which has the following form:

PRINT__OUT (variable);

FORMAC permits several LET statements to be combined into one statement and the same thing for ATOMIZE and for PRINT__OUT statements, as illustrated below:

LET (A = B; C = 1; D = X/Y);
ATOMIZE (P; Q; R);
PRINT__OUT (A; B; C);

12.3. EXAMPLE

The code given below is a complete FORMAC program for expanding the fourth-degree polynomial

$$(1) \qquad P(x) = [(Ax + B)^2 + Ax + C] [(Ax + B)^2 + D] + E$$

---

[3]*Exception*: The EXPAND option does not cause a completely factored denominator to be expanded. Thus the denominator in the fraction $A/(B*(C + D)**2)$ would not be expanded, whereas the denominator of $A/(2 + (B + C)**2)$ would be expanded because it is not factored.

where A, B, C, D, and E are given below:

$$A = \sqrt[4]{a_4}$$

$$B = \frac{a_3 - A^3}{4A^3}$$

$$D = 3B^2 + 8B^3 + \frac{a_1 A - 2a_2 B}{A^2}$$

$$C = \frac{a_2}{A^2} - 2B - 6B^2 - D$$

$$E = a_0 - B^4 - (C + D)B^2 - CD$$

The result of this algebraic effort should be

(2) $$P(x) = a_0 + a_1 x + a_2 x^2 + a_3 x^3 + a_4 x^4$$

(The significance of this is that a fourth-degree polynomial given in the form (2), where $a_4 > 0$, can be converted into the form (1) by means of the formulas for A, B, C, D, and E, in which form the polynomial can be evaluated in only three multiplications.)

Note that in this code the EXPAND option has been used to cause all parentheses to be removed.

```
/* CHECK FORMULAS FOR ECONOMICAL EVALUATION METHOD */
GO: PROC OPTIONS (MAIN);
    FORMAC_OPTIONS;
    OPTSET (EXPND);
    OPTSET (LINELENGTH=72);
    LET (A = A4**(1/4));
    LET (B = (A3 − A**3)/(4*A**3));
    LET (D = 3*B**2 + 8*B**3 + (A1*A − 2*A2*B)/A**2);
    LET (C = A2/A**2 − 2*B − 6*B**2 − D);
    LET (E = A0 − B**4 − (C+D)*B**2 − C*D);
    LET (P = ((A*X+B)**2 + A*X + C)*((A*X+B)**2 + D) + E);
    PRINT_OUT (P);
    RETURN;
    END GO;
```

The output from this FORMAC program is the following:

$$P = A0 + A1\ X + A2\ X^2 + A3\ X^3 + A4\ X^4$$

12.4. FORMAC BUILT-IN FUNCTIONS

FORMAC has a number of built-in functions that can be used in LET statements for purposes such as (1) controlling the form of an algebraic expression, (2) isolating part of an expression, and (3) making substitutions. Some of the most important of these functions are briefly described and illustrated below. The reader should consult the PL/I reference manual for additional information on these functions and other built-in functions. We shall discuss in Section 12.6 some of the FORMAC mathematical functions, such as SQRT and COS.

(1) The CODEM function forces fractions to be combined. A reference to it has the form CODEM(e), where e denotes an expression. The value of this is the expression e transformed so that all fractions have been combined over common denominators[4] at all levels of the expression. The CODEM of an expression never contains more than one slash (division), if rational constants are not counted.

Example:

$$\text{LET } (T = A/B + C/(D + E/F));$$
$$\text{LET } (T = \text{CODEM}(T));$$

After this code is executed, the value of T is

$$\frac{A(DF + E) + BCF}{B(DF + E)}$$

(2) The EXPAND function removes parentheses. A reference to it has the form EXPAND(e), where e denotes an expression. The value of this is the expression e transformed so that all products have been multiplied out in order to remove parentheses.[5] The main difference between the EXPAND function and the EXPAND option (Section 12.2) is that the function can be used more selectively than the option. (Some additional remarks on the use of CODEM and EXPAND together are given in the next section.)

Example:

$$\text{LET } (P = A + B);$$
$$\text{LET } (Q = C + D);$$
$$\text{LET } (R = P*E + \text{EXPAND}(Q*F));$$

After this code is executed, the value of R is $(A + B) E + CF + DF$.

(3) The functions NUM and DENOM extract the numerator and denominator of a fraction. References to these functions have the forms NUM(e) and DENOM(e), where e denotes an expression. If e is a fraction a/b, the value

---

[4]Not necessarily least common denominators. There is no least-common-denominator function in FORMAC.

[5]*Exception*: The EXPAND function does not expand completely factored denominators appearing in its argument (see the remarks in Section 12.2 on the EXPAND option).

of NUM(e) is a, and the value of DENOM(e) is b. If e is not a fraction or if it is a rational constant, the value of NUM(e) is e, and the value of DENOM(e) is 1. (A rational constant is not decomposable.)

Example:

```
LET (P = A + B/C);
LET (Q = CODEM(P));
LET (NP = NUM(P); DP = DENOM(P));
LET (NQ = NUM(Q); DQ = DENOM(Q));
```

After this code is executed, NP has the value A + B/C; DP, the value 1; NQ, the value AC + B; and DQ, the value C.

(4) The COEFF function extracts from an expression the coefficient of a specified term. A reference to the function has the form COEFF(e_1, e_2), where the arguments denote expressions. The value of this is the coefficient of e_2 in e_1. If e_2 is not a subexpression of e_1, then the function value is 0. In its analysis of e_1, COEFF does not look inside parentheses. In other words, it examines e_1 only at the topmost level.

Example:

```
LET (P = A*X**2 + B*X**2 + C*Y — D*Y);
LET (Q = COEFF(P,X**2)*X**2 + COEFF(P,Y)*Y);
LET (R = A*X + B*(X + Y));
LET (T=COEFF(R,X));
```

After this code is executed, the value of Q is $(A + B)X^2 + (C - D)Y$, and the value of T is A.

(5) The REPLACE function performs substitutions. A reference to it has the form REPLACE(e_1, e_2, e_3), where the arguments are expressions. The value of this is the result of substituting e_3 for each occurrence of e_2 in e_1.

Example:

```
LET (P = A*(X+1)**2 + B*(X+1) + C);
LET (Q = REPLACE(P,X+1,Y));
```

After this code is executed, the value of Q is $AY^2 + BY + C$.

(6) The IDENT function compares two expressions to see if they are identical. A reference to it has the form IDENT(e_1; e_2). This function is unlike

the functions discussed previously in this section in that it is used in PL/I statements rather than in FORMAC statements. IDENT(e_1; e_2) is a bit string of length one whose value is '1'B if e_1 is identical to e_2 and '0'B if e_1 is not identical to e_2. A bit-string value is used because the function is mainly used in IF clauses (see Section 9.15).

Example:

```
LET (P = A + B);
IF IDENT(P; 0) THEN GO TO LB3;
```

When this code is executed, the THEN clause is skipped, because A + B is not identical to 0.

Several of the functions discussed above are used in combination in the next example.

Example: Suppose that it is desired to make the substitution $x = y + 1$ in the quadratic $ax^2 + bx + c$ and then to express the result as a quadratic in powers of y. The following code does this:

```
LET (P = A*X**2 + B*X + C);
LET (P = REPLACE(P,X,Y+1));
LET (P = EXPAND(P));
LET (P = COEFF(P,Y**2)*Y**2 + COEFF(P,Y)*Y + REPLACE(P,Y,0));
```

After this code is executed, the value of P is the expression

$$AY^2 + (2A + B)Y + A + B + C$$

A general rule concerning the use of FORMAC functions, including all of those discussed in this section, is that, before the function routine is called, FORMAC always evaluates an expression used as an argument with whatever options are in effect.

12.5. ADDITIONAL REMARKS ABOUT BUILT-IN FUNCTIONS

It is often difficult for a FORMAC programmer to know just what built-in functions he must use to get an algebraic expression into some special form. Commonly some experimentation is required to discover just what code is needed. The programmer should not always expect to be able to write a program at one sitting, even a short program. Only after he sees some preliminary output can he know that that a CODEM, say, is called for at some point in a program.

Both experimentation and debugging can be facilitated by use of the PRINT option, which is turned on by execution of the statement

$$\text{OPTSET (PRINT)};$$

This option causes the value assigned to a variable to be printed on SYSPRINT every time a LET statement is executed. The option can be turned off by executing the statement

$$\text{OPTSET (NOPRINT)};$$

A few remarks on the use of the CODEM and EXPAND functions may be helpful to beginning FORMAC programmers: It is often a mistake to try to expand the CODEM of an expression. One can learn the reason for this observation by examining the following statement:

$$\text{LET } (P = \text{EXPAND}(\text{CODEM}(A/B + C/(D + E))));$$

The value of CODEM(A/B + C/(D + E)) is

$$\frac{A(D + E) + BC}{B(D + E)}$$

The result of expanding this is not

$$\frac{AD + AE + BC}{BD + BE}$$

as might be thought, but is just the original expression

$$\frac{A}{B} + \frac{C}{D + E}$$

again. The reason for this is that FORMAC thinks of

$$\frac{A(D + E) + BC}{B(D + E)}$$

in the form $B^{-1}(D + E)^{-1}(A(D + E) + BC)$, which simplifies to

$$B^{-1}A + (D+E)^{-1}C = \frac{A}{B} + \frac{C}{D + E}$$

when it is expanded.

As this illustration shows, the EXPAND function can undo the work of CODEM. The EXPAND option has, of course, the same effect, and it is often ineffective to use CODEM while this option is turned on.

In spite of the problem with EXPAND and CODEM that was explained above, one can still expand the numerator and denominator of a fraction, as is illustrated below.

```
LET (T = CODEM(A/B + C/(D + E)));
LET (P = EXPAND(NUM(T))/EXPAND(DENOM(T)));
```

Here T has the value

$$\frac{A(D + E) + BC}{B(D + E)}$$

Since the numerator and denominator of T are expanded independently, no difficulties arise, and the value of P is

$$\frac{AD + AE + BC}{BD + BE}$$

Example: Consider the following continued fraction approximation to tanh x:

$$\cfrac{x}{1 + \cfrac{x^2}{3 + \cfrac{x^2}{5 + \cfrac{x^2}{7 + \cfrac{x^2}{9 + \cfrac{x^2}{11 + \cfrac{x^2}{13 + \cfrac{x^2}{15}}}}}}}}$$

Suppose that is desired to express this continued fraction in fractional form, that is, as a polynomial divided by a polynomial. The code given below does that. Note that the PRINT option is used so that intermediate as well as final results can be studied.

```
/* CONVERT CONTINUED FRACTION INTO FRACTIONAL FORM */
GO: PROC OPTIONS (MAIN);
    FORMAC_OPTIONS;
    OPTSET (LINELENGTH=72);
    LET (Z = X**2);
    OPTSET (PRINT);
    LET (TANHX=X/(1+Z/(3+Z/(5+Z/(7+Z/(9+Z/(11+Z/(13+Z/15)))))))) ;
    LET (TANHX = CODEM(TANHX));
    LET (TANHX = EXPAND(NUM(TANHX))/EXPAND(DENOM(TANHX)));
    RETURN;
    END GO;
```

The output of this code is like this:

ΓANHX $=X/(X^2/(X^2/(X^2/(X^2/(X^2/(1/15\,X^2 + 13) + 11) + 9) + 7) + 5) + 3) + 1)$
TANHX $= (3\,(5\,(7\,(9\,(11\,(1/15\,X^2 + 13) + X^2) + (1/15\,X^2 + 13)X^2) + (11\,(1/15\,X^2 + 13) + X^2)\,X^2) + (9\,(11\,(1/15\,X^2 + 13) + X^2) + (1/15\,X^2 + 13)\,X^2)\,X^2) + (7\,(9\,(11\,(1/15\,X^2 + 13) + X^2) + (1/15\,X^2 + 13)\,X^2) + (11\,(1/15\,X^2 + 13) + X^2)\,X^2)\,X^2)X/(3\,(5\,(7\,(9\,(11\,(1/15\,X^2 + 13) + X^2) + (1/15\,X^2 + 13)\,X^2) + (11\,(1/15\,X^2 + 13) + X^2)\,X^2) + (9\,(11\,(1/15\,X^2 + 13) + X^2) + (1/15\,X^2 + 13)\,X^2)\,X^2) + (5\,(7\,(9\,(11(1/15\,X^2 + 13) + X^2) + (1/15\,X^2 + 13)\,X^2) + (11\,(1/15\,X^2 + 13) + X^2)\,X^2) + (9\,(11\,(1/15\,X^2 + 13) + X^2) + (1/15\,X^2 + 13)\,X^2)\,X^2)\,X^2 + (7\,(9\,(11\,(1/15\,X^2 + 13) + X^2) + (1/15\,X^2 + 13)\,X^2) + (11\,(1/15\,X^2 + 13) + X^2)\,X^2)\,X^2)$
TANHX $= (135135\,X + 18018\,X^3 + 462\,X^5 + 12/5\,X^7)/(63063\,X^2 + 3465\,X^4 + 42\,X^6 + 1/15\,X^8 + 135135)$

12.6. MATHEMATICAL FUNCTIONS

In addition to the functions described in the preceding section, FORMAC also has a number of built-in mathematical functions, such as SIN, LOG, and COSH. These functions can be used with either numeric or symbolic arguments in LET statements.

The functions for which FORMAC has built-in routines are the following:

SIN	ATAN	LOG10
COS	ATANH	LOG2
SINH	ATAN(x, y)	ERF
COSH	LOG	

As with algebraic expressions, FORMAC performs a number of automatic transformations on expressions involving these transcendental functions. For example, COS(-X) is always simplified to COS(X), and LOG (A**B) is always transformed to B*LOG(A). A complete description of these transformations is given in the FORMAC reference manual.

If the argument to one of the transcendental functions listed above has a numeric value, FORMAC automatically computes a double-precision floating-point value for the function. Thus, if LOG(2) appears in an expression, the natural logarithm of 2 is calculated, and its value in floating-point replaces the function in the expression. The programmer can inhibit this action by executing the statement

OPTSET (NOTRANS);

This turns off the TRANS option and thus causes the functions listed above to be retained symbolically and not to be evaluated for numeric arguments. The TRANS option can be turned back on by executing the statement OPTSET (TRANS).

FORMAC also recognizes several other mathematical functions not included in the list given above. These functions are handled by substituting other expressions for them automatically. The main functions in this category are the following, which are shown with the substitutions used for them:

$$
\begin{aligned}
\text{EXP(X)} &= \#E**X \\
\text{SQRT(X)} &= X**(1/2) \\
\text{TAN(X)} &= \text{SIN(X)}/\text{COS(X)} \\
\text{TANH(X)} &= \text{SINH(X)}/\text{COSH(X)} \\
\text{ERFC(X)} &= 1 - \text{ERF(X)}
\end{aligned}
$$

(The term #E used in the expression for EXP(X) is a FORMAC *systems constant* representing the transcendental constant *e*.)

Evaluation of functions like TAN, TANH, and ERFC for numeric arguments is subject to control of the TRANS option, since the expressions substituted for these functions are under control of that option. EXP and SQRT are both expressed, on the other hand, in terms of the double asterisk (**) operator, which is not subject to TRANS control. (An expression of the form A**B in which both A and B have numeric values is always evaluated in floating-point arithmetic by FORMAC.) Therefore, the SQRT of a numeric argument is always computed in floating-point, and there is no option that will prevent this action.

The same would be true for EXP if it were not for the fact that the systems constant #E does not automatically have a numeric value in FORMAC. If the programmer wishes to have the EXP of a numeric argument evaluated in floating-point, he must substitute a numeric value for the systems constant #E by means of the EVAL function, which is a built-in function that we did not discuss in Section 12.4. For example, a value could be assigned to #E in an expression named T by writing

LET (T = EVAL(T, #E, 2.71828182));

The following example illustrates the use of some of the mathematical functions recognized by FORMAC.

Example: The code given below is a complete program for establishing the trigonometric identity

$$\frac{1}{\cos x} - \tan x - \frac{\cos x}{1 + \sin x} = 0$$

```
/* TRIGONOMETRIC IDENTITY */
GO: PROC OPTIONS (MAIN);
     FORMAC__OPTIONS;
     OPTSET (PRINT);
     OPTSET (LINELENGTH=72);
     LET (E = 1/COS(X) — TAN(X) — COS(X)/(1 + SIN(X)));
     LET (E = CODEM(E));
     LET (E = EXPAND(NUM(E))/DENOM(E));
     LET (E = REPLACE(E, SIN(X)**2, 1—COS(X)**2));
     LET (E = EXPAND(E));
     RETURN;
     END GO;
```

The output from this code is the following:

```
E = — COS(X)/(SIN(X) + 1) — SIN(X)/COS(X) + 1/COS(X)
E = (COS(X)(— SIN(X)(SIN(X) + 1) — COS²(X)) + COS(X)(SIN(X) + 1))/
     COS²(X) (SIN(X) + 1)
E = (— COS (X)SIN²(X) — COS³(X) + COS(X))/COS²(X)(SIN(X) + 1)
E = (— COS (X)(— COS²(X) + 1) — COS³(X) + COS(X))/COS²(X)(SIN(X) + 1)
E = 0
```

FORMAC also has integer-valued built-in functions for evaluating factorials and binomial coefficients. The value of FAC(n) is $n!$, and the value of COMB (n, k) is the binomial coefficient[6]

$$\binom{n}{k} = \frac{n!}{(n - k)!k!}$$

We shall illustrate the use of FAC in Section 12.8.

12.7. PROGRAMMER-DEFINED FUNCTIONS

The FORMAC programmer can define functions himself to supplement those that are built into the system. This is done by means of the FNC statement. To define a function named, say, F in terms of n variables, we write

LET (FNC(F) = expression);

In the expression defining F, the symbols $(1), $(2), ..., $(n) are used to denote the n variables. After F has been defined in this way, it can be referenced

---

[6]COMB can also be used to compute multinomial coefficients.

in LET statements in the form $F(e_1, e_2, \ldots, e_n)$, where the arguments are arbitrary FORMAC expressions.[7]

Example: The following statement defines a function named FEXPAND, with which one can expand independently the numerator and denominator of a fraction:

LET (FNC(FEXPAND) = EXPAND(NUM($(1)))/EXPAND(DENOM($(1))));

Thereafter, we might use this function as follows:

LET (T = FEXPAND(T));

This would be equivalent to writing

LET (T = EXPAND(NUM(T))/EXPAND(DENOM(T)));

A programmer-defined function can be named in the same way as any FORMAC variable, but it cannot have the same name as a FORMAC variable used in the same program. Ordinary FORMAC variables can be used in an FNC function definition. The values of such variables *at the time of definition* are the values used when the function is invoked. Programmer-defined functions cannot be redefined.

Example: The code given below is a complete program for establishing the trigonometric identity

$$\csc^6 x - \cot^6 x - 1 - 3(\csc^2 x)(\cot^2 x) = 0$$

The functions csc x and cot x must be defined, because they are not known to FORMAC.

```
/* TRIGONOMETRIC IDENTITY */
GO: PROC OPTIONS (MAIN);
    FORMAC_OPTIONS;
    OPTSET (PRINT);
    OPTSET (LINELENGTH=72);
    LET (FNC(CSC) = 1/SIN($(1)));
    LET (FNC(COT) = 1/TAN($(1)));
    LET (E = CSC(X)**6 — COT(X)**6 — 1 — 3*(CSC(X)**2)*(COT(X)**2));
    LET (E = CODEM(E));
    LET (E = REPLACE(E, COS(X), SQRT(1 — SIN(X)**2)));
    LET (E = EXPAND(NUM(E))/DENOM(E));
    RETURN;
    END GO;
```

---

[7]FORTRAN programmers will note the similarity between FORMAC FNC-type functions and FORTRAN arithmetic-statement functions.

The output of this code is the following:

$CSC = 1/SIN(\$(1))$

$COT = COS(\$(1))/SIN(\$(1))$

$E = - COS^6(X)/SIN^6(X) - 3 COS^2(X)/SIN^4(X) + 1/SIN^6(X) - 1$

$E = (SIN^6(X)(- COS^6(X) SIN^4(X) - 3 COS^2(X)/SIN^6(X)) + SIN^{10}(X) - SIN^{16}(X))$
$/SIN^{16}(X)$

$E = (SIN^6(X)(- 3 SIN^6(X)(- SIN^2(X) + 1) - SIN^4(X)(- SIN^2(X) + 1)^3) + SIN^{10}(X)$
$- SIN^{16}(X))/SIN^{16}(X)$

$E = 0$

12.8. EXCHANGING DATA BETWEEN PL/I AND FORMAC

It is sometimes useful to be able to refer to a PL/I variable in a FORMAC statement or to a FORMAC variable in a PL/I statement. We shall explain below how to do both of these things.

A PL/I variable can be referenced on the right hand side of a FORMAC LET statement by enclosing the name of the variable in double quotation marks.[8] When the LET statement is executed, the value of the PL/I variable is converted to FORMAC format. The PL/I variable can be either fixed-point or floating-point.

Example:

$$LET (K = "K");$$
$$LET (A = B + "X");$$

In the first statement K is the name of both a FORMAC variable and a (different) PL/I variable. The statement causes the value of the PL/I K to be assigned to the FORMAC K. In the second statement the value of the PL/I variable X is converted into FORMAC format and added to B, and this result is assigned to the FORMAC variable A.

A FORMAC variable can be referenced in a PL/I statement by making it the argument of either the ARITH or INTEGER functions. Each of these is a PL/I function that takes a FORMAC variable (not an expression) as an argument. An argument of ARITH is converted into a PL/I value with the attributes FLOAT BIN (53), or, in other words, into a PL/I double-precision floating-point value. An argument of INTEGER is rounded to an integer and converted into a PL/I value with the attributes FIXED BIN (31). Use of

---

[8]A "double quotation mark" is one character, not two single quotation marks side by side.

ARITH and INTEGER is not limited to assignment statements; they can appear wherever functions with their attributes are valid in PL/I statements.

> **Example:** The code given below is a complete program for computing the elements of the matrix H_5^{-1}, where $H_5 = (1/(i + j - 1))$ is the 5×5 segment of the Hilbert matrix. The elements of H_5^{-1} are all integers that can be computed by means of a formula involving factorials. These elements are converted to PL/I values by means of the INTEGER function so that the output can be formatted with a PUT EDIT statement. Note that the numerical results obtained with this program are exact, since the FORMAC arithmetic used to compute them is exact.

```
/* COMPUTE INVERSE OF HILBERT SEGMENT OF ORDER 5 */
GO: PROC OPTIONS (MAIN);
     FORMAC OPTIONS;
     DCL T(5, 5) FIXED BIN (31);
     N = 5; LET (N = "N");
L1:  DO I = 1 TO N;
     DO J = I TO N;
     LET (I = "I"; J = "J");
     LET (T = (- 1)**(I+J)*FAC(N+I-1)*FAC(N+J-1)/
             ((I+J-1)*(FAC(I-1)*FAC(J-1)**2*FAC(N-I)*FAC(N-J))));
     T(I, J) = INTEGER(T);
     END L1;
     PUT EDIT (((T(I, J) DO J=I TO N) DO I=1 TO N))
                            (SKIP, (I-1)X(10), (N-I+1)F(10));
     RETURN;
     END GO;
```

The output of this code is the following. Since the matrix is symmetric, the program prints out only the upper right side of it.

25	−300	1050	−1400	630
	4800	−18900	26880	−12600
		79380	−117600	56700
			179200	−88200
				44100

12.9. EXAMPLE

In this section we give another example to illustrate some of the FORMAC programming principles discussed so far in this chapter.

The polynomial of degree 15 obtained by truncating the Chebyshev series for arctan x is

$$P(x) = \sum_{0}^{7} \frac{(-1)^k \, 2 \, (\sqrt{2} - 1)^{2k+1}}{2k + 1} T_{2k+1}(x)$$

Here $T_n(x)$ denotes the Chebyshev polynomial of degree n, which is defined by the following recursion relation:

$$T_0(x) = 1, \qquad T_1(x) = x$$
$$T_n(x) = 2xT_{n-1}(x) - T_{n-2}(x), \qquad n = 2, 3, \ldots$$

In the code below, we obtain $P(x)$ in power-series form. This is done by forming recursively the Chebyshev polynomials through $T_{15}(x)$ and then computing the coefficients of $P(x)$ in floating-point form.

```
/* EXPAND ARCTAN X IN CHEBYSHEV SERIES */
GO: PROC OPTIONS (MAIN);
    FORMAC_OPTIONS;
    OPTSET (LINELENGTH=72);
    OPTSET (EXPND);
    LET (T(0) = 1 ; T(1) = X);
L1: DO K = 2 TO 15;
    LET (K = "K");
    LET (T(K) = 2*X*T(K—1) — T(K—2));
    END L1;
    LET (C = SQRT(2) — 1);
    LET (P = 0);
L2: DO K = 0 TO 7;
    LET (K = "K");
    LET (CFCT = ((— 1)**K)*2*(C**(2*K+1))/(2*K+1));
    LET (P = P + CFCT*T(2*K+1));
    END L2;
    PRINT_OUT (P);
    RETURN;
    END GO;
```

The output of this program is the following:

P = .99999924 X — .33329538 X^3 + .19943081 X^5 — .13892041 X^7
    + .09601656 X^9 — .05538169 X^{11} + .02150925 X^{13} — .00396025 X^{15}

12.10. DIFFERENTIATION

Analytic differentiatiation of FORMAC variables can be accomplished by use of the DERIV built-in function. Suppose, for example, that F is a FORMAC variable whose value depends on an atomic variable X. Then the value of DERIV(F,X) is the first derivative of F with respect to X.

FORMAC knows the chain rule of differential calculus and knows formulas for the derivatives of its own built-in functions.

Example:

```
LET (F = EXP(X**2));
LET (D = DERIV(F,X));
```

After this code is executed, the value of D is 2 X EXP(X^2).

A reference to DERIV can be of the more general form

$$DERIV(e, v_1, n_1, v_2, n_2, \ldots, v_r, n_r),$$

where e denotes the expression to be differentiated, the v's denote atomic variables, and the n's denote nonnegative integers. The value of this function is the partial derivative

$$\frac{\delta^{n_1+n_2+\cdots n_r} e}{\delta v_1^{n_1} \delta v_2^{n_2} \ldots \delta v_r^{n_r}}$$

Example:

```
LET (P = EXP(X**2)*SIN(Y));
LET (Q = DERIV(P,X,1,Y,2));
```

After this code is executed, the value of Q is - 2 X EXP(X) SIN(Y).

A use of DERIV in a complete program is given in the next example, and another example involving DERIV appears in the next section.

It may be mentioned here that FORMAC has no facilities for analytic integration.

Example: The code given below is a complete program for finding the limit

$$\lim_{x \to a} \frac{F(x)}{G(x)}$$

by means of l'Hospital's rule. This rule from differential calculus can be briefly stated as follows: If $F(a) = G(a) = 0$, then the limit above can be obtained by differentiating the numerator and denominator an equal number of times until at least one of the derivatives is not zero at $x = a$. The desired limit is the quotient of the two derivatives evaluated at $x = a$, provided that a nonvanishing derivative in the numerator does not appear sooner than in the denominator. For the sake of simplicity, we ignore in this example the possibility that the denominator vanishes when the numerator does not. The limit computed by this program is

$$\lim_{x \to 0} \frac{24 - 12x^2 + x^4 - 24 \cos x}{\sin^6 x}$$

It requires six differentiations of numerator and denominator to find that the value of this limit is $\frac{1}{30}$.

```
/* L'HOSPITAL'S RULE */
GO: PROC OPTIONS (MAIN);
    FORMAC_OPTIONS;
    LET (F = 24 — 12*X**2 + X**4 — 24*COS(X); G = SIN(X)**6; A = 0);
    DO K=1 TO 10;
    LET (N = REPLACE(F, X, A));
    LET (D = REPLACE(G, X, A));
    IF ¬(IDENT(N; 0) & IDENT(D; 0)) THEN GO TO OUT;
    LET (F = DERIV(F, X); G = DERIV(G, X));
    END;
OUT: LET (LIMIT = N/D);
    PRINT_OUT (LIMIT);
    RETURN;
    END GO;
```

12.11. INPUT/OUTPUT OF FORMULAS

Unlike PL/I, FORMAC has the capability of reading in a formula during object-program execution and using it immediately. This is possible because FORMAC LET statements are executed interpretively, and a formula read in during execution time is treated in the same way as a formula built into a FORMAC source program.

The technique of reading in and using a formula is illustrated in the following code:

```
DCL FORMULA CHAR (80);
GET EDIT (FORMULA) (A(80));
LET (F = "FORMULA" + 3);
```

The data read in from SYSIN is a formula written just as it would be written if it were actually part of a FORMAC program. This formula is assigned to the PL/I character-string variable FORMULA. The double quotation marks in the LET statement indicate that the character-string value of FORMULA (in other words, the formula itself) should be converted to an internal form suitable for use by FORMAC. If, for example, the formula in the data card were

SIN(X)/X — SQRT(X)

then the effect of the LET statement in the code given above would be equivalent to that of the following statement:

LET (F = SIN(X)/X — SQRT(X) + 3);

The procedure just described can be reversed so that formulas are written out instead of read in. This process requires use of the CHAREX statement, which has the following general form:

CHAREX (PL/I VARYING character-string variable = FORMAC variable);

The effect of this statement is to cause an equation stating the value of the FORMAC variable to be represented as a character string and assigned to the PL/I character-string variable. Consider the following illustration:

```
DCL EQUATION CHAR (100) VAR;
LET (Y = A + 5 — SIN(X));
CHAREX (EQUATION = Y);
PUT EDIT (EQUATION) (A);
```

Here the character-string value assigned to EQUATION would be 'Y = A + 5 — SIN(X)', and that string is what would be printed.

The technique discussed in the foregoing illustration can easily be modified to punch out an equation on a card so that it can be used as an assignment statement in a PL/I program.

The following example shows how the technique of reading in a formula during execution time can be applied.

Example: The code given below is a complete program for reading in a formula for a function $F(x)$ and solving the equation $F(x) = 0$ by means of Newton's method. This method consists of choosing a starting value x_0 and computing a sequence of values $x_1, x_2, x_3, \ldots$ by means of the recursion relation

$$x_{k+1} = x_k - \frac{F(x_k)}{F'(x_k)} \qquad k = 0, 1, 2, \ldots$$

Under certain conditions the sequence converges to a root of the equation $F(x) = 0$. For the sake of simplicity, we take $x_0 = 1$ and stop the calculations when $|F(x_k)/F'(x_k)| < 10^{-5}$. The COPY option is specified in the GET statement so that the formula for $F(x)$ is printed just as it appeared on the data card.

```
/* NEWTON'S ITERATION FOR FINDING ROOT OF F(X) = 0 */
GO: PROC OPTIONS (MAIN);
      FORMAC__OPTIONS;
      DCL F CHAR (80);
      GET EDIT (F) (A(80)) COPY;
      LET (F = "F");
      LET (FP = DERIV(F, X));
      X = 1;
L1: DO K = 1 TO 20;
      LET (P = REPLACE(F, X, "X"));
      LET (Q = REPLACE(FP, X, "X"));
      DELTA = ARITH(P)/ARITH(Q);
      X = X - DELTA;
      IF ABS(DELTA) < 1E-5 THEN GO TO L2;
      END L1;
      PUT LIST ('TOO MANY ITERATIONS');
      RETURN;
L2: PRINT__OUT (F);
      PUT SKIP EDIT ('K = ', K, 'X = ', X) (A, F(2), X(5), A, F(10,6));
      RETURN;
      END GO;
```

The output of this code is the following:

$$SIN(X) - X + 1$$
$$F = -X + SIN(X) + 1$$
$$K = 5 \quad X = 1.934568$$

EXERCISES

1. Establish each of the trigonometric identities given below. *Hint*: Transpose everything to the left so that an identity of the form $f(x) = 0$ is obtained. Then use FORMAC to simplify $f(x)$ and to show that $f(x)$ is indeed identically zero.

(a) $\cos^4 x - \sin^4 x = 1 - 2 \sin^2 x$ *Hint*: $\sin^2 x + \cos^2 x = 1$

(b) $\dfrac{3 \sin x + \cos x}{3 \tan x + 1} = \cos x$

(c) $\dfrac{\sin x}{\cos x} + \dfrac{\cos x}{\sin x} = (\sec x)(\csc x)$ *Hint*: $\sec x = 1/\cos x$
                                                    $\csc x = 1/\sin x$

2. Write code to read in a formula for $F(x)$ during program execution and to compute the following approximation to $\int_0^1 F(x)\,dx$:

$$\frac{1}{10}\left[\frac{1}{2}F(0) + \sum_{k=1}^{9} F(k/10) + \frac{1}{2}F(1)\right]$$

(This is the trapezoid rule with 11 points.)

3. Write code to read in a formula for $F(x)$ during program execution, differentiate $F(x)$ to obtain $F'(x)$, and then punch out the formula for $F'(x)$ in the form of a PL/I assignment statement suitable for compilation. *Hint*: Use CHAREX.

4. Consider the power series expansion for tan x.

$$\tan x = \sum_{n=0}^{\infty} t_{2n+1} x^{2n+1} = t_1 x + t_3 x^3 + t_5 x^5 + \cdots$$

Let the sequence $r_1, r_3, r_5, \ldots$ be defined by the following recursion relation:

$$r_1 = 1$$

$$r_{2n+1} = (-1)^n\left[1 + \sum_{k=1}^{n}(-1)^k\binom{2n+1}{2k-1}r_{2k-1}\right], \qquad n = 1, 2, 3, \ldots$$

Then

$$t_{2n+1} = \frac{r_{2n+1}}{(2n+1)!} \qquad n = 0, 1, 2, \ldots$$

Using the facts just given, compute exact (rational) values for $t_1, t_3, t_5, \ldots, t_{21}$.

ANSWERS TO
SELECTED EXERCISES

Chapter 1

1. Valid are (a), (b), (f), (h), and (i)

Chapter 2

1. A REAL FIXED DEC (5,0), B REAL FLOAT BIN (21), (C, D) REAL FLOAT DEC (16), E CPLX FLOAT DEC (16)

2. (a) REAL FIXED BIN (4,4), (b) REAL FIXED DEC (4,3), (c) REAL FLOAT DEC (4), (d) REAL FIXED DEC (2), (e) CPLX FIXED DEC (1), (f) CPLX FLOAT DEC (3)

3. (c), (e)

4. (a) REAL FIXED DEC (11,0), (b) REAL FIXED BIN (16,0), (c) REAL FIXED DEC (6,0), (d) REAL FIXED DEC (15,0) with FOFL possible, (e) REAL FIXED DEC (11, 0) with SIZE possible, (f) REAL FIXED DEC (15,5) with FOFL possible, (g) REAL FIXED DEC (11,0)

5. (a), (b), (g), (h), single; (b), (c), (e), (f), double

6. Zero in both cases

Chapter 3

1. A = 2, B = 0

2. P = 0, Q = 1

3. C = 2

Chapter 4

2.   ISUM = 0;
     LP: DO I = 1 TO N—1;
          DO J = I TO N—1;
          ISUM = ISUM + I∗J;
          END LP;

3. T = 0;
   DO K = 1 TO 8, 10 TO 25;
   T = T + K**3;
   END;

4. Zero

5. T = 0;
   DO K = 1 BY 1 WHILE (T <= 2500);
   T = T + K**5;
   END;
   N = K;

Chapter 5

1. DCL T(4,4), A(2,2) DEF T, B(2,2) DEF T(1SUB, 2SUB−2), C(2,2) DEF
   T(1SUB−2, 2SUB), D(2,2) DEF T(1SUB−2, 2SUB−2);

2. DCL T(28), A(10,10) DEF T(2*1SUB+2SUB−2);

3. DO K = 1 TO 25 WHILE (A(K) ¬= 0);
   END;
   A(K) = 1;

4. DCL A(3,3) INIT (1,4,7,2,5,8,3,6,9);

5. LP: DO I = 1 TO 25;
   DO J = 1 TO 25;
   A(I,J) = 2*B(I,J) + 3*A(1,4);
   END LP;

Chapter 6

1. (a) PUT EDIT (((A(I, J) DO J = 1 TO 5) DO I = 1 TO 5)) (SKIP(2), (5)E(14,6));
   (b) PUT EDIT (((A(I, J) DO J = I TO 5) DO I = 1 TO 5)) (SKIP(2), (I−1)X(14),
   (I)E(14,6));

2. (a) GET LIST (A);
   (b) GET LIST (((A(I,J) DO J = 1 TO 5) DO I = 1 TO 5));

3. (a) GET EDIT (A) (COL(41), F(10));
   (b) GET EDIT (((A(I,J) DO J = 1 TO 5) DO I = 1 TO 5)) (COL(41), F(10));

4. GET EDIT (A, B, C) (COL(1), E(10,0), COL(21), F(10), SKIP, COL(41), F(5));

5. Invalid are (b) and (g)

Chapter 7

1.   DCL A(100);
   LP: DO K = 1 TO 100;
       ON CONV SNAP BEGIN; PUT LIST (ONSOURCE); GO TO LBL; END;
       GET LIST (A(K));
   LBL: END LP;

2. ON ENDPAGE(SYSPRINT) BEGIN;
       K = K + 1;
       PUT EDIT (K) (PAGE, COL(110), F(4));

```
        END;
  K = 0;
  SIGNAL ENDPAGE(SYSPRINT):
  PUT EDIT ((N, 1/N DO N = 1 TO 1000)) (COL(1), F(4), X(5), F(10,6));
```

Chapter 8

```
1. AMAX: PROC (A);
         DCL A(*);
  LP:    DO K = 1 TO HBOUND(A,1);
         END LP;
         RETURN(T);
         END AMAX;

2. TRACE: PROC (A);
         DCL A(*, *);
         IF HBOUND(A,1) ¬= HBOUND(A,2) THEN SIGNAL ERROR;
  LP:    DO K = 1 TO HBOUND(A,1);
         T = T + A(K,K);
         END LP;
         RETURN(T);
         END TRACE;

3. POLAR: PROC (Z,R,THETA);
         DCL Z CPLX;
         R = ABS(Z);
         THETA = ATAN(REAL(Z)/IMAG(Z));
         RETURN;
         END POLAR;
```

Chapter 9

```
2. ALPHA: PROC (X) RETURNS (BIT(1));
         DCL X CHAR (*);
         IF VERIFY(X, 'ABCDEFGHIJKLMNOPQRSTUVWXYZ') ¬= 0 THEN
             RETURN('0'B);
         RETURN('1'B);
         END ALPHA;
```

4. (a) '567',   (b) 5

6. Beginning in print position one of line 30: PI=b3.14

7. 3

Chapter 10

1. 25

2. 2

3. 6

4. The following code replaces the Euclidean-norm calculation in the example of Section 10.3:

```
NROW = 1; RNORM, SUM = 0;
P = START;
L3: DO WHILE (P ¬= NULL);
    I = (K−1)/100;
    IF NROW = 1 THEN DO; NROW = I; RNORM = MAX(SUM, RNORM);
        SUM = 0; END;
    SUM = SUM + ABS(A);
    P = CHAIN;
    END L3;
    RNORM = MAX(SUM, RNORM); PUT DATA (RNORM);
```

Chapter 11

1. 6

2. CONVERSION error

3. 5

4. ZERODIVIDE error

5. FIXEDOVERFLOW error

6. 6

7. 0

8. $1.1 - 11\epsilon$ (that is, nearly 1.1)

9. 5

Chapter 12

2.
```
    DCL F CHAR (80);
    GET EDIT (F) (A(80));
    LET (F = "F");
    LET (SUM = 0);
LP: DO K = 0 TO 10;
    IF (K = 0) | (K = 10) THEN LET (SUM = SUM + EVAL(F, X, "K"/10)/2);
    ELSE LET (SUM = SUM + EVAL(F, X, "K"/10));
    END LP;
    PRINT__OUT (INTEGRAL = SUM/10);
```

3.
```
DCL F CHAR (80), DF CHAR (71) VAR, PUNCH OUTPUT FILE;
GET EDIT (F) (A(80));
LET (DF = DERIV("F", X, 1));
CHAREX (DF = DF);
DF = DF || ';';
OPEN FILE(PUNCH) LINESIZE(80);
PUT FILE(PUNCH) EDIT (DF) (COL(2), A(71));
```

(This solution is based on the assumption that the statement to be punched is no more than 71 characters long.)

INDEX

A format item 108, 140
A picture character 91, 137, 156
Abbreviations of keywords 4
ABS built-in function 40, 46, 49, 65, 124
ADD built-in function 26
Addition 18–24
ADDR built-in function 183
Aggregates, data 65
   arrays 53–65
   structures 65–68
ALL built-in function 62, 65
ALLOCATE statement:
   used with BASED variables 174, 175, 177, 181, 183, 184, 187, 188
   used with CONTROLLED variables 58, 59, 126, 139, 187, 188
Allocation (see Storage allocation)
Alphabetic characters 2
"and" operation 37, 160
ANY built-in function 62
Arcsine function 116
Area:
   arguments 185
   assignment 181, 182
   function values 185
   parameters 185
   variables 180–183
AREA attribute 180, 181
AREA condition 181, 186
Argument list 111–113, 130
Arguments 111, 113 (see also Parameters)
   area 185
   array 123–125, 134

Arguments (cont.):
   based 185
   constants as 111
   controlled 127
   dummy 112, 117–119, 134, 135
   entry name 122
   expressions as 112
   label 121
   of mathematical functions 16, 17, 119, 120
   offset 185
   parentheses around 135
   pointer 185
   relationship to parameters 112–114, 116–119, 123, 132, 150, 201
   string 150
Arithmetic data 8, 154, 164
   attributes for 8, 9
   comparison of 34, 35
   constants 11, 12
   defaults for 10
Arithmetic mean 62
Arithmetic operations 14–29
   conversion in 15, 18–20
   operators 17, 167
   results of 17–25
Array:
   arguments 60, 123-125
   arithmetic 59–61, 69
   assignment 59–61
   asterisks for bounds 124, 125
   built-in functions for manipulating 61, 62
   character-string 137, 148
   cross sections 62–64, 68

Array (cont.):
   dimensions 53, 54
   dynamic storage allocation for 58–60
   functions with array values 124
   initialization 55, 59, 201
   input/output 75–77
   of statement labels 55, 56
   structure containing an 67
   use of CHECK on 196
Arrow notation for pointer qualification 172
Assignment:
   area 181, 182
   array 59–61
   CHECK condition raised for 195
   conversion caused by 15, 19, 22, 166, 167
   element 14–16
   FORMAC 206
   label 33
   multiple 16
   pointer 174
   structure 67
Asterisk notation:
   for bounds in dimension specifications 59, 124, 125, 134, 183, 188
   for string length 139, 151, 188
   for subscripts 62, 63
Attributes:
   of built-in function arguments 17
   of built-in function values 17, 20
   of constants 11, 12

Attributes (*cont.*):
  default 10
  factoring of 11
  of results in arithmetic
    operations 18-25
  of target in conversions
    18–20
Automatic storage 126, 127,
    129, 133, 139, 187,
    188

B format item 158
B picture character 89
Backspacing tapes 97
Base 8–10
  in arithmetic conversion
    18–20, 166
  of arithmetic expression
    18–20
  binary 8–10
  conversion 19–23, 25,
    27, 166
  decimal 8–10
  default attribute for 10
  in exponentiation 19
  of numeric-character data
    156
Base-subscript list 57
Base variable of DEFINED
    attribute 14, 56,
    130, 156, 196
Based storage 171, 187, 188
  allocation of 173–175,
    181, 187
  freeing of 174, 175, 181
  overlaying of 183
BASED variables 171–173,
    187, 188
  associated with pointers
    171–173
  CHECK not permitted 196
  input/output 184
BEGIN block 102, 103,
    132–135, 187
  compared with subpro-
    gram 133
  END statement for
    102, 132
  as on-unit 103
BEGIN statement 102, 103,
    132–134
  condition prefixes to
    102, 195
BIN (*see* BINARY attribute)
BINARY (abbr.: BIN) attribute
    9, 10
BINARY (abbr.: BIN) built-in
    function 25, 164, 200
Bisection method 48
BIT built-in function 164

Bit-string data 154, 157–163
  attributes for 158
  concatenation of 158
  constants 158
  conversion of 163–165
  input/output 158
  operators 160, 167, 168
  variables 158
Blanks 5, 75, 158
  in constants 3, 75, 136
  in data-directed input/
    output 78
  in edit-directed input/
    output 86, 96
  in list-directed input/
    output 75
  in operators 5
  padding strings with
    138, 141, 142, 147
  significant 5, 136
  in structure declarations
    65
Block structure 132, 133, 184
Boolean operations 160
Boundaries, card and line 73
Bounds (in array dimen-
    sions) 53, 54, 68
  in ALLOCATE statement 59
  of array parameters
    123–125
  asterisk notation for 59,
    124, 125, 134, 183,
    188
  expressions for 59, 124,
    152
Branch (*see* GO TO
    statement)
Built-in functions 16, 17
  with array arguments
    60, 64, 134
  array manipulation 61,
    62, 64, 124
  attributes of arguments 17
  attributes of function
    values 17, 20, 24, 25
    124, 134
  based storage 178, 181,
    183
  causing SIZE errors 27
  with complex arguments
    17, 49
  for controlling attributes
    of arithmetic expres-
    sions 25–27
  FORMAC (*see* FORMAC)
  generic 17
  mathematical 16, 17, 24,
    25, 119, 120
  string manipulation
    143–146, 164
BY NAME option in structure
    assignment 43

C format item 85
CALL statement 111–113
Card format 4, 5
Carriage control 73, 74, 84
Chaining technique for
    lists 176
CHAR (attribute) (*see*
    CHARACTER attribute)
CHAR built-in function 164
CHARACTER (abbr.: CHAR)
    attribute 137, 146
  in ALLOCATE statement
    139
Character sets 2–4
Character-string data
    136–170
  arrays 137
  assignment of 141
  comparison of 142, 143
  concatenation 142
  constants 136, 137
  conversion of 163–165
  defined on numeric-
    character data 156
  initialization 138
  input/output 139–141
  length 137
  picture specification for
    137, 138
  storage allocation 138,
    139
  truncation and padding
    138, 141, 142
  variable-length (*see*
    VARYING attribute)
  variables 137
Character-string value of
    numeric-character
    data 155
Chebyshev series 221
CHECK condition 195–197
Chi-square 62
Ciphers 149
CLOSE statement 72, 93–97
Closing of files 72, 93–97
Closure, multiple, of nested
    loops 45
Coded arithmetic data
    154, 164, 166, 167
COL (*see* COLUMN format
    item)
Collating sequence 3, 143
COLUMN (abbr.: COL) format
    item 82–84, 96,
    153, 202
Comma picture character
    89, 154
Comments 7
Comparison:
  of arithmetic data 34, 35
  attributes of result of 161
  conversions in 35, 143
  operators 34, 37, 142,
    167–169

Comparison (*cont.*):
  priority of 167, 168
  of pointers 175, 184
  of string data 142
COMPLEX (abbr.: CPLX)
  built-in function
    29, 113
Complex data 9, 10, 28, 29,
    49, 85, 113, 116,
    129
  input/output 75, 85
COMPLEX (abbr.: CPLX)
  pseudo-variable 29
Concatenation:
  bit-string data 158
  character-string data
    142, 148
Condition 99–110 (*see also*
    Interrupt)
  arithmetic codes for
    107, 195
  enabling and disabling
    100–102, 106
  in input/output 91–93
  investigation of, by
    programming 107,
    109, 195
  programmer-defined 107
  action for 103–105
  standard system action
    92, 103
  in subprogram 128
CONDITION condition 107
Condition prefix 101, 102,
    192, 193, 195
  scope of 128, 131
Conditional expression 161,
    201 (*see also* Com-
    parison)
  in IF statement 34, 37,
    38, 142
  in WHILE clause 47
CONJG built-in function 29
Constants:
  arithmetic 11, 12, 156
  bit-string 158
  blanks in 5, 136
  character-string 136, 137
  label 34
Continuation of state-
    ments 4, 5
Control:
  flow of 33
  interrupt of 99
  return of:
    from on-unit 104
    from subprogram
      113, 115
Control-format items 81,
    82, 84, 86
Control variable in DO
    42–47, 50, 51
Controlled arguments 127,
    188

CONTROLLED (abbr.: CTL)
  attribute 58–60, 62,
    126, 127, 129, 133,
    139, 175, 187, 188
Controlled parameters 127,
    188
Controlled storage 58–60,
    126, 127, 171, 187,
    188
  allocation of 58, 126,
    175, 187
  freeing of 58, 126,
    187, 188
  stacking of 59, 187
Controlled variables 58–60,
    62, 126, 127, 129,
    133, 139, 175, 187,
    188
CONV (*see* CONVERSION
    condition)
Conversion:
  arithmetic 15, 27, 35, 168
  arithmetic to bit string
    163–165
  arithmetic to character
    string 163–167, 200
  in arithmetic operations
    18–20
  bit string to arithmetic
    163–165
  bit string to character
    string 163–165
  bit string to hexadecimal
    159
  character string to arith-
    metic 143, 163–167
  character string to bit
    string 163–165
  in comparison operations
    35, 143
  error conditions 15 (*see
    also* CONVERSION
    condition)
  in exponentiation opera-
    tions 19
  in expression evaluation
    18–25
  fixed to floating 23, 24
  of function argument 17
  in input/output 82
  offset to pointer 185
  pitfalls 27, 165–167
  pointer to offset 185
  resulting from assignment
    15, 19, 22, 166
  resulting from INITIAL 16
CONVERSION (abbr.: CONV)
    condition 86, 91, 93,
    104, 107, 143, 201
  in assignment to picture
    156
  in character-string to
    arithmetic conversion
    143, 165

CONV condition (*cont.*):
  in character-string to bit-
    string conversion 165
  in comparisons 143
  in E-format input 86
  ONSOURCE used in 109
  in P-format input 91, 141
  in stream input 86, 91, 93
COPY option of GET state-
    ment 190, 191, 226
CPLX (*see* COMPLEX)
Cross sections of arrays
    62–64, 69
CTL (*see* CONTROLLED
    attribute)

Data:
  aggregates 65
  arithmetic 8, 154
  bit-string 154
  character-string 136–168
  coded-arithmetic 154
  conversion (*see*
    Conversion)
  label 33, 34
  locator 182, 184
  numeric-character
    154–157
  offset 182–185
  pointer 171–173
  problem 34, 154, 196
  program-control 34
  string 136
Data-directed input/output
    75
  input 78, 79
  output 80
Data interrupt 201
Data list:
  for data-directed input/
    output 78–80
  for edit-directed input/
    output 80, 81, 83
  for list-directed input/
    output 75, 77
DATE built-in function 148
DCL (*see* DECLARE statement)
Debugging 106, 190-203
  list-processing programs
    197–199
  programming pitfalls
    199–203
  use of CHECK condition
    195–197
  use of COPY option 190,
    191
  use of FINISH condition
    194, 195
  use of SIZE condition
    193, 194
  use of SNAP option 190,
    191
  use of STRINGRANGE con-
    dition 191, 192

Debugging (*cont.*):
use of SUBSCRIPTRANGE
condition 191, 192
DEC (*see* DECIMAL attribute)
DECIMAL (abbr.: DEC) attribute 9, 10
DECIMAL (abbr.: DEC)
built-in function 25,
26, 164, 198
Decimal point picture character 89, 91, 155
DECLARE (abbr.: DCL) statement 8–11, 68
default rules for 10
position of, in program 11
use of factoring 11
DEF (*see* DEFINED attribute)
Default:
attributes for arithmetic
variables 10
attributes of function
values 114
conditions disabled, en-
abled by 100
first-letter rule 10
DEFINED (abbr.: DEF) attribute 14, 59, 69
for arrays 56–58, 125
with BASED 183
for character strings 148,
149, 156
CHECK not permitted 196
with EXTERNAL 130
for numeric-character
variables 156
and storage classes 127
Diagnostic aids (*see*
Debugging)
Dimension:
in ALLOCATE statement 59
in BEGIN block 133
bounds of 53, 68, 124,
125, 134, 183, 188
extent of 54, 68
maximum number of 69
Disabling conditions
100–102
compared to use of null
on-unit 106
DIVIDE built-in function 28,
200
Division:
by zero 99 (*see also*
ZERODIVIDE)
fixed-point 28, 200, 202
remainder of 57
DO group 38, 39, 45
DO loop 5, 38, 39, 42–51,
203
"backward" loop 43, 51
control variable 42–47,
50, 51
iterative 42, 43
multiple closure 45

DO loop (*cont.*):
noniterative 43, 50
skipping over 43, 51
termination 38, 42, 44,
45, 50
transfer into range of
44, 108
transfer out of 44
WHILE clauses 47, 48, 50
DO in repetitive specification 76
Double-precision floating-
point arithmetic 12,
13, 23–25, 48
Dummy arguments 112,
117–119, 134, 135
Dynamic storage allocation
58, 59, 69, 126, 127,
133, 171, 173–175,
187, 188

E format item 81, 84, 86, 96
Edit-directed input/output
75
format items for 81, 82
84–91
FORMAT statement 85
input 80–83
output 83–85
ELSE clause 35–37, 40
EMPTY built-in function 181
Enabling conditions 99–102
END statement 6, 38, 39, 42
for BEGIN block 132, 133
for DO group 38, 42, 43,
45, 50
multiple closure by 45
for procedure 6, 112, 114,
132
statement label in 39,
44, 132
ENDFILE condition 92, 97,
100, 107, 109
ENDPAGE condition 73, 92,
100, 104
ENTRY attribute 113,
117–119, 121, 134,
150, 151, 164
Entry name 112, 113
as argument 122
explicit declaration of
114, 121
ENTRY statement 122
Equivalencing variables
183
ERF built-in function 88
ERROR condition 100, 104,
116, 192–194, 201
causing program termina-
tion 104, 192–194
use with ONCODE 107,
195

Euclidean norm 124, 125,
179, 180
EXP built-in function 40,
46, 49
Explicit opening and closing
of files 72, 94–96
Explicit pointer qualification 172, 173, 177,
198
Exponentiation operations
19, 21
Expression 14, 17–27
arithmetic:
base attribute of 19
mode attribute of 19
precision attribute of
20–25
scale attribute of 19
array 59–61
for array bound 59, 124,
152
data conversions in
evaluation of 18–20
evaluation of 17–25
in format 87, 97
in RETURN statement 115
for string length 152
structure 67
as subscript 55
use of parentheses in 17,
18, 38, 143, 161, 167
EXT (*see* EXTERNAL attribute)
Extent of dimension 54, 68
EXTERNAL (abbr.: EXT)
attribute 128–130,
132, 135
with DEFINED attribute 129
with INITIAL attribute 129
with storage-class attri-
bute 129, 183, 188
External procedure 111,
130, 134

F format item 81, 84, 86, 96
Factor:
iteration 87
repetition 55, 137, 158
Factoring of attributes 11
File:
closing 72, 93–96
nonstandard 93–96
opening 72, 93–96
standard 71, 72, 93, 97
FILE attribute 94, 95
FINISH condition 194, 195
FIXED attribute 9, 10
FIXED built-in function 25,
26
Fixed-point arithmetic:
compared with integer
arithmetic 202, 203
constants 11, 12
conversions to floating
point 23, 24

Fixed-point arithmetic (*cont.*):
division 27, 28, 200, 202, 203
expressions 20–23
pitfalls 27, 28, 193, 194, 200
use of FIXEDOVERFLOW, SIZE conditions 193, 194
variables 9
FIXEDOVERFLOW (abbr.: FOFL) condition 22, 23, 28, 100, 104, 109
compared with SIZE condition 193, 194
FLOAT attribute 9, 10
FLOAT built-in function 25
Floating-point arithmetic 12, 13
constants 11, 12, 23–25
double precision 12, 13, 23–25, 48
expressions 23–25
single precision 12, 13, 23–25
variables 9
FOFL (*see* FIXEDOVERFLOW condition)
FORMAC:
arrays 207
assignment statement 206
atomic variables 207, 208
ATOMIZE statement 208, 209
automatic simplification 208, 213
built-in functions 210–218
ARITH 220, 221
CODEM 211, 214, 215
COEFF 212
COMB 218
DENOM 211, 212
DERIV 223, 224
EVAL 217
EXPAND 211, 214, 215
FAC 218, 221
IDENT 212, 213
INTEGER 220, 221
mathematical functions 216–218
NUM 211, 212
REPLACE 212
CHAREX statement 224
constants 207
conversions 207
differentiation 223, 224
double quotes 220, 221
exchanging data with PL/1 220, 221
floating-point data 207, 216
FNC function definition 218, 219

FORMAC (*cont.*):
FORMAC OPTIONS statement 206
LET statement 206
options:
EXPND 209, 214, 215
LINELENGTH 206
PRINT 214
TRANS 216, 217
OPTSET statement 206
parenthesis removal 208, 209, 214, 215
preprocessor 205
PRINT OUT statement 209
rational data 207
reading in formulas 224–226
subscripts 207
substitutions 208, 212, 217
systems constants 217
user-defined functions 218, 219
Format:
conditional expressions in 87, 88, 97
control-format items 81, 82, 84, 86
data-format items 81, 84, 85
iteration factors 87
reading in 97
remote-format item 85
scanning rules 83, 97
variables in 87, 97
FORMAT statement 85
Fortran 1, 15, 29–31, 40, 50, 51, 68, 69, 96–98, 109, 134, 135, 168, 169, 202, 203, 207
48-character set 3
FREE statement 58, 126, 174, 175, 177, 181, 184, 187, 188
Freeing of storage:
based storage 174, 175, 177, 181, 184, 187, 188
controlled storage 58, 126, 187, 188
Function 111, 113–116
arguments 114
array-valued, not permitted 124
built-in (*see* Built-in functions)
generic 119, 120
name 113
recursive 120, 127, 134
termination of 115
value returned by 113–115, 124, 150, 152
without arguments 121

Gamma function 121
Gaussian integration 122
Generation, storage:
of BASED variable 175, 187
of CONTROLLED variable 175, 187
Generic functions 17, 119, 120, 134
Geometric mean 62
GET statement 71, 73, 75, 78, 80
COPY option 190, 191
GET STRING statement 153
for internal data movement 153
with nonstandard input file 95
GO TO statement 5, 33, 40
out of BEGIN block 133
computed 40
LABEL variable in 33, 40
out of on-unit 104
out of procedure block 122

HBOUND built-in function 125
Hex conversion 159
Hierarchy of operations (*see* Priority of operators)
High-order digits (*see* SIZE condition)
Hilbert matrix 221

IF statement 34, 35, 40
ELSE clause 35–37, 40
nested 36, 37
IMAG built-in function 29
IMAG pseudo-variable 29
Implementation dependence 3, 4, 6, 9, 20, 21, 23, 24, 55, 72, 77, 94, 100, 112, 113, 117, 119, 121, 143, 156, 158, 172, 176, 181–184, 193, 195
Implicit pointer qualification 172, 173, 177, 198
IN option of ALLOCATE and FREE statements 181
INDEX built-in function 144
Infix operators 18
INIT (*see* INITIAL attribute)
INITIAL (abbr.: INIT) attribute 13, 14, 29, 138
in ALLOCATE 59
for arrays 55, 201
for AUTOMATIC variables 127, 188
for BASED variables 183, 188

INITIAL attribute (*cont.*):
  for CONTROLLED variables 59, 127, 188
  for DEFINED variables 14
  for EXTERNAL variables 129
  for LABEL variables 33
  for locator variables 184
  for STATIC variables 127, 188
Initialization of variables (*see* INITIAL attribute)
INPUT file attribute 95
Input/output 71–98
  of areas 182
  of BASED variables 184
  conversions in 76
  data-directed 78–80, 139, 184
  edit-directed 80–85, 140
  list-directed 75–78, 139
  of lists 182
  locate mode 171
  nonstandard files 93–96
  of pointers 184, 198
  record type 1, 71, 171
  standard files 71
  statements for 71
  stream type 1, 71
  of strings 139, 141
Interest-rate calculation 48
Internal procedure 111, 130–132, 135
Interrupt 99–110 (*see also* Condition)
  enabling and disabling 100–102, 106
  in input/output 91–93
  investigation of, by programming 107, 109, 195
  programmer-defined 107
  action for 103–105
  standard system action for 92, 103
  in subprogram 128
iSUB variables 57, 58, 125
Iteration factor (*compare* Repetition factor):
  in format list 87
  in INITIAL attribute 55

Keypunching PL/1 source program 4
Keywords 4, 5, 9
  abbreviations for 4
  blanks in 5
Kronecker delta 161

Label 3, 4, 55
  argument 121

Label (*cont.*):
  assignment 34
  constants 34
  parameter 121
  procedure 6
  use of CHECK on 196
  variable 33, 121
    in GO TO statement 33, 55
    initialization of 34
LABEL attribute 33, 55
Layout of pages 72, 73
LBOUND built-in function 125
Length:
  attribute 136
  of external names 128
  of file names 94
  of identifiers 3
  of procedure names 6
  specified in ALLOCATE statement 139
  of string parameters 151
  of strings 136–138, 144, 147, 200
LENGTH built-in function 144, 151, 152
Level numbers in structures 65
L'Hospital's rule 223
LIKE attribute for structures 67
LINE format item 84, 153
Line number 73
LINE option of PUT statement 74, 105, 153
LINENO built-in function 73, 75, 93
LINESIZE option 72, 73, 94, 95
List-directed input/output:
  input 75–77
  output 77, 78
Lists 171, 176–182
  building 176–178
  copying 181, 182
  debugging 197–199
  freeing 181
  input/output of 182
  limiting space for 181
  terminating 176, 178
Locate-mode input/output 171
Locator data 182
  arguments 185
  comparison 184
  conversion 185
  function values 185
  input/output of 184
  parameters 185
  variables 182, 184
    BASED 184
    initialization of 184
LOG built-in function 49

Logical operators 37, 38, 160, 167, 169
Long-precision floating-point (*see* Double-precision floating-point arithmetic)

MAIN option of PROCEDURE statement 6
Main program 6
Major structure variable 66, 177
Mathematical built-in functions 16, 17, 24, 25, 119, 120
Matrix multiplication 64, 123, 124
Matrix norm 124, 125, 179, 180
MAX built-in function 125
Maximum precisions 9
Minor structure variable 66, 177
Minus-sign picture character 89, 156
MOD built-in function 57, 149, 203
Mode 8–10
  of arithmetic expression 19
  complex 8–10, 28, 29
  conversion of 18, 19, 26, 28, 29
  default for 10
  in exponentiation 19
  real 8–10
Multiple assignment statement 16, 201
Multiple closure 45
Multiplication 21, 26
MULTIPLY built-in function 26, 27

Nested IF statements 36, 37
Nested multiplication method 54
Nested procedures 130
Newton-Raphson method 39, 46, 49, 225
9-picture character 89, 137, 154
NO in condition prefix 102
Nonstandard files 92–96
Normal probability table 88
"not" operation 34, 37, 161
NULL built-in function 178
Null on-unit 106
Null pointer value 178
Null string 138, 158
Numeric-character data 154–157
  arithmetic value of 155

Numeric-character data (*cont.*):
character-string value of 155
compared with coded arithmetic data 154, 200
conversion to character-string data 167, 200
picture characters for 88–91, 154, 155
position of decimal point in 155
signs in 157

OFFSET attribute 182–185
OFL (*see* OVERFLOW condition)
ON statement 103–105
position of 105, 203
scope of 128
SNAP option 106, 190, 191
in subprograms 128
On-condition (*see* Condition)
On-unit 103, 104
BEGIN block as 103, 106, 108
GO TO statement in 104
null 106
return from 104, 107
RETURN statement in 104
single-statement 103
stacking of 128
ONCODE built-in function 107, 195
ONSOURCE built-in function 109
OPEN statement 72, 93–96
Opening files 72, 93–96
Operators:
arithmetic 17, 167
bit-string 38, 160, 167, 168
blanks in 5
comparison 34, 37, 142, 167
concatenation 142, 148, 158
infix 18
logical 37, 38, 160, 167, 168
prefix 18
priority of 18, 38, 167–169
OPTIONS (MAIN) specification 6
"or" operation 34, 37, 161
Output (*see* Input/output)
OUTPUT file attribute 95
OVERFLOW (abbr.: OFL) condition 100, 104
(*see also* FIXED-OVERFLOW)

Overlaying variables 183

P format item 88–91, 96, 141, 154, 155, 157
Padding of strings 138, 141, 142, 147, 158, 160
PAGE format item 84, 96, 97, 153
Page layout 72, 73
PAGE option of PUT statement 74, 153
PAGESIZE 72, 74, 84, 92, 94
Parameter lists 112, 114
Parameters (*see also* Arguments):
area 185
array 123–125
CHECK on, not permitted 196
CONTROLLED 127, 188
default attributes for 118
entry name 122
label 121
matching with arguments 112–114, 116–119, 123, 134, 201
offset 185
pointer 185
storage allocation for 127, 188
string 150, 151
Parentheses:
around arguments 135
in expressions 17, 38, 143, 167
PIC (*see* PICTURE attribute)
Picture:
characters:
for character-string data 91, 137, 138, 147, 156
for numeric-character data 88-91, 154–157
format item 88–91
summary of uses 156, 157
PICTURE (abbr.: PIC) attribute 137, 147, 154, 155
Pitfalls with fixed-point arithmetic 27, 28, 193, 194, 200
Point, position of, in numeric-character data 89, 91, 155
Point picture character 89, 91, 155
Pointer:
argument 185
assignment 174
associated with BASED variable 171–173
comparisons 175

Pointer (*cont.*):
contextual declaration of 171, 185
null value 178
parameter 185
qualification 172–173, 177, 198
variable 171-175, 185, 198
POINTER (abbr.: PTR) attribute 171
Polynomial evaluation 54, 209
POS (*see* POSITION attribute)
POSITION (abbr.: POS) attribute 148
Power method 64, 197
PREC (*see* PRECISION built-in function)
Precision:
of arithmetic expression 20–25
attribute 8–10
in base conversions 200
conversion of 15, 20–25, 27, 200
default for 10
determination in conversions 20–22, 164–167, 200
in exponentiation 21
of fixed-point expressions 20–23
of floating-point expressions 23–25
maximum 9, 20, 21
of target in assignment statement 22, 166
PRECISION (abbr.: PREC) built-in function 25, 26
Prefix (*see* Condition prefix *and* Label)
Prefix operators 18
PRINT files 94, 99, 140
(*see also* Printer layout)
Printer layout 73, 74
Priority of operators 18, 34, 38, 143, 166, 167, 169
in comparisons 38, 143, 166, 167, 169
Problem data 34, 154, 196
Procedure 6
block 133
END statement for 6, 112, 114, 132
external 111, 130
function 111, 113–116
initial 6
internal 111, 130–132, 135
invocation of 111, 113

Procedure (*cont*.):
main 6
name 6, 112, 114
nesting of 130–132
sharing variables 111
subroutine 111–113
PROCEDURE statement 6,
112, 114, 152
CHECK prefix for 195
label of 6, 112, 114
PROD built-in function 61,
62, 64, 124
Program-control data 34
Programmer-named condi-
tion 107
Pseudo-variables 29, 145,
158
PTR (*see* POINTER attribute)
Punched-card output 72,
94, 95
"Pushed-down" storage 59,
187
PUT statement 71, 73, 77,
79, 83
ENDPAGE condition raised
for 73, 92, 100, 104
with nonstandard output
file 94
PUT SKIP DATA state-
ment 7
PUT STRING statement 153

Qualification (*see* Pointer)
Qualified names 66, 67
Quote in character-string
constant 163

R format item 85
Random number generation
121
READ statement 71
REAL attribute 9, 10
REAL built-in function 29
REAL pseudo-variable 29
RECORD attribute 71, 171,
182
Record size, logical 95
RECORD type input/output
1, 71, 171, 182
Recursive procedure 120,
127, 134
Remote format item 85
Repetition factor (*compare*
Iteration factor):
in bit-string constants 158
in character-string con-
stants 137
in INITIAL attribute 55
Repetitive specification 76,
77

Return of control:
from function 115, 164
from on-unit 104, 107
from subroutine 113
RETURN statement 6, 104,
107, 113, 115, 164,
194
expression in 115
for function termination
115, 164
in on-unit, not permitted
104
for subroutine termina-
tion 113
Returned function value:
of arithmetic built-in
functions 26
attributes of 114, 115,
124
conversion of 115
of mathematical built-in
functions 17, 24, 119
RETURNS attribute 115, 119,
134, 152
RETURNS option of PROCE-
DURE statement 114,
152
REVERT statement 128
Rewinding tapes 97
Rounding errors 35, 45
Rounding of output 78, 86,
87, 90
Row-major order 55, 75,
77, 98
Row norm 125

S picture character 89, 155,
156
Scale 8–10
of arithmetic expression
19
conversion of 20–23, 25
default for 10
in exponentiation 19
fixed-point 8–10
floating-point 8–10
Scope:
of condition prefix 128,
131
of ON statement 128
of variables 130
Scratch file 72, 95, 96
Secondary entry point 122
Semicolon:
in data-directed input/
output data 79, 80
statement delimiter 5
SET option of ALLOCATE
statement 174
Sharing variables between
procedures 130

Short-precision floating-
point (*see* Single-
precision floating-
point arithmetic)
Sign picture characters 89,
155, 156
SIGNAL statement 106, 116
Significant digits, loss of
(*see* SIZE condition)
Simulation of an interrupt
106
Single-precision floating-
point arithmetic 12,
13, 23–25
60-character set 2–4
SIZE condition 15, 23, 142,
193, 194, 200 (*com-
pare* FIXEDOVERFLOW
condition)
in base conversion 21
caused by built-in func-
tions 27
compared with FIXED-
OVERFLOW 193, 194
in F-format output 193
in precision conversion
15, 200
SKIP format item 81–84,
86, 96, 97, 153, 202
SKIP option:
in GET statement 73, 74,
82, 153
in PUT statement 74, 153,
202
Skipping of records 73, 82
Slashing of zeros 146
SNAP option of ON statement
190, 191
Source program, keypunch-
ing 4
Spacing format item 81, 84,
86
Spacing of lines in printed
output:
double 74, 78, 97
single 74, 97
space suppression 74, 97
Sparse matrix 108, 180
Special characters 3
SQRT built-in function 16,
17, 119, 124
Stacking:
of controlled storage 59,
187
of on-units 128
Standard files 71, 93, 97
Start of execution 6
Statement label (*see* Label)
STATIC attribute 126, 127,
129, 187, 188
Static variables:
allocation of storage 126,
127, 187
initialization of 127

Static variables (*cont.*):
in recursive procedures 127
Storage allocation (*see also* Storage classes):
for DEFINED variables 127, 149, 188
dynamic 58–60, 126, 127, 133, 139, 171, 173–175, 187, 188
for EXTERNAL variables 129, 183, 188
for parameters 127, 188
in recursive procedures 127
in subprograms 126, 127, 184
Storage classes 187–188
attributes for 126, 127, 149
automatic 126, 127, 134, 139, 187, 188
based 171–188
controlled 58–60, 126, 127, 134, 139, 187, 188
static 126, 127, 134, 187, 188
STREAM attribute 71, 73, 75, 76, 96, 202
STRG (*see* STRINGRANGE condition)
String data (*see* Bit-string data *and* Character-string data)
String-handling built-in functions 143–146, 164
String length 136–138, 144, 200
expressions for 152, 184, 188
of subprogram parameters 151
varying 147
STRING option of GET, PUT statements 153, 154
STRINGRANGE (abbr.: STRG) condition 143, 191, 192
Structures 65–68, 176–178, 188
blanks in declaration 66
identical 67, 68
structure arithmetic 67
structure assignment 66
Subprograms 111-135
arguments and parameters (*see* Arguments)
END statement for 112, 114, 132
external 111, 130, 134
function (*see* Function)

Subprograms (*cont.*):
internal procedure 111, 130–132, 135
interrupts in 128
invocation of 111, 113
nesting of 130
recursive 120, 127, 134
return from 113, 115, 164
storage allocation 126, 127, 184
SUBRG (*see* SUBSCRIPTRANGE)
Subscript 53, 55, 69
asterisk as 62–64, 69
checking of range (*see* SUBSCRIPTRANGE)
expression as 55
fractional 55
Subscripted qualified structure names 67
SUBSCRIPTRANGE (abbr.: SUBRG) 55, 58, 101, 102, 104, 191, 192
SUBSTR built-in function 143, 145, 148, 158, 192
SUBSTR pseudo-variable 145, 146, 192
Substring (*see* SUBSTR built-in function)
SUM built-in function 61, 62, 64, 124
SYSIN standard input file 71
SYSPRINT standard output file 71
SYSTEM specification for ON statement 104, 105, 195

Tab positions for printing 77, 80
Target in assignment statement 15, 19, 22, 166
Termination (*see also* Return of control):
of BEGIN blocks 132, 133
of DO group 38, 42, 43, 45, 50
of execution 6
of procedure 6, 112, 114, 132
THEN clause in IF statement 34, 35
Transfer (*see* GO TO statement)
TRANSLATE built-in function 145
Triangular matrix 58
Trigonometric identities 217–220
TRUNC built-in function 202

Truncation:
of high-order digits (*see also* SIZE condition *and* FIXEDOVERFLOW condition) 15
of low-order digits 16
of output 78, 87, 90
of quotients 202
of strings 138, 141, 142, 158

UFL (*see* UNDERFLOW condition)
UNDERFLOW (abbr.: UFL) condition 100–102, 104, 105
UNSPEC built-in function 158, 198
UNSPEC pseudo-variable 158

V picture character 89, 155
compared with point picture 91, 155
VAR (*see* VARYING attribute)
VARYING (abbr.: VAR) attribute 146–149, 152, 153
for arguments and parameters 153
for arrays 148
for BASED variables, not permitted 183, 188
for DEFINED variables 149
VERIFY built-in function 144
Vigenère cipher 149

WHILE clause of DO statement 47, 48, 50, 77
WRITE statement 71

X format item 81, 84, 96
X picture character 91, 156

Y picture character 89

Z picture character 89
ZDIV (*see* ZERODIVIDE condition)
Zero suppression:
in E-format output 84
in F-format output 84
in P-format output 89, 90
ZERODIVIDE (abbr.: ZDIV) condition 100, 104, 109, 203
Zeros, padding with 158